Saving the Gray Whale

Society, Environment, and Place

Series Editors: Andrew Kirby and Janice Monk

Saving the Gray Whale

People, Politics, and Conservation in Baja California

Serge Dedina

The University of Arizona Press Tucson

First printing
The University of Arizona Press

♾ This book is printed on acid-free, archival-quality paper.
Manufactured in the United States of America
05 04 03 02 01 00 6 5 4 3 2 1

Library of Congress Cataloging-in-Publication Data
Dedina, Serge, 1964–
Saving the gray whale : people, politics, and conservation in
Baja California / Serge Dedina.
p. cm. — (Society, environment, and place)
Includes bibliographical references (p.) and index.
ISBN 0-8165-1845-9 (cloth : alk. paper)
ISBN 0-8165-1846-7 (paper : alk. paper)
1. Gray whale — Mexico — Baja California Sur. 2. Wildlife
conservation — Mexico — Baja California Sur. I. Title. II. Series.
QL737.C425 D44 2000
333.95′952216′091641 — dc21 99-6766
CIP

British Library Cataloguing-in-Publication Data
A catalogue record for this book is available from the British Library.

Publication of this book is made possible in part by grants from the Homeland
Foundation and the Wallace Research Foundation.

For Daniel, Israel, Emily, and my parents

Gray Whale

Gray whale,
once there is no more left of you than an image
of a dark shape that moved on the waters
in animal paradise
once there is no memory
no legend to log your life and its passage
because there is no sea where your death will fit
I want to set these few words
on your watery grave:
"Gray whale,
show us the way to another fate."

—*Homero Aridjis*

Contents

Illustrations

Maps

Tables

Acknowledgments

There is nothing more pathetic than a couple of over-educated *gabachos* floundering around in the wind and nothing more likely to arouse the sympathy of even the most hardened *choyero*. The only reason that my wife, Emily Young, and I survived our year in San Ignacio Lagoon and Magdalena Bay was that our neighbors adopted us. Without the help and friendship of the Aguilar Osuna, Ruelas, Mayoral González, Fisher Liera, and Ayala, Romero and Rodríguez Zavala families, we would still be digging our Ford F-150 pickup out of the mud somewhere on the road between San Ignacio Lagoon and Magdalena Bay.

A special thanks to Baja Discovery, Ecoturísmo Kuyíma, Acuendi Tourism Cooperative, Unión de Lancheros Turísticos de Puerto Adolfo López Mateos, Special Expeditions, Blue Waters Ocean Kayak Tours, and Baja Air Ventures for their logistical support and for allowing me to tag along on trips. Thanks also to the members of my San Diego technical supply and support team (especially Bill Spencer and Greg Abbott). My dad, Michel Dedina, kept us supplied in the field. He also reviewed the manuscript and made many helpful suggestions. Kara Mills helped prepare the final manuscript.

The following people in Baja California Sur facilitated research for this book and answered endless questions: Alejandro Ostos García, Ignacio Peña, Marco Antonio Girón García, Carlos Ramírez Cruz, Benjamín Ballesteros, Jorge Jiménez López, Guadalupe Camargo, Carlos Cota López, Guillermina Espinoza Cota, Wenceslao Nieblas Sandoval, Octavio Maravilla, German Ponce Díaz, Hernán Ramírez, Jorge Urban, Leonardo Reyes Silva and the staff of the Pablo Martínez Archives in La Paz, Aradít Castellanos, Victor Ramos, Manuel Vázquez, Manuel Gardea, Raul López, Jorge Peón, Eduardo Sedano, and José de Jesús Varela.

Guillermina Bautista Gómez, Lucilya Neyra González, Elías Gutiérrez Núñez, Betty Ferber, Homero Aridjis, and Maria Elena Sanchez facilitated research in Mexico City. I greatly appreciate the assistance of Luis

Echeverría and his staff for explaining the historical and political context of gray whale conservation in Mexico. Joel Reynolds and Jacob Scherr of the Natural Resources Defense Council, Holly Payne of World Wildlife Fund–Mexico, Mark Spalding, and Juan Bremer of Exportadora de Sal provided information on the San Ignacio Lagoon saltworks. The staffs at the San Diego Natural History Museum and the Scripps Institute of Oceanography facilitated access to the papers of Raymond Gilmore and Carl Hubbs. Thanks also to Luis Fleischer, Steven Swartz and Bruce Mate for answering my questions on gray whales.

The Association of American Geographers, American Cetacean Society–Los Angeles Chapter, Charlie and Hallie Jackson, California Coastal Conservancy, Cetacean Society International, Pro Esteros, Southwest Wetlands Interpretative Association, Surfers' Environmental Alliance, University of Texas at Austin Institute of Latin American Studies, and U.S. Marine Mammal Commission provided funding for field research. Thanks to the anonymous donor of computer equipment and to Lee Moore and Roswitha Mueller for arranging the use of Roswitha's home in Todos Santos, where most of this book was written.

Jorge Eloy was kind enough to grant permission to use his political cartoons, although he does not endorse my opinions on politics in Mexico or the San Ignacio Lagoon saltworks. Thanks to Granate Sosnoff of the Public Media Center in San Francisco for providing a copy of the Group of 100 advertisement. Thanks to Homero Aridjis for granting permission to use his poem "Ballena Gris" and George McWhirter for providing the translation.

My former colleagues at The Nature Conservancy and in Mexico provided insight into the possibilities of nature protection in Mexico, especially Brian Houseal, Susan Anderson, Joe Quiroz, Juan Bezaury, Joe Keenan, Bob McCready, Antonio Cantú, Benito Bermúdez, Carlos Castillo, Patricia and Laura Martínez, and Alejandro Hernández. Thanks also to my mother, Josephine Dedina, and to Michelle Blumenberg, Eric Penner, George Henderson, Diana Liverman, Rabbi Stephanie Aaron, Sallie Marston, Marian Modrak, Gabe Aguirre, Jamie Mitchell, Greg Tate, Robin Doughty, Jeff Knox, Mercedes Sironi, Mark Tourtellote, John Trimble, Pat and Mike McCoy, and the entire Young family for all their support. My brother Nick and Irene Zuñiga kindly lent us their dog Chip who braved howling winds, coyotes, scorpions, stingrays, rattlesnakes, and oatmeal.

Whether she was enduring all-day fishing excursions in a cramped panga without a bathroom break or hiding her discomfort while observing the slaughter of sea turtles, Emily was always an inspiration. I could not have completed this project without her love, patience, and encouragement.

Finally, thanks to Daniel, Israel, and the beautiful surf at La Pastora, Punta Perfecta, Cabo San Lázaro, Santa María, the Sloughs, and North Bird Rock for reminding me why I began this project.

Abbreviations

CIB	Center for Biological Research (later CIBNOR)
CIBNOR	Northwest Center for Biological Research (previously CIB)
CROM	Regional Confederation of Mexican Workers
GEF	Global Environmental Facilities program
IFAW	International Fund for Animal Welfare
INE	National Institute of Ecology
IWC	International Whaling Commission
NRDC	Natural Resources Defense Council
PAN	National Action Party
PRI	Institutional Revolutionary Party
PROFEPA	Federal Attorney General's Office for Environmental Protection
SCT	Ministry of Communications and Transportation
SEDUE	Ministry of Urban Development and Ecology
SEDESOL	Ministry of Social Development
SEMARNAP	Ministry for the Environment, Natural Resources, and Fisheries
UABCS	Autonomous University of Baja California Sur

Saving the Gray Whale

1 Mexican by Birth

Midmorning. Early January. Sunny. The surface of San Ignacio Lagoon in Baja California is like a sheet of glass as I paddle my kayak across the main channel. Making my way through the water, I hear a rippling sound and immediately turn to my right. About a hundred yards away a gray whale is suspended in the air for a brief moment. Suddenly the whale crashes down on its side. The splash reverberates throughout the lagoon.

Seconds later I feel the ripple of the water again. I turn to my left. My view of the ocean is blocked by two whales, one spyhopping—lifting itself out of the water with its tail and looking around—the other breaching—leaping completely out of the water. The spyhopper slips back into the lagoon. His companion comes down hard. I continue paddling. A pair of whales glides by me, with bottlenose dolphins in chase. I quickly cross the channel and watch from the safety of shore.

Less than ten days after my encounter with the world of gray whales in San Ignacio Lagoon, American whalewatching outfitters set up their camps. These companies bring in hundreds of tourists a year, who pay thousands of dollars each to watch the spectacle of the annual gray whale migration up close. After they arrive, the lagoon is filled with skiffs searching the lagoon for gray whale mothers and calves making their morning rounds, adult whales engaged in frenzied mating rituals, and others leaping out of the water like spent rockets.

About a thousand whales visit San Ignacio Lagoon from January to April. Many of them enter for a few days and continue their migration southward to Magdalena Bay and around the tip of the Baja California peninsula into the Sea of Cortez. Others stay longer and take care of their newborn calves in the shallow, saline waters of the upper portion of the lagoon known as El Remate.

Until the 1930s, whalers sailed the coast of Lower California in search of gray whales, a species they often referred to as "devil-fish" because of the ferocious attacks on any boat-riding man who tried to harpoon them. Today, the animals show little fear of the tourist skiffs that chase them in their winter playgrounds. The devil-fish is now the "friendly whale." During the nineteenth century, when the commercial harvest of gray whales reached its peak, whalers were terrified of gray whales. An American whaler, Captain Charles Scammon, reported that "The casualties from coast and kelp whaling are nothing to be compared with the accidents that have been experienced by those engaged in taking the females in the lagoons. Hardly a day passes but there is upsetting or staving of boats, the crews receiving bruises, cuts, and, in many instances, having limbs broken; and repeated accidents have happened in which men have been instantly killed, or received mortal injury."[1]

Although whalers suffered in their encounters with gray whales, the whales suffered even more. Thousands of gray whales were slaughtered along the coast of the Californias, reducing a once plentiful population to a few thousand by the time the International Whaling Commission banned the harvest of the species in 1946.

Today, for the multimillion-dollar whale tourism industry, the question is not whether tourists will see whales but how close they will get to them. Tourists hug, kiss, stroke, and put their hands in the mouths of gray whales in the lagoons of Baja California Sur. This turnaround is remarkable, considering that in 1970 the gray whale was listed as an endangered species under the U.S. Endangered Species Act. International efforts to protect the gray whale—a species that is watched by millions of people each year along its Pacific coast migratory route—helped bring it back from the brink of demographic disaster.

There is no doubt that international efforts to stop the commercial harvest of the gray whale played a large role in its recovery, but other factors also helped. Most notable were the efforts of the Mexican government to establish two important gray whale lagoons in Mexico's state of Baja California Sur as sanctuaries. Scammon's Lagoon and San Ignacio Lagoon were declared protected areas in the 1970s.[2] While the United States was busy destroying its Pacific coastal wetlands, Mexico set aside two of the largest remaining wetlands on the Pacific coast of North America as gray whale refuges. It was a remarkable achievement for a country not known to have a positive environmental record.

As a result of actions taken by Mexico and the international whaling community to protect the gray whale, the population recovered enough for the U.S. Fish and Wildlife Service to remove the eastern North Pacific stock of this marine mammal from the U.S. List of Endangered and Threatened Wildlife in 1994. This decision was based on a determination by the Fish and Wildlife Service and the U.S. National Marine Fisheries Service that the population had recovered to its pre-exploitation size of between fifteen thousand and twenty-four thousand animals.[3] The gray whale population has climbed from near extinction to full recovery in less than a century.

But the world of the gray whale today is not the world that it was in 1800—before whalers began to wipe the species off the face of the earth. In 1800, the gray whale lagoons of Baja California Sur remained virtually free of boat traffic. Gray whales are now chased up and down the lagoons by tourist boats.

Today, Scammon's Lagoon is the site of the largest salt harvesting facility in the world. Almost ten thousand people live around the shores of Magdalena Bay where an electric power plant and a deep-water port line the mangrove-fringed shoreline of Mexico's "Chesapeake of the Pacific." The Mexican government and Mitsubishi, the Japanese firm, plan for a larger salt harvesting facility to be located about 120 miles south of Scammon's Lagoon, along the shore of San Ignacio Lagoon, the world's last undeveloped gray whale lagoon.

To read about conservation in the Third World is to enter a world of doomsday scenarios. Clearly, the case of the gray whale is an exception. Whereas other, more industrialized countries such as the Soviet Union, Norway, and Japan were doing their best to clear the ocean of a range of large cetaceans after the 1950s, Mexico was moving in the opposite direction. The decision by President Luis Echeverría in 1971 to set aside Scammon's Lagoon as a whale reserve initiated a seventeen-year period in Mexico of laws designed to protect gray whale lagoons in Baja California Sur. While many of the wealthy nations of the world were turning a blind eye to the fate of the world's whales, Mexico, a country beset by rampant poverty but with a wealth of natural resources, helped protect a species it considers "Mexican by birth."[4]

Efforts to protect gray whales in Mexico were a postrevolutionary response to gain control over valuable resources previously exploited by foreigners. Gray whale conservation is a product of national views regarding sovereignty and the need for political control over potentially valuable resources, which include gray whales and their habitat. Although rural

Baja California Sur is as far as you can get in Mexico from the national political scene, the structure of the national political system connects even the most remote areas. In Mexico, gray whale conservation is a microcosm of national, regional, and local politics.

It is impossible to live in Mexico without being thrown into a cauldron of political activity. At every level of government, a hierarchy of power and politics permeates and transcends everyday life. This corporate structure of the Mexican state means that even the smallest cooperative and the poorest *ejido* are part of a paternalistic system that needs the electoral support of the rural sector to maintain the illusion of democracy. Symbolism is all-important in a country where the ruling party has kept a tight grip on political activities for more than seventy years. Although the power of the current ruling party, the Institutional Revolutionary Party (PRI) is weakening, it continues to tightly control Mexico. It is within this system that decisions are made and policies enacted. These decisions greatly affect the habitat that the gray whales return to in Baja California Sur year after year.

This book explores the reasons behind Mexico's efforts to protect the gray whale and its habitat in Baja California Sur. I discuss the historical reasons behind gray whale protection and track conservation policies from Mexico City into San Ignacio Lagoon (which forms part of the 6.2 million hectare Vizcaíno Biosphere Reserve) and Magdalena Bay, one of the largest remaining wetlands along the Pacific coast of North America.

My intent has been to determine whether policies and programs developed in distant cities and bureaucracies have any relation to what occurs in the remote areas gray whales travel to each winter in Mexico. By providing an in-depth look at the battle over the proposal to build an industrial salt production facility on the shore of San Ignacio Lagoon, I illuminate the contradictions of past and present gray whale conservation policies. The controversy highlights how the need to defend national sovereignty and territorial integrity, which is deeply embedded within the postrevolutionary Mexican political system, has come face-to-face with the present and future of globalization and resource extraction by multinational corporations.

Most of the research for this book was carried out during a two-year period from 1993 to 1995. Historical information was obtained through interviews with longtime gray whale lagoon residents and from archives in

Pondering the beached whales, the man observes: "They lost the fear of dying, and they were more afraid of living. . . . I wonder if whales also form political parties."

San Diego (the Carl Hubbs Papers at the Scripps Institution of Oceanography and the Raymond Gilmore Papers at the San Diego Natural History Museum), La Paz (the Pablo Martínez State Historical Archives), and Mexico City (National Archives, Pesca Library, and SEDESOL archives). Information on politics was obtained through interviews with government officials in La Paz and Mexico City and on trips with them to the field.

Although I examine the historical and political aspects of gray whale conservation in Mexico, a fundamental part of my approach is to put a human face on wildlife conservation. To do this I spent five months living in San Ignacio Lagoon and six months in the fishing village of Puerto Adolfo López Mateos. I have returned periodically to both places since 1994. I also lived in the town of San Carlos on Magdalena Bay during the summer of 1997. While in the field I accompanied local residents on their daily activities, including fishing and whalewatching. With my wife, Emily Young, I interviewed about sixty residents of San Ignacio Lagoon and Magdalena Bay about their attitudes toward wildlife conservation and Mexican politics.

The success of gray whale conservation depends on the people who live around the gray whale lagoons of Baja California Sur. To respect the confidentiality, privacy, and friendship of many of the people I spoke with, especially those who talked to me about the San Ignacio saltworks, I changed many of the names used in this book.

Gray whales form part of the culture, history, politics, and geography of one of Mexico's most isolated states. These animals have helped to shape the world around them and the lifeways of the people who share the Pacific lagoons of Baja California Sur with them. Gray whales represent our destructive past and a hopeful future.

2 The Natural History and Human Exploitation of the Gray Whale

After evading the civilized whaler and the instruments of destruction, and perhaps while they are suffering from wounds received in their southern haunts, these migratory animals begin their northward journey.

— CAPTAIN CHARLES M. SCAMMON

The annual journey of gray whales from their feeding grounds near Alaska brings them into contact with Alaska, Canada, the mainland United States, and the Baja California peninsula. While the whales and their young calves are oblivious to the political boundaries through which they pass, they daily confront obstacles produced by three nations.

Gray whales are like the thousands of undocumented workers who, while migrating into the United States on their way to an imagined economic and political utopia, duck under fences that protect international boundaries, dart across open fields and freeways, and evade the Border Patrol at every step of the way. Heading south from the frigid waters close to the Arctic Circle, gray whales embark on an 8,000-mile ocean migration that requires similar know-how: avoiding tanker traffic, fishing nets, oil spills, and sewage discharged into the ocean from the megacities of Vancouver, Seattle, San Francisco, Los Angeles, and San Diego–Tijuana. The animals evade the frenzy of whalewatching boats that chase them while they make their long journey from Alaska to three coastal lagoons tucked away on the Pacific coast of Baja California Sur in Mexico (see map 2.1). It is within these sheltered and warm lagoons that the whales mate, socialize, give birth, and suckle their newborn calves.

Natural History

Although the gray whale is probably the most studied of the world's great whales, biologists who have spent years close to the animals are the first to admit that there is still much to learn about gray whale behavior. Gray whales are cetaceans, an order of mammals that includes whales, dolphins, and porpoises. Similar to fish, cetaceans spend their lives in the water, but they are warm-blooded rather than cold-blooded. Their body

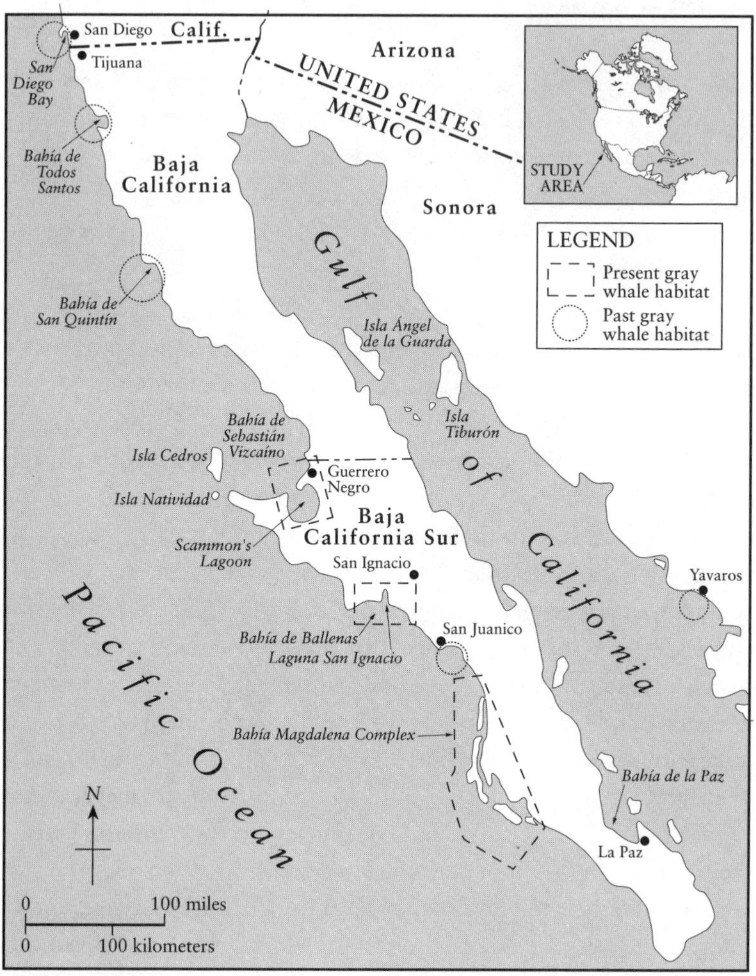

Map 2.1. The Baja California peninsula and gray whale habitat. Scammon's Lagoon includes Laguna Manuela and Laguna Guerrero Negro. Gray whales have also been sighted in Bahía de la Paz and throughout the Gulf of California.

temperatures are stable year-round. Whales, like all cetaceans, breathe through their lungs.

Scientists are not sure about the origins of gray whales. Originally it was thought that they evolved from an extinct family of whales, the Catotheridae, that lived on earth 30 million years ago and contained up to fifty different species of medium and small whales. However, more recently the lack of a fossil record linking the whales to that extinct family has placed the origin of the gray whale in doubt. As a result, gray whales are the only member of the Eschrichtidae family.

Fossil remains indicate that gray whales once had a much wider range, including the eastern and western North Atlantic, as well as the Pacific Ocean. Experts recognize two populations of gray whales: the western North Pacific (Korean) and the eastern North Pacific (California). While the eastern herd has rebounded from very low numbers (about forty-four thousand), the western stock remains endangered.[1] Gray whales found in Baja California Sur belong to the eastern Pacific population. The North Atlantic gray whales are extinct.

There are two general categories of whales: baleen and toothed whales. The gray whale is a member of the baleen or Mysticete family of whales. They differ greatly from the toothed whales, or Odontecetes, because rather than teeth, they have a baleen brush made of keratin inside their mouth. These baleen plates allow gray whales, which grow up to 50 feet in length and weigh up to 35 tons, to scoop up and filter the amphipods, krill, and tiny fish they find at the bottom of their feeding grounds near Alaska. In these summer areas they consume abundant benthic amphipods between May and November. It is estimated that each animal consumes approximately 65 tons of food annually, mostly during the five months the animals spend in their northern migratory range. The animals dive to depths of up to 248 feet to bottom-feed, around 27 feet more than their dives during the annual migration.[2] However, they usually swim at shallower depths on migration.

Gray whales are not gray. A newborn calf is coal black. The barnacles that quickly grow on gray whales and the depigmented skin tissue caused by barnacles that fall off give the species a discolored gray and even white appearance. Gray whales are not particularly beautiful or sleek animals. Even up close it is hard to get a sense of what they look like and how big they are. Pitted skin, barnacles, and sea lice distort the natural and smooth appearance of their skin. Their annual 8,000-mile migration to and from their feeding grounds near Alaska takes its toll on animals that can live up to seventy-five years. The hulk of a Chinese immigrant slave-trading ship confiscated by the Mexican Navy and rotting off the port of San Carlos in Magdalena Bay bears a close resemblance to many of the gray whales that visit the area each winter—old, tired, and roughed up from barnacles.

The unique discoloration and physical features of gray whales allow individuals to be identified year after year by research scientists and whale-watching guides. Whale researchers use these markings to make photo-identification records of each animal to help track migration patterns across the oceans. Steven Swartz and Mary Lou Jones spent six consecutive winters studying the behavior of gray whales at San Ignacio Lagoon. They assembled a photographic record of five hundred individual whales. The photos are compared with those of other researchers to determine where individual whales travel each year.[3]

Nicknamed "the desert whale," it is the only whale that regularly takes refuge from the open sea by entering lagoons during its annual migration from the north. Historically, the relatively warm and protected lagoons of Baja California Sur and mainland Mexico have served as breeding grounds and nurseries for gray whales. Guerrero Negro Lagoon, Scammon's Lagoon, San Ignacio Lagoon, and Magdalena Bay are the most important habitats for gray whales between December and April. The warm, protected waters of these lagoons are safe places for whales to mate and for mothers to raise their calves. The whales mate either along their migratory route or in and around the lagoons. The mothers and their newborn calves, which can weigh up to 1 ton and average about 15 feet at birth, remain in the shallow inner lagoon areas, while single and mating whales frequent the deeper, more turbulent, rougher waters around lagoon entrances. The period of gestation for gray whales is approximately thirteen months.

Each spring, gray whales depart from the lagoons, swimming approximately 3,600 to 4,800 miles northward to reach feeding grounds in the Bering and Chukchi Sea in Alaska. During the migration these mammals travel in pods of up to sixteen animals but are also observed swimming alone, in pairs, or in trios. The configuration of pods constantly changes over the migratory route. Once they arrive in their summer feeding grounds, the whales tend to congregate in the Bering Sea—the richest

The dunes and mangroves of Magdalena Bay.

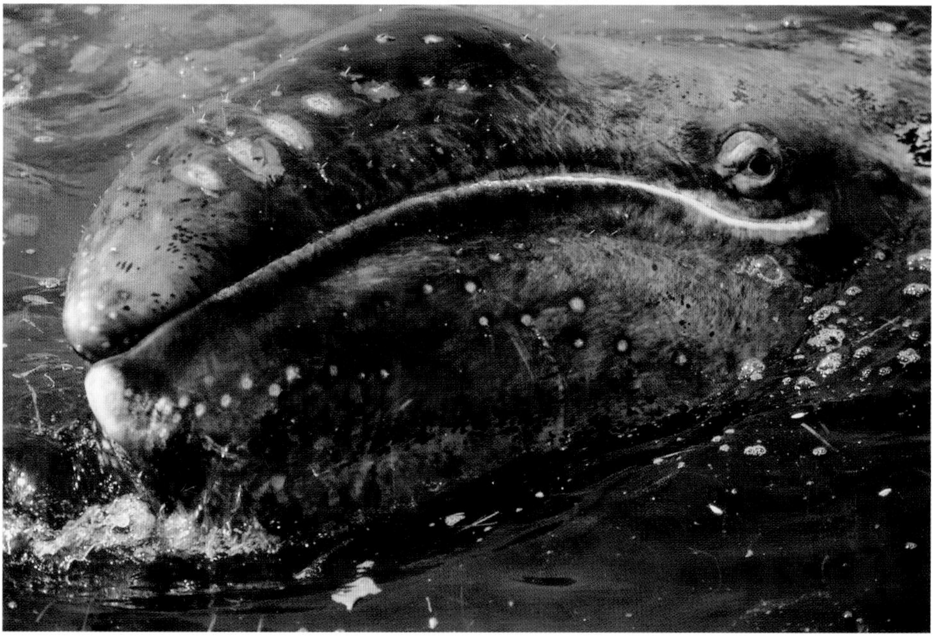

A friendly gray whale calf in Magdalena Bay. Local whalewatching guides in Baja California Sur are concerned that renewed indigenous whaling could change the behavior of these marine mammals.

A breaching gray whale calf at the Boca de Soledad in Magdalena Bay. The Boca de Soledad, just north of Puerto Adolfo López Mateos, is the most popular and accessible location for whalewatching, making the management of the whalewatching skiffs especially contentious there.

A gray whale calf interacting with whalewatching skiffs at the Boca de Soledad. Calves are generally accompanied by their mothers. Friendly behavior is learned and is generally more prevalent toward the end of the January–April season.

An adult gray whale at the Boca de Soledad.

A gray whale raising its tail fluke to dive in Magdalena Bay.

A gray whale aggregation at the mouth of Bahía Almejas in the southern end of Magdalena Bay.

feeding grounds. The animals travel throughout the region in search of food. Mothers and their calves often swim farther north to the less rich Chukchi Sea, where they are less likely to encounter predators, such as killer whales.

During the winter, some gray whales swim around the cape of the Baja California peninsula, into the Gulf of California (also known as the Sea of Cortez), and along the coasts of Sonora, Sinaloa, and Nayarit on mainland Mexico. The number of gray whales present in the Gulf of California is small in relation to the overall population. The relative importance of this—and other coastal habitats—for gray whales in their southernmost range has received considerably less attention than their activities in the lagoons of Baja California Sur.

The greatest number of gray whales occupy Scammon's Lagoon, followed by San Ignacio Lagoon and then Magdalena Bay (see table 2.1). Approximately one thousand whales are counted in Scammon's Lagoon from January to April. Scientists have found that the number of calves peaks around the middle of February. This is in contrast to San Ignacio Lagoon, where due to the arrival of calves from Magdalena Bay to the south, the number of calves peaks about a month later. San Ignacio Lagoon is more heavily populated by single whales rather than female-calf pairs, compared with Scammon's Lagoon and Magdalena Bay.[4] Jones and Swartz found that from late December to late February, about 150 to 200 whales (female-calf pairs and single whales) congregated in San Ignacio Lagoon near the Boca del Surgidero ocean entrance up to Punta Piedra (see map 2.2). Twenty percent frequented the middle of the lagoon from Punta Piedra to La Fridera. The remaining 80 percent were distributed in the upper lagoon from La Fridera to the north end of Isla Garzas. Mother-calf pairs seem to use this upper part the most.

Although Magdalena Bay harbors fewer gray whales than other lagoons, they congregate more densely there, especially in the narrow confines of the Boca de Soledad (see map 2.3). The narrow width of the main channel in this area results in a higher density of whales per square mile than in other lagoons.[5] The northern part of Magdalena Bay provides refuge for the third highest number of gray whales in Baja California Sur and is the third most important location for female-calf pairs.[6] Aerial censuses conducted during the 1980s reveal that the northern part of the bay had a high count of 363 gray whales in 1985. The central zone had a

Table 2.1 Censuses of Gray Whales in Baja California Sur Lagoons, 1947–1985[1]

Year[2]	Scammon's Lagoon	San Ignacio Lagoon	Magdalena Bay[3]
1947	101	69	—
1952	440	173	106
1953	259	70	193
1954	489	142	90
1955	190[4]	86	251
1956	347	76	393
1957	312	97	97
1959	1,005	91	26
1960	760	261	27
1961	427	108	27
1962	681	140	—
1964	923	258	—
1970 (1/31–2/1)	252[5]	158	—
1970 (3/4)	221	156	—
1973	517	94	33
1980	1,301	450	254
1981	1,527	489	255
1982	1,589	544	135
1983	1,225	494	241
1984	1,399	—	158
1985	1,354	—	363

[1] Includes total number of whales counted outside and inside Scammon's and San Ignacio lagoons. These are daily counts and do not represent the total number of whales that use each lagoon (which has not been quantified).

[2] The count for 1947 is from Hubbs 1947b. Counts for 1952–1973 are from Gard 1974:138–39. Counts for 1980–1985 are from Fleischer and Beddington 1985:11.

[3] For Magdalena Bay the counts are for inside the bay for 1952–1973. For 1980 and 1983–1985 the counts are for the North Zone. For 1981 and 1982 the counts are for the Central Zone and were obtained from Fleischer 1990:18.

[4] Count is for inside the lagoon only.

[5] Count is for inside the lagoon only.

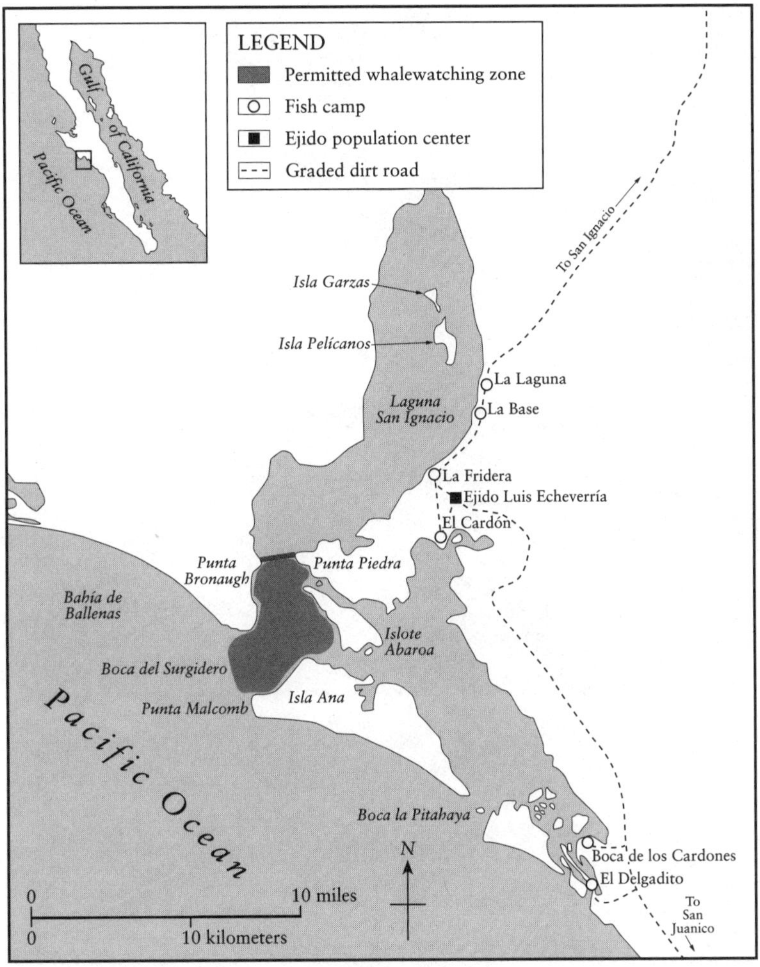

Map 2.2. San Ignacio Lagoon

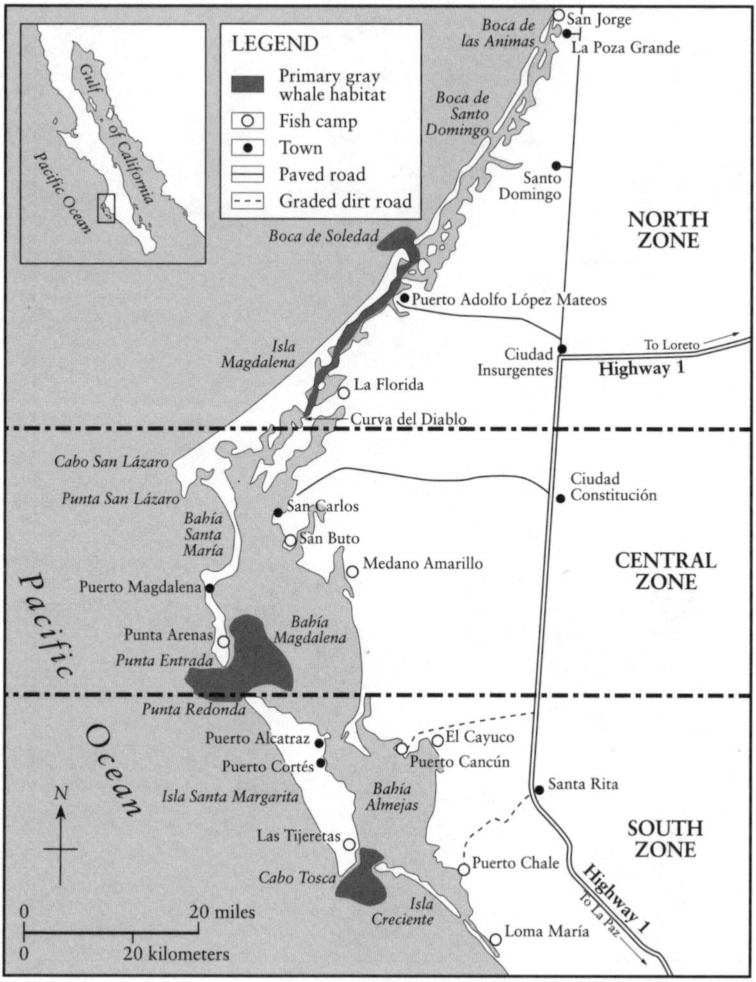

Map 2.3. Magdalena Bay

high of 255 in 1981. Biologists counted 139 in the southern entrance of the bay in 1980.[7]

What becomes apparent after reviewing studies on the use of the Baja California Sur lagoons by gray whales is that less than a third of the total population uses the lagoons during the period from January to April. The majority of the population is spread out between Alaska and the upper portion of the Sea of Cortez. The fact that many animals do not enter the lagoons does not diminish their importance for maintaining the long-term health of the population. The long-term viability of the eastern Pacific population of gray whales is dependent on the protection of their core reproduction and mating habitats—Scammon's Lagoon, San Ignacio Lagoon, and Magdalena Bay—and feeding habitats in the Bering and Chukchi Seas.

Gray whales display a number of behaviors in the lagoons not often observed in the open sea. They often "breach"—leap out of the water—from two or three times to twenty times in a row. Explanations of why they breach include attempts to get rid of parasites, courtship displays, or merely "playfulness." Gray whales often appear to "play" in the surf at the lagoon entrances, so much so that an observer in Magdalena Bay noted that the animals surf "just as a man would . . . in front of the crest of the waves."[8] Captain Charles Scammon, a whaling captain and frequent visitor to the lagoons of Baja California during the mid to late 1800s, observed gray whales at the mouth of Scammon's Lagoon playing in the breakers and "going through the surf."[9]

A second behavior that gray whales often engage in is "spyhopping"—pushing themselves vertically out of the water for up to thirty seconds. When they are spyhopping, gray whales appear to be observing the area around them. In many cases, however, the eyes of spyhoppers remain underwater when they surface.[10] A third behavior frequently observed in the lagoons is bubble blasting—the release of large amounts of air underwater. As the bubbles rise to the surface they turn into a "circular mass of bubbles."[11] Bubble blasting may be an avoidance or disturbance response to human activities or noise, or perhaps a method of regulating buoyancy. By expelling large amounts of air, the mammals can sink to lower depths and avoid detection.[12]

The time gray whales spend inside and directly outside the Mexican lagoon entrances is most often utilized for mating, and sometimes for other activities. Up to twenty animals at a time will engage in sexual activity, making it impossible for a human observer to determine paternity.[13] Foreplay is particularly frenzied, with groups of two to three whales rolling about and splashing the surface for hours. When calves are old enough to explore the lagoon with their mothers and to begin to socialize, they often participate in "play groups" of up to twenty mothers and their calves. In these groups the whales rub against each other, blowing giant bursts of bubbles.[14]

The behavior that whales are best known for is the curiosity some demonstrate toward humans. One of the first accounts of such behavior was by researcher Raymond Gilmore. Writing to a colleague in 1976, he mentioned "the Friendly Whale of San Ignacio Lagoon which for two weeks solicited care and attention from people in skiffs." According to Gilmore, tourists rubbed and petted the head of the whale "for hours at a time."[15]

"Friendly" whale behavior has increased since that first report in 1976. According to Jones and Swartz, the friendly-whale phenomenon rapidly expanded during the course of their research. Only a few whales engaged in such behavior in 1977 and 1978. Five years later scientists noted over two hundred such encounters with whales. That same year tourists from all thirty excursion boats that visited the lagoon touched whales.[16] Although it was initially in San Ignacio Lagoon where observers noted these whales, "friendlies" are now also encountered in Magdalena Bay and Scammon's Lagoon. There have even been reports of similar behavior along the west coast of Vancouver Island, British Columbia, and in the Bering Sea.[17]

Friendly behavior usually occurs around small tourist skiffs with outboard motors. Researchers speculate that the whales are attracted to the noise of the submerged engine running in neutral—the same frequency range as the sounds that whales make.[18] These whales will generally not follow skiffs operating at high speeds, preferring to approach them when they are either idling or traveling at low speeds. According to Antonio Aguilar, a longtime San Ignacio Lagoon whalewatching guide, "They often come up from behind, right near the outboard. I keep the engine idling, and then the whale moves over to the side of the skiff for a good look at the passengers." Whales generally avoid nonmotorized watercraft such as kayaks and canoes.

An encounter with a friendly whale is a remarkable experience. In many cases a calf will visit a tourist skiff with its mother. Tourists pet or rub the whales, and in many cases the whales rub against or lift the skiffs partially out of the water. The presence of one friendly whale may attract others, so at times tourist skiffs are surrounded by up to twenty curious animals.

Although researchers have noted both gray whale food resources and feeding behavior in the lagoons and along the coastal migratory corridor, these areas are not important to the nutritional needs of the population. Gray whales in the lagoons have been observed swimming against the tide with their mouths wide open, sieving plankton through their baleen and skimming the bottom of the lagoon.[19] During extreme low tides, exposed shoals in the middle of San Ignacio Lagoon, adjacent to the main channel near Rocky Point, reveal deep scooped-out pits that could be the result of whales filtering bottom sediment. However, the coastal lagoons of Baja California Sur do not provide sufficient food for the gray whales. Feeding in these areas seems to be opportunistic.

Researchers report a high level of acoustic activity among gray whales in their winter lagoons. Lower levels occur on their feeding grounds. Marilyn Dalheim argues that vocal signaling is important to achieve successful mating and to maintain contact between cows and calves in southern grounds.[20] Moreover, lowered acoustic activity outside the lagoons makes them less conspicuous to potential predators such as killer whales. Because killer whale predation is infrequent along the Pacific coast of Baja California Sur, vocalization in the lagoons does not appear to pose the same risk as in the northern reaches of gray whale range, such as the Bering and Chukchi Seas.

Human Exploitation

Because they tend to migrate close to the coastline, gray whales were easily hunted for subsistence by indigenous people in the Arctic Ocean and Okhotsk Sea and by other aboriginal groups in the Pacific. Although there are early Spanish reports of Cedros Island inhabitants hunting gray whales, native peoples in Baja California apparently did not engage in any systematic exploitation of these large marine mammals. Stranded and dead whales along the shoreline and within shallow lagoons did provide native groups with an occasional source of food.[21]

The colonization of Baja California by Jesuit missionaries during the eighteenth century had little impact on the gray whale population, which probably numbered around twelve thousand (see table 2.2).[22] Although Spaniards did not kill gray whales, detailed observations by Hispanic explorers and Jesuit missionaries along the coast of the peninsula alerted other European and American whalers to the abundance of commercially valuable whales.

Magdalena Bay was the first lagoon in Baja California to be invaded by whalers. Whaling inside Magdalena Bay began in the winter of 1845–46 with the arrival of the Stonington ship *United States,* under Captain Joshua Stevens, and the New London ship *Hibernia,* under Captain James Smith. During that first season, whalers learned that taking mothers and their calves in the shallow enclosed lagoons could be dangerous. The death of the second mate and severe injuries to the first mate of the *United States* and numerous deaths and accidents in following years resulted in "devil-fish" being the most common term applied to this cetacean that is now called the "friendly whale."[23] Whalers also referred to grays as hard-heads, mussel-diggers, gray-backs, and rip-sacks.[24] In that first season, Stevens and Smith harpooned a total of thirty-two whales, for a yield of 1,440 barrels of oil based on the nineteenth century estimate of thirty-five barrels of oil per gray whale.[25]

Reports of the abundance of grays filtered back to whalers around the world. This initiated an era in which Magdalena Bay became the most important center for this lucrative trade. The gray whale population was severely damaged. From 1845 through 1874, American and European whalers killed approximately 3,300 gray whales in the lagoons and bays of Baja California (see table 2.3). More than half, approximately 2,100, were taken in Magdalena Bay—more than any other single location along the Pacific coast of the peninsula. In their search for whales, whalers did not just restrict themselves to the lagoons and bays of Baja California. Ships spread along the eastern Pacific coastline, killing approximately 8,100 whales after 1845.[26] Despite the initial interest in whaling inside the peninsula's lagoons, whalers soon learned that it was difficult and dangerous work. A Mexican government official estimated that the 42 or so whaling vessels that arrived in Magdalena Bay from 1845 to 1848 captured about 338 whales, for an average of 8 per ship.[27] Whaling in the bay was discontinued from 1848 to 1851. During the 1852–53 season, when

Table 2.2 Population Estimates for the Eastern Pacific Gray Whale, 1800–1988

Year	Population Estimate
1800	12,000[1]
1845	15,000–20,000[2]
1875	4,400
1952–1953	2,894[3]
1954–1955	3,603
1956–1957	4,454
1967–1968	12,921[4]
1968–1969	12,070
1969–1970	12,597
1970–1971	10,707
1971–1972	9,760
1972–1973	15,099
1973–1974	14,696
1974–1975	12,955
1975–1976	14,520
1976–1977	15,304
1977–1978	16,879
1978–1979	13,104
1979–1980	16,364
1980–1981	—
1981–1982	16,000
1982–1983	—
1983–1984	—
1984–1985	21,443
1985–1986	20,113
1986–1987	—

[1] Estimate is from Reilly 1981 cited in Reeves and Mitchell 1988:378. Low population figure is based on aboriginal removal rate of approximately 600 per year.

[2] Estimate is from Henderson 1972:185.

[3] The 1952–1957 data are from Gilmore 1960:26.

[4] The 1967–1988 data are from Buckland et al. 1993:247 with the exception of the 1981–1982 data, which is based on an estimate from Reilly et al. 1983 cited in Jones and Swartz 1986:47.

Table 2.3 Summary of Gray Whales Killed by Whalers in Baja California Sur Bays and Lagoons, 1846–1926

Location	Date	Whales Killed
Scammon's Lagoon	1855–1865	606
	1866–1874	30
San Ignacio Lagoon and adjacent waters	1855–1865	374
	1866–1874	55
Magdalena Bay	1846–1854	550–605
	1855–1865	1,375
	1866–1874	165
	1924–1926[1]	141[2]
Total		3,296–3,351

Sources: The 1846–1874 data are from Henderson 1972:256–257. The 1924–1926 data are from Reeves 1984:191.

[1] Specific catch data for lagoons are not available after 1926, although whaling ships continued to catch whales off the coast of Baja California Sur until 1935.

[2] Includes up to 10 whales from Cabo San Lucas.

whaling resumed, Captain Curry of the San Francisco–based *Aquetnet* harpooned only four whales from late-December to mid-February. Other whalers reported no catches at all.[28]

The boom years of whaling at Magdalena Bay occurred from 1845 to 1847 and from 1851 to 1865, when 125 whaling vessels killed approximately fifteen hundred gray whales.[29] According to Scammon, the years 1856 to 1861 were most productive for Magdalena Bay: 34,425 barrels of oil brought $516,375.[30]

Scammon sailed to Magdalena Bay during his first whaling voyage to Baja California in 1855 on the *Leonore,* a 370-ton, square-sail, three-masted ship. He returned in 1856, the peak year for whaling.[31] Seventeen ships harpooned 250 whales, by far the largest number harvested in any single year.[32] Killing that many whales was not easy. Scammon reported that devil-fish were so dangerous that before one was captured, "two skiffs were entirely destroyed while the others were staved fifteen times."

Of his crew of eighteen, "six were badly jarred, one had both legs broken, another three ribs fractured, and still another was so injured internally that he was unable to perform duty during the rest of the voyage."[33]

Residents of Magdalena Bay found work flensing discarded carcasses and selling the oil they retrieved to the whaling ships. This process, called "carcassing," involved rendering discarded or "stinker" whales by "trying out the fat" from the intestines, hearts, and lungs. Up to three to four barrels of oil could be obtained from each carcass in this manner.[34]

The impact of the slaughter of so many gray whales throughout their migratory route and the recklessness of killing mothers and calves — the core reproductive stock of any animal population — was never a concern to an industry focused on maximizing profits for investors. In January 1867, however, when American adventurer and reporter J. Ross Browne visited Magdalena Bay, there were only two whaling ships present. According to Browne, gray whales were "becoming scarce, so much, indeed, as to render their pursuit no longer profitable."[35] Indeed, after 1865 few whaling ships ventured inside Magdalena Bay. They harpooned gray whales offshore instead.

Whalers expanded their search for gray whales and soon discovered other lagoons to the north. The first whaler to scout San Ignacio Lagoon was Captain Pool of the bark *Sarah Warren,* who unsuccessfully attempted to pass through the main entrance in 1858.[36] During the summer of 1859, the *Sarah Warren* and another ship found a safe passage into the lagoon. The *Sarah Warren* returned in December to hunt whales, accompanied by the schooner *Kate* and the barks *Ocean Bird* and *Carib.* The *Kate* was the first ship that "passed the bar" into the main part of the lagoon. In a few days all four ships had entered safely.[37]

During that first season, a total of eight ships took about thirty-five hundred barrels of gray-whale oil from the lagoon.[38] The following season (1860–61) four ships and a small shore party filled forty-seven hundred barrels. The name La Freidera (now known as La Fridera) was given to a site on the southern shore of the lagoon used as a tryworks. The same name was given to a beach at the mouth of the Boca de Soledad in Magdalena Bay just opposite the site where Puerto Adolfo López Mateos sits today.

Oil obtained for the first two-year period was worth an estimated $123,000. From 1859 to 1874 approximately 440 whales were killed inside the lagoon and in the waters of Ballenas Bay.[39] However, the lagoon did not sustain intensive whaling. Scammon reported in 1869 that, "this limited whaling-ground very soon gave out, and . . . the place [San Ignacio Lagoon] is no longer regarded as valuable for that purpose."[40]

The Best Gunnery Range in the Pacific

The gray whale population experienced a sharp decline after the 1870s. During the first few years, the population probably reached its lowest levels. It was during this time that the United States government made at least one of the Baja California Sur whale lagoons completely uninhabitable for whales. From 1904 to 1910 the U.S. Navy used Magdalena Bay as a practice gunnery and bombing range during the months when gray whales were present.

Gray whales are extremely sensitive to noise. Acoustical experiments conducted in San Ignacio Lagoon in 1984 by researcher Marilyn Dalheim highlighted the threats of man-made noise in the enclosed lagoons. After a month of experiments in which 120 hours of prerecorded sounds were played in the lagoon (ranging from industrial noise to killer whale sounds), Dalheim found that the whale count in early March was 81 percent lower than the mean count of 223 whales for the five-year period from 1978 to 1982.[41] If the playback of prerecorded sounds caused gray whales to abandon San Ignacio Lagoon, one can only imagine the effect that the intensive shelling of Magdalena Bay had on them.

There does not appear to be any logical reason for the Mexican government to have permitted this activity. Perhaps dictator Porfirio Díaz felt that allowing the U.S. Navy to destroy a bay already owned by American speculators was a way to further ingratiate himself with the U.S. government.[42] Permission for the activities of U.S. naval ships came directly from Don Porfirio himself.

From 1904 to 1907, the Mexican government provided permission for many of the boats of the navy's Pacific Fleet to use the bay for target practice. Magdalena Bay was only a short trip from California ports. San Diego–and San Francisco–based ships made frequent use of Mexico's open invitation to engage in target practice. In January 1904, the U.S.S. *Adams,* under Commander Charles E. Fox, shelled the bay with large cannons and guns. On March 2, 1906, the port captain counted seven U.S.

naval ships inside the bay. They ranged from the 1,000-ton U.S.S. *Princeton,* under Captain J. F. Marshall, to the 6,220-ton supply ship U.S.S. *Saturn,* under Captain J. W. Merill.[43]

The use of Magdalena Bay as a gunnery range by the U.S. Navy became known throughout the Pacific. In May 1904, an Italian battleship sailed in and requested permission to engage in gunnery practice. The request was denied.[44] Two years later, in August 1906, the Mexican government relented and gave the Italians permission to shell the bay as long as no land camps were made and guns were not pointed landward.

Ironically, although Díaz appeared to be unconcerned about the impact of gunnery activities on the bay, he seemed perturbed by the potential damage that sailors could have on the waterfowl of the area. In a response to the request from the U.S. Ambassador to Mexico that American sailors be allowed to hunt ducks, Díaz replied that only individuals with rifles could hunt.[45] Díaz also ordered naval ships not to fire on land nor allow troops to disembark, although that rule was not enforced.[46]

On December 16, 1907, Teddy Roosevelt's White Fleet — sixteen battleships strong — left Hampton Roads, Virginia, on the start of a 14,000-mile Latin American tour. Four months later, in March 1908, the fleet arrived at Magdalena Bay near the end of a tour that included stops in Trinidad, Rio de Janeiro, Punta Arenas, and Callao. By the time the fleet arrived in Magdalena Bay, it contained a total of twenty-eight ships and more than thirteen thousand sailors. Mexican government officials reported that from March 14 to 18, the fleet bombed the bay day and night.[47]

One can only imagine the impact of twenty-eight coal-burning ships, including sixteen of the largest battleships in the U.S. Navy. Scammon noted that whales left the bay as a result of the noise associated with whaling. The noise generated by whalers in the 1850s could not have come close to approximating the disturbance of the twenty-eight naval ships. Chief Turret Captain Roman J. Miller of the U.S.S. *Vermont* wrote, "All day long and half the night, the big guns boomed on the target ranges, the great hissing shells tore out across the smooth, unruffled waters of the bay. Guns of all sizes were fired, from the sharp, barking three-pounders to the ponderous, reverberating eight and twelve-inch turret guns."[48] The following year (1909), twenty-nine U.S. naval ships anchored inside the bay from March 16 to April 29.[49] Today, fishermen from around the bay talk of finding shells while fishing and diving.

Modern Whaling

Thirty years after American whalers withdrew and five years after the U.S. Navy left Magdalena Bay, Europeans took over the gray whale fishery. Modern commercial pelagic whaling with factory ships fueled a new round of gray whale exploitation, dominated by Norwegians after 1900. In 1913, the Mexican government granted a Norwegian factory ship and four catchers a license to operate in Magdalena Bay.[50] The first modern whaling vessel to do so was the *Capella I.* Norwegians took a total of nineteen whales off the coast of Baja California in 1914.[51]

The second "wave" of whaling occurred during the 1920s, when the Norwegian factory ships *Kommanddoren I* and *Mexico* killed 129 whales inside Magdalena Bay.[52] Raymundo Lucero of Puerto Adolfo López Mateos remembers Norwegians killing many whales in the 1920s with "exploding harpoons," which resulted in "lots of blood in the water."[53] Those two ships—along with another floating factory, the *Esperanza*—slaughtered a total of 181 gray whales, 1,568 humpbacks, 870 blue whales, 74 sei whales, 34 Bryde's whales, 8 fin whales, and 8 sperm whales off the Baja California coastline between 1924 and 1929.[54]

Juan Zuñiga, a fisherman from Punta Abreojos, north of San Ignacio Lagoon, told Scripps biologist Carl Hubbs in 1948 that he observed the Norwegian *Esperanza* hunting whales at the mouth of San Ignacio Lagoon around 1926 or 1927.[55] Foreign companies continued to harvest grays along the Baja California peninsula under Mexican concessions until 1937. Overhunting, combined with the collapse of the oil market and problems with financial allocations, contributed to the demise of whaling in Mexico. Commercial interests had shifted to the Antarctic Ocean.

The Current Status of Gray Whales

Beginning in 1946, gray whales rebounded, thanks to an international ban on harvesting the species and subsequent protective measures taken by Mexico. The current eastern Pacific stock is estimated at about twenty-one thousand and is probably increasing. The decision in 1994 to take the gray whale off the U.S. List of Endangered and Threatened Wildlife was made despite concerns that such an action was premature. Although gray whales are no longer hunted commercially in the Mexican lagoons, some potential threats have emerged in the past few years that could change their future status. New threats include renewed indigenous hunting of grays, Russian commercialization of gray whale products under the guise of indigenous subsistence whaling, development threats in Baja California Sur, and habitat degradation in summer feeding habitat.

In light of the gray whale's recovery, the International Whaling Commission (IWC) reclassified the gray whale from a protected to a sustained management stock in 1978 and set an annual quota of 169 whales to be taken by Siberian Natives in the Russian Federation in 1992, 1993, and 1994. No whales were harvested in 1992 or 1993. However, despite opposition from environmental groups, the Makah Indians of northern California have been granted permission by the IWC to harvest five gray whales annually. Some environmental groups believe that the renewed interest in Makah whaling forms part of a larger strategy by Japanese whaling interests to reverse the international ban on commercial whaling.[56]

Renewed Makah whaling is occurring at the same time that indigenous people in Siberia are commercializing gray whale products. One report confirmed that gray whales harvested for subsistence means are being fed to foxes raised for their fur. Villagers also sell gray-whale oil for industrial use.[57]

However, the biggest threat to gray whales is the degradation of their feeding, calving, and birthing habitats in the Bering and Chukchi Seas and in Baja California Sur. There is no other large cetacean that depends on such well-defined near-shore habitat for its survival. The biggest conservation challenge for the gray whale will be to coordinate habitat protection efforts and programs with three nations and regulate the predatory actions of Japanese and Russian whaling interests. Mitsubishi, a large Japanese company, is the main proponent and source of finance capital for a proposal to develop the world's largest salt harvesting facility at San Ignacio Lagoon. So far the world's biggest multinational corporation is being held back by a coalition of American and Mexican environmental groups. The gray whale is safe—for now. It will require a more concerted effort to insure that this marine mammal remains a "friendly whale" far into the future.

3 People and Gray Whales in Baja California Sur

During my first year here, I was out getting scallops one afternoon when I saw a big animal in the water. So I asked what it was, and someone told me it was a whale. Well, in Michoacán, where I'm from, everyone says that whales eat people. So I was kind of afraid of the whales. Now I know that whales don't eat people and I like them.

—WOMAN FROM SAN IGNACIO LAGOON

The last thing on the minds of the children from the two-room elementary school near San Ignacio Lagoon is the war in Chiapas, or the assassination of presidential candidate Luis Donaldo Colosio. These future guardians of the last undeveloped whale lagoon in Mexico live with their families in ramshackle houses without running water or electricity. The children sitting beside me in a small skiff want a closer look at the whales they have watched breaching and spyhopping all winter long.

As we round Rocky Point, one of the children jumps up and down in his seat shouting, "Look, there's a whale! Look, there's a whale!" An adult whale slowly surfaces, spouting. Alongside is a coal-black calf. The skiff driver idles the engine, and the young calf sticks its head out of the water.

Screaming with delight, the children rush to the front of the boat and take turns patting the calf—its mouth and eyes wide open—while the mother floats nearby. The whales have initiated a lifelong friendship with the future guardians of a habitat vital to their long-term survival.

The Gray Whale as a Symbol of a Coastal State

It is impossible to travel in Baja California Sur without running across someone who has interacted in one way or another with gray whales. The cetaceans inhabit more than the physical boundaries of the coastal lagoons they travel to each winter. They form part of the cultural geography of Baja California Sur, a desert state almost entirely surrounded by the ocean. Understanding the importance of gray whales to the identity of Baja California Sur provides insight into why the issue of their conservation has such a high profile there. Gray whales are part of the past and present everyday lives of the states' inhabitants.

Whales have been symbolically represented in Baja California for thousands of years. Pre-Columbian Indian populations painted their images in the caves and on the rocks in the Sierra de San Francisco northeast of San Ignacio Lagoon. Today, the annual arrival of gray whales in Baja California Sur reminds politicians and policy makers that gray whale conservation is a top priority. Because gray whales are so visible, these cetaceans receive considerably more attention than other more threatened and endangered animals such as sea turtles, pronghorn antelope, and bighorn sheep.[1]

The giant statue of a gray whale tail at the entrance to La Paz highlights the symbolic importance of the gray whale in Baja California Sur. The statue illustrates the ties the state has to the sea and is a reminder that the mammals encircle the state during their annual migration, often swimming into the beautiful but polluted Bay of La Paz during their travels north into the Sea of Cortez. During the months of February and March 1989, researchers Luis Fleischer and Octavio Maravilla counted fifty-four gray whales in the Bay of La Paz, some of which swam near the city's *malecón,* or boardwalk.[2] The visits of gray whales to the capital of Baja California Sur is a reminder that La Paz is the center for marine mammal research and conservation in Mexico. One of the few museums in La Paz is the Community Gray Whale Museum, a small facility at the edge of a cultural complex in the heart of the city. Founder and director Victor Ramos actively involves La Paz residents in all aspects of museum operations.

The arrival of whales to Baja California Sur has become an annual spectacle for tourists and the residents of the state. On weekends during the winter months, the residents of La Paz flock to Magdalena Bay to observe whales, an activity once enjoyed only by foreign tourists. Whalewatchers include Boy Scouts, nuns, grandmothers, politicians, and even the bishop of La Paz. Busloads of politicians and their wives arrive from the capital every weekend during the whale season to catch a glimpse of whales and picnic among the dunes of Magdalena Island. Decisions about gray whale conservation cannot be conveniently forgotten in Mexico's least-populated state. These marine mammals' yearly arrival en masse is a conspicuous reminder that the fishermen and the state's economy share the habitat with the gray whale.

The fact that relatively undeveloped and unaltered wetlands that provide critical habitat for thousands of migratory cetaceans exist within a day's drive of southern California is testament to the inaccessibility of the peninsula's Pacific coast. While Californians were busy dredging, diking, and filling in the bays of San Francisco and San Diego, the lagoons of Baja California Sur escaped much of the habitat destruction that caused the loss of more than 90 percent of California's coastal wetlands.

Baja California Sur has only four hundred thousand residents,[3] and only a few of them live around whale lagoons, but any increase in tourism and industrial development there could have an adverse impact on the gray whale population. If existing development proposals for Baja California Sur's coastal lagoons are realized, these once isolated areas will become centers for industry and tourism rather than whale refuges. The town of Guerrero Negro and the adjacent Scammon's Lagoon is the headquarters of the Exportadora de Sal Company, the largest producer of salt in the world. Ironically, the company, which harvests salt from the area around Scammon's Lagoon and plans to expand its operations to San Ignacio Lagoon, uses a gray whale as its logo. Proposals to build a paved road along the Pacific coast from the town of San Ignacio southward to Magdalena Bay could open up the coast to development. Today that would be unthinkable due to the area's isolation and vehicle-destroying dirt roads.

In the last ten years, the stretch of coastline between Cabo San Lucas and San José del Cabo at the southern tip of the peninsula has become an unplanned urban disaster. The Los Cabos tourist corridor is a parody of everything that is wrong with mega-resort coastal development. The stunning physical setting of Cabo San Lucas has been lost to the hotels, condos, and marinas that blot the view of Land's End. A four-lane highway connects Cabo San Lucas with the mission town of San José del Cabo. Shantytown *colonias* stand adjacent to high-end hotels. Gray whales and humpback whales that once spent peaceful winters here now dodge sportfishing boats and giant luxury liners.

Fishing Communities and Gray Whales

During the gray whale season, the residents of fishing communities along the Pacific coast often come into daily contact with gray whales. Families stand along the beach listening for spouts and observing the spectacle of breaching and spyhopping whales. One morning in January, my neighbor at San Ignacio Lagoon, Angel Ruelas, a lifelong fisherman and whale-watching guide, asked me excitedly, "Did you hear them spouting last night—whooooosh!"

Although tourism and industrial development are changing the coast-line on both coasts from La Paz around to Los Cabos, the rest of the state's Pacific coast is characterized by small fishing communities and the fisher-men and families who inhabit them. While many Baja California Sur coastal residents live next to the sea, many have their hearts in the moun-tainous Sierra *ranchos* where relatives remain.

The life of ranching, with its no-nonsense approach to wildlife and nature, greatly influences coastal people's attitudes toward whales. While he was dropping off fresh *carne asada* at his brother Antonio's house at San Ignacio Lagoon, Tatito Aguilar, a Sierra de Guadalupe rancher and former fisherman, talked to me one day about how to come up on a whale. "Of course we know how to approach whales here," he said. "It's just like dealing with a cow. You never come up on them from behind. Always from the side."

From the economic and political stronghold of the fishing coopera-tives of the Vizcaíno Peninsula north of San Ignacio Lagoon to the much weaker and smaller cooperatives and independent fishermen that dot the Pacific coast, earning a living from the sea has become a way of life in Baja California Sur. Pacific fishermen moved to the coastline only in the past sixty years. The establishment of cooperatives in the 1930s by President Lázaro Cárdenas was an attempt to promote the settlement and develop-ment of a Pacific coastline rich in fish and shellfish. Today the state is the most important supplier of abalone and Pacific lobster in Mexico. The high wholesale value of these species provides the economic basis for the majority of fishing settlements on the Pacific coast.

The residents of Bahía Tortugas, Bahía Asunción, La Bocana, Punta Abreojos, San Ignacio Lagoon, San Juanico, La Poza Grande, Puerto Ado-lfo López Mateos, San Carlos, Puerto Chale, and Bahía Magdalena are almost entirely dependent on fishing revenues. Farther south in Todos Santos, fishermen harvest lobster and dive for rock oysters. With a plum-meting economy and declining yields of fish and shellfish, many residents of coastal communities view whalewatching as one of the few alternatives to fishing.

Although the establishment of cooperatives promoted the growth of towns along the Pacific coast, it was the movement of ranchers from the mountains into the coastal area around San Ignacio Lagoon and Magdalena Bay during the 1920s that initiated fishing activities.[4] These ex-ranchers established small fish camps close to water holes throughout the coast. They survived by harpooning turtles and selling the meat to inland towns and ranching communities. They also traded with American and European whalers.

Some of these early fishermen, who descended from the settlements high in the Sierra de San Francisco, just north of San Ignacio, were probably already familiar with whales and other marine life of the Pacific and the Sea of Cortez. Pre-Columbian paintings in the mountains depict sea turtles, pelicans, bat rays, and whales.[5] The residents of mission towns and ranches around San Ignacio and Comondú fanned out to form the powerful fishing cooperatives of the Vizcaíno Peninsula and the fish camps and settlements strung out along the Pacific coast.

Today, hidden among the nooks and crannies of the coast are a profusion of tiny fish camps where fishermen and their families eke out a living harvesting pismo clams, mangrove oysters, corvina, sierra, and shark. These fishing communities are in remote coastal areas without paved access roads, sewers, electricity, running water, telephones, or mail service. Families spend much of their income, time, and energy obtaining basic necessities such as food, water, and propane. Life in remote coastal areas is symbolized by driving old Ford or Chevy pickup trucks with fifty-gallon water containers tied to their beds over suspension-destroying dirt roads ten or fifteen miles to the nearest ranch or town where water is available.

Often the presence of gray whales adds to the difficulties of making a living from the sea. One story relates the hardships of a father and son surrounded by a pod of whales in Scammon's Lagoon while tending lobster traps. Terrified for their lives, the fishermen held on to each other while waves from breaching whales engulfed their skiff. After what seemed like hours, the whales slowly moved away from the boat. But before they could catch their breath and relax, a giant whale emerged next to their panga, with its mouth wide-open and mischievous eyes flashing. Hugging each other in terror, they watched the animal sink back into the lagoon and swim away. The lobstermen quickly counted their blessings—and the lobsters remaining in the boat—thankful that their family, waiting patiently for them to return with the day's catch, would never realize what they went through every day to support them.[6]

Not all the residents of Baja California Sur believe that whales are a danger. Older fishermen, who remember accounts of devil-fish attacking whaling skiffs, generally keep their distance. Some enjoy the whale show while they tend their lobster traps or hand-line fish for *cabrilla*. Victor Arce, a fisherman who has spent more than sixty years at San Ignacio Lagoon, said, "I like to watch whales leaping, jumping, and playing around, but I'm far enough away to avoid trouble. No point in risking my boats, nets, outboard, and my life."

Although gray whales are not the only animals that inhabit the lagoons of Baja California Sur, they symbolize the lagoons to the outside world. Whales crowd the lagoon during the two or three short winter months. Their spirit remains when they are gone. Gray whales are like relatives home for the holidays. Lagoon residents are glad to see them arrive and sad but relieved after they leave so that the business of everyday life can get back on track.

The Magdalena Bay Gray Whale Festival

Similar to the ways in which Cajun communities in Louisiana celebrate their relationship with alligators and the bayous they live on, fishing communities in Magdalena Bay have adopted the gray whale as a symbol of their ties to the sea. The Magdalena Bay gray whale festival is a confirmation of the ways in which gray whales have become part of the cultural landscape of Baja California Sur. The annual event is an opportunity for politicians, fishermen, and tourists to celebrate the return of the gray whale to Baja California Sur each winter.

Gray whales have been a part of the lives of the non-Indian residents of Magdalena Bay since at least the 1850s, when local ranchers traded with American and European whalers. Many of the residents of the bay are descendants of American and European whalers who married local women from the mission towns or the mission settlements of the Comondú area.

Even after the initial round of whalers left the bay in the 1880s, the bones of the thousands of whales slaughtered were daily reminders of the legacy of whaling and the presence of gray whales. On December 7, 1914, when the *Mary Dodge*, under Captain A. H. Moore, sailed into

Magdalena Bay in search of guano, the people of Magdalena Island must have been elated. However, the *Mary Dodge* was not interested only in guano. Captain Moore offered to buy whale bones at ten pesos a ton. That was a good salary in the days when manual laborers were lucky to receive a peso a day in wages.

Moore's offer initiated a flurry of activity. Soon there were 125 tons of bones waiting on the beach. Captain Moore and his crew collected them and promised that when the *Mary Dodge* returned in a few months he would purchase any remaining bones. After the vessel set sail, islanders collected 200 tons of bones and left them on the beach of Magdalena Island's tiny port. By March 29, 1915, the *Mary Dodge* still had not returned. The giant pile remained waiting. The customs chief of Magdalena Bay wrote to the governor in La Paz wanting to know what he should do. "Are people allowed to sell bones without the permission of the government?" he asked.[7] The response from Brigadier General Felix Ortega was clear: the governor had no objection to poor people collecting bones as long as they paid the proper export duties.[8] A group of island residents asked the governor to allow them to collect all the bones they could, as it was the "only hope they had to alleviate their difficult situation."[9] The *Mary Dodge* never returned, and the bones remained on the beach—a testament to the legacy of destruction of the gray whales of Magdalena Bay.

Today, the gray whale festival is an opportunity to celebrate the abundance of gray whales rather than fight over their bones. The gray whale festival is a chance for the long-isolated residents of Mexico's largest gray whale habitat to remind state residents and politicians in La Paz and Mexico City that they are the custodians of the country's animal superstar.

Since 1994, the county of Comondú has sponsored the gray whale festival in Magdalena Bay with fireworks, concerts, and a Miss Gray Whale beauty pageant. The event draws residents from all over the state. According to Juan Rodríguez, a whalewatching guide from the town of Puerto Adolfo López Mateos, the mayor of La Paz originally lobbied to have the festival in the state capital. "How is La Paz going to celebrate a gray whale festival?" said Juan. "We're the ones surrounded by whales. This is where the festival should take place."

During the 1995 festival, children from the towns of Puerto Adolfo López Mateos and San Carlos were deputized by government officials to be voluntary "eco-inspectors" to safeguard the local environment of the bay and its gray whales. A quarrel between local whalewatching outfitters on the one hand and federal officials and foreign outfitter companies on the other over rights of access to whales was set aside. A youth whale conservation corps was created to show that whale protection is a community affair.

Choyeros, or cactus people, as native-born Baja California Sur residents refer to themselves, are proud to host gray whales and to participate in the gray whale festival. Visitors travel from afar to observe the gray whales. The festival illustrates that gray whales connect the isolated state of Baja California Sur with the Pacific Rim and the rest of the world. This became especially apparent during the first year of the festival in 1994, when it was held prior to the annual meeting of the IWC in Puerto Vallarta. Although gray whales are currently safe from commercial whalers, the proposal by Norway that year to resume the commercial harvest of minke whales was a threat, in the minds of Baja California Sur residents, to the survival of their whales. Suddenly it became clear that the gray whale was no longer just an animal whose winter home is Mexico but a species that depends on global cooperation for its survival.

Indignant about the apparent lack of First World concern for whales, Juan Rodríguez said, "If Mexico can refrain from killing whales, then I think Norway should be able to as well. I bet there is not one town in Norway that is as poor as Puerto Adolfo López Mateos is. If we don't kill whales, they shouldn't. Besides, whales are a lot more valuable alive than dead. Who is going to pay to see a dead whale?"

Whales are not the only attraction at the annual festival. According to a young Bimbo-bread truck driver from La Paz who gave me a lift on the empty road between Ciudad Constitución and Puerto Adolfo López Mateos, "The festival is great. There are lots of women and *cerveza*. This is the place to be. But *sabes una cosa*? [you know what?] They need to have cameras filming the whales hooked up to giant television screens. Then we could hang out here on the beach, drink beer, and watch the whales on TV without having to go out in pangas to watch them swim around."

The best evidence that gray whales are part of the state's cultural identity is that the locally famous smuggling clan, the Tomateros (Tomato boys), traveled to Puerto Adolfo López Mateos during the festival in 1994 with their solid-gold finger covers, gold chains and rings, 10-gallon hats, alligator shoes, and $30,000 custom four-by-four pickups—to go whale-watching. Whether or not the Tomateros and the rest of the state's inhabitants are concerned with the fate of gray whales is irrelevant. As a result of their participation in the festival, they have become de facto supporters of gray whale conservation.

The Gateway to the Gray Whale Lagoons

The forces of modernization are slowly transforming Baja California Sur from its historical isolation, but there is an exception: San Ignacio, an eighteenth-century date-palm oasis at the northern end of the state, where the native residents, or *panzas dulces,* passively resist the rapid pace of the twentieth century.[10]

Although San Ignacio is located in the middle of the peninsula, halfway between the Sea of Cortez and the Pacific Ocean, it is the historical gateway to the lagoons of Baja California Sur. The Cochimí Indians who inhabited this area prior to the arrival of the Spanish traveled to Scammon's and San Ignacio Lagoons from Kadakaaman, now known as San Ignacio, the largest oasis and source of water in the region. Before the transpeninsular highway was paved, local trucks used the dirt road that skirted San Ignacio Lagoon and Magdalena Bay along the Pacific coast, a route that today is used only by ranchers, fishermen, and tourists traveling to San Ignacio Lagoon and farther south to the fishing village of San Juanico.

The San Ignacio area, inhabited by about two thousand people, is famous throughout the peninsula. Mention a visit to the town to any native choyero, and a round of jokes about the town's idle inhabitants is told. San Ignacio is where burros wear tennis shoes and the vocal chords of roosters are severed to avoid waking up an entire town of *dormilones* (sleepyheads). In reality, the residents of San Ignacio are far from lazy. The town derives its reputation from the fact that many of its inhabitants are fishermen, who earn good wages by collecting abalone and lobster and spend a few months each year in their adobe and concrete-block houses in San Ignacio. Other residents are retired from a hard life of fishing in San Ignacio Lagoon or diving for abalone at Punta Abreojos. While at home, people putter around their gardens and invariably head toward the tree-shaded plaza dominated by a 200-year-old church to gossip. In the plaza you'll hear about Ricardo Aguilar, who boarded a Norwegian whaling vessel in the 1930s; the German mechanic who doused himself with gasoline and immolated himself after losing his patience with a difficult engine ("*Muy corrajudo,*" very short-tempered); or the postal clerk who has unsuccessfully attempted suicide four times — the last time by jumping off the top of a windmill. If you're thirsty, ask one of the *rancheros* waiting around the plaza in their beat-up Ford pickups if they have any date tequila or homemade wine.

To understand the relationship among choyeros, whales, and conservation, one must travel off the main highway to the ranchos set in palm-fringed canyons surrounded by cactus and mesquite. Here friends and family sit together in the shade and talk. Some days there is a visiting relative from *el otro lado* (the other side of the border — the United States), nursing his hangover, listening to *corridos* and talking about the old days when whalers sailed the coast and fishermen harpooned sharks and sea turtles with whales swimming around with them.

One afternoon I visited Ricardo Aguilar in his palm-thatched house a few blocks from the main plaza. Ricardo had been born and raised in Cadeje, an oasis village located in a palm-filled canyon about 7 miles north of San Juanico (halfway between Magdalena Bay and San Ignacio Lagoon). As we spoke he continued to work on a pair of two-tone leather *zapatones*. He told me the story of his visit to the Norwegian whaling ship sixty years earlier.

"In May 1935," he said, "I had just returned from my father's ranch in Cadeje after a week of loading salt near San Ignacio Lagoon. One day, while tending cattle a few kilometers from the ranch, I spotted a couple of strangers walking in from the south. They were hot and thirsty and could barely speak Spanish. They managed to tell me that they came from a ship anchored off San Juanico and wanted to buy some beef. I offered them water, loaded them up on my horse, and brought them back to the ranch, where my father sold them six head of cattle. They were pretty happy and invited me and my brothers to visit their ship."

The next day, the Aguilar brothers stood on the cliffs of San Juanico and spied the largest ship they had ever seen. They had no inkling that this was the last whaling vessel to work the southern Baja coastline. Ricardo caught the attention of the crew, who sent over a skiff to bring them aboard. Once on deck, the Aguilars watched dumbfounded as the hundred-member crew cut up the whales they had just harpooned.

The vessel boarded by the Aguilar brothers was probably the *Esperanza,* a Norwegian-Mexican factory ship that in the spring of 1935 made a final voyage, bringing 3,821 barrels of whale oil home to Norway.[11] It is fitting that the *Esperanza* was the first and last whaling ship Ricardo ever saw. He was a witness to the end of whaling in Baja California. It was a good omen for his future nephew, Antonio Aguilar, who works as a whalewatching guide at San Ignacio Lagoon.

On a hot late afternoon in October, I found Elario Gutiérrez at Tota's Restaurant, just off the plaza. Don Elario is seventy-eight and has the handsome and fit look of a lifelong fisherman. Although no longer a resident of San Ignacio, Don Elario was visiting his birthplace for a few days to relive old memories, play the guitar, and fill his pickup with dates, which he will give to his neighbors back north in Ensenada.

Over beer and shrimp, the retired fisherman told me about life in San Ignacio. "It was a hard life when I was a child here," he said. "There was no work, and if you were lucky enough to find a job, it only paid a peso a day. Once in a while, my father would load up our burro with supplies and plenty of water and we'd walk to La Laguna to catch sea turtles. On one trip we arrived when the whales were still there. I had never seen a whale before and I was amazed. They were all over the lagoon, jumping around and playing. I spent most of my life fishing and watching whales, but I'll never forget my first sight of those creatures. They were big—they sure were big."

Álvaro ("Varo") Aguilar, a stocky, bearlike diver who works as a whalewatching guide during the winter, walked over to me one morning while I waited in the plaza for the bus to Ensenada. When Varo is not fishing on the coast, he passes the time in town playing dominoes and visiting with his friends at the plaza. The previous year he had worked for an American scientist conducting radio-tracking research on gray whale calves. "They had some really expensive equipment," Varo said while kicking a soccer ball to his nephew on the other side of the square. "Transmitters cost thousands of dollars, and losing one is a real problem. We managed to attach one to a calf, but the thing fell off after a few hours. The scientist couldn't afford to replace it, so we searched all over the lagoon for that thing. Finally, around the time it was getting dark, we found it somewhere along the mangroves. He was pretty lucky."

Gray whales are living symbols of the rugged, changing world that the fishing people of Baja California Sur inhabit. While older fishermen still avoid the migrating whales, their sons and grandsons who work as tourist outfitters get as close to them as possible. Their relationship with whales, however, underscores the ability of choyeros to accept and negotiate the changing world they live in. It also reflects the importance of symbolism and cultural values in conservation. Conservation is more than a political process. It intersects with the way people live, perceive, and interact with the animals and landscape around them. It is that world that conservation inhabits as it leaves the offices of bureaucrats, policy makers, and politicians in Mexico City and La Paz. The ways in which people share their lives with whales pave the way for gray whale conservation.

4 The Origins of Gray Whale Conservation in Mexico

We found nothing on the shore save an old leathern vat for straining oil, and the carcass of a whale, over which myriads of buzzards were hovering. The air was heavily laden with the stench. Two or three half-breeds, who contrive to live in some mysterious way, were lazily reclining under the bushes, as if time and business were matters of no concern to them.

—J. ROSS BROWNE, 1868

On December 6, 1971, Mexican President Luis Echeverría made an important and unprecedented contribution to the conservation of marine mammals internationally: he established a gray whale reserve at Scammon's Lagoon. The declaration of Scammon's Lagoon as a protected area initiated a seventeen-year period in Mexico (1971–1988) that resulted in four pieces of legislation for gray whale habitat protection. This culminated in the establishment of the Vizcaíno Biosphere Reserve on November 30, 1988, by President Miguel de la Madrid. This reserve includes Scammon's and San Ignacio Lagoons, as well as the entire central portion of the peninsula from the Pacific Ocean to the Sea of Cortez. No other habitat is so vital to the survival of a cetacean as the Vizcaíno Biosphere Reserve.

The passage of whale protection legislation was a remarkable achievement for a less-developed country. While its rich and powerful neighbors to the north squabbled over hunting quotas for scientific purposes, Mexico accepted the responsibility for the protection of animals it viewed as "Mexican by birth."

Were the actions taken by three successive Mexican presidents to protect gray whales a unique series of events that truly reflected an altruistic concern for the survival of whales? Were they part of a larger historical trend toward protecting economically important species? The answer to both questions is yes. Efforts by Mexico's postrevolutionary governments to protect endangered marine mammals in Baja California Sur culminated in the establishment of the first whale reserves. The wave of legislation catalyzed by Echeverría in 1971 fits into a larger historical pattern, which began after the Mexican Revolution, of using conservation laws to reestablish national sovereignty over economically important wildlife species and identifying resources predominantly exploited by foreigners. Gray whale protection was a postrevolutionary response to resource extraction and depletion by foreigners that reveals how nationalism plays a powerful role in the way governments perceive natural resources. The conservation of natural resources in Baja California Sur and their legal protection was "an act of the purest form of national sovereignty."[1]

Formal gray whale conservation in Mexico is a legacy of the state-sponsored conservation that began toward the end of the rule of dictator Porfirio Díaz (1900–1910) and continued through the revolutionary period (1911–1920) and into the 1970s, when gray whale reserves were established. These historical forces resulted from: (1) attempts to identify and assess economically important natural resources, including flora and fauna in Baja California, from the turn of the century into the revolutionary period; (2) postrevolutionary conservation measures designed to protect useful mammals in danger of extinction and establish national control over important resource zones; (3) Mexico's representation on the IWC and its participation in the international ban on the commercial harvest of gray whales; and (4) the influence of Mexican and American scientists and government officials who initiated a three-decade campaign to have gray whale lagoons in Mexico declared protected areas.

Surveys and Science

In 1861, Teodoro Riveroll, the governor of the southern district of Baja California, reported to President Benito Juárez that although the peninsula was an excellent location for fishing, there was not one large Mexican commercial fishing boat in the entire territory. The problem of not having a fishing fleet, according to Riveroll, was compounded by the fact that "Every year more than twenty whaling ships arrive at the bays, wetlands, lagoons, and coast of the territory, especially Magdalena Bay, without permission." Riveroll did not want to stop whaling, however. He wanted to permit it to be undertaken "by Mexican boats whose captain and crew are Mexican."[2]

Riveroll's letter illuminates a particular problem associated with the history of Mexican economic development: much of the nation was unknown to the government officials who controlled the political and economic life of the country. This ignorance about the nation's resources by those charged with promoting development enabled foreigners to exploit Mexico's natural heritage. How could Mexico initiate whaling to compete with its American neighbors if no one knew how many whales swam along its coastline? Such a dearth of information became particularly obvious during the Porfiriato (the rule of dictator Porfirio Díaz from 1876 to 1910) and even more so during the postrevolutionary period. Faced with a nation devastated by war, government officials promoted the development of Mexico for Mexicans.

With respect to conservation, what was unknown could not be saved. In Baja California, whales and a wide range of plants, animals, and minerals were exploited almost exclusively by foreigners. To ensure the future of resources, such as marine mammals, they would have to be "saved" from foreign hands. The results of surveys carried out would be cataloged by administrators serving the needs of the nation. Resources could then be exploited by Mexicans who would help to promote national economic development.

These surveys provided the foundation for future conservation actions designed to protect marine mammals, and they illustrate how conservation endeavors are tied to issues beyond the boundaries of the environment. It is this nationalist response to the plunder of Mexico's natural resources that ultimately led Mexico to establish the first gray whale reserve in 1971.

The Porfiriato

It must have been frustrating for government officials at the turn of the century in Mexico City. They were charged with devising economic plans, initiating development projects, facilitating the modernization of a booming but foreign-dominated economy, but they lacked the facts and statistics on which to base their "scientifically" derived decisions about the nation's resources. To resolve the dearth of information about natural resources, in 1909 the Ministry of Industry formed the Exploratory Commission of National Flora and Fauna. In November of that year, the commission sent letters to governors throughout Mexico requesting information on all known animals and plants. In the southern district of Baja California, this request led the governor to delegate the responsibility of collecting data to the district's mayors.[3]

The mayor of Comondú, whose jurisdiction included Magdalena Bay, reported an abundance of whales, sharks, dolphins, groupers, crabs, swordfish, clams, shrimp, and sardines.[4] In San José del Cabo, whales of all classes were reported to be abundant, along with dolphins, sea turtles, yellowtail, lobsters, and bat-rays.[5] The mayor of La Paz wrote to the governor that there was no information on the flora and fauna of the peninsula because, "if any foreign naturalists have gone through the peninsula and made studies over particular species, they are only known in the United States and France, where they were probably published."[6]

This comment is particularly revealing. Not only were foreign industrialists and pirates exploiting the resources of the country, but foreign scientists and naturalists—cataloging and reporting on the exotic and valuable species—were viewed as advance scouts of the industrial world. The legacy of this resentment by Mexican politicians and policy makers toward foreign scientists continues to this day.

The Revolution

Although President Francisco Madero had a difficult time dealing with conflicts between factions in the country, his administration organized the conservation and utilization of the nation's resources. By 1912 it had become clear that despite the attempt to catalog flora and fauna, little was known about Mexico's resources. As a result, the Ministry of Industry declared that the state of "useful animals" was deplorable due to the overexploitation of animal stocks by foreign concessionaires. To rectify this situation, the ministry called for information on potential lands available for parks and forest reserves, along with the useful birds and mammals that inhabit them and "that are worthy of protection and conservation."[7] To initiate this project, the federal government determined that a total of 15,803,528 hectares were available throughout the entire country for the establishment of national parks. These included 1.5 million hectares in the southern district of Baja California (see table 4.1).

In response to the request for information, the governor asked the mayors to comment on the species and resources of each county that might be in need of protection. The mayor of Todos Santos told the governor that carrying out such a project "would be quite difficult." A different perspective came from Comondú and Triunfo, where mammals such as deer,

Table 4.1 Location and Size of Proposed National Parks and Forest Reserves in Mexico, 1912

Region	Area (in hectares)
Baja California Distrito Sur	1,500,000
Campeche	1,344,000
Chiapas	97,400
Chihuahua	3,103,000
Coahuila	219,000
Durango	1,164,854
Guerrero	1,100,000
Quintana Roo	0
San Luis Potosí	92,476
Sierra de la Parida (in Zacatecas, Jalisco, Tepic)	55,040
Sinaloa	108,000
Sonora	5,350,000
Tabasco	118,580
Istmo de Tehuantepec	1,400,000
Tepic	0
Veracruz	9,682
Yucatán	55,691
Zacatecas	85,805
Total	15,803,528

Source: Secretario de Estado 1912.

jackrabbits, pronghorn antelope, and quail were deemed worthy of protection. The mayor of Mulege informed the governor that there were no appropriate lands for parks or forest reserves. Nor were there any useful animals at the point of extinction, because "nobody is dedicated to their destruction."[8]

Various responses were undertaken after the overthrow of President Madero by Victoriano Huerta in February 1913. Remarkably, despite intensive and often violent political conflict during the revolutionary period, bureaucrats in Mexico City still concerned themselves with resource management and the nation's wildlife. Despite foreign military intervention and general strikes, the bureaucracy forged ahead with resource surveys. Under President Venustiano Carranza, who overthrew Victoriano Huerta in 1914, agencies continued the collection of information about the nation's riches. Given the upheaval in Mexico, it is doubtful that data gathered by previous administrations were available for new policy makers. As a result, in July 1917 President Carranza authorized the Ministry of Development to form the Agency of Land, Water, Forest and Archaeological Inspections. The new agency would provide "immediate and efficient" information and furnish statistics about the location and means of exploiting the nation's resources.[9] An agency office was opened in La Paz.[10] It is no coincidence that Carranza's new agency formed after the creation of the Constitution of 1917. Under Article 27 of that revolutionary document, the Mexican state had ownership over water and mineral resources as well as the right to regulate private property. In addition, Article 27 of the Constitution also granted only native-born or naturalized Mexicans the right to own property in Mexico. The Constitution of 1917 established the nationalist foundation of future environmental policies, programs, and legislation.

After the Revolution

With the fall of President Carranza and the rise of the government of Álvaro Obregón in 1920, a period of semistabilization appeared in Mexican politics. Information on the biological and natural resources was still needed. In 1920, the Office of Biological Studies of the Ministry of Agriculture announced an ambitious plan to incorporate resource data into a general map of Mexico that the Office of Geographic and Climatological Studies would prepare. The map would help "discover and exploit the natural products" of Mexico. The governor of southern Baja California was asked to assist by funding the costs of an expedition to report on the "forests, coasts, lakes and minerals" of the peninsula.[11]

Six years later, the Office of Biological Studies sent out researchers to study the "marine riches of the Republic, especially those that are exploited on a large-scale and whose conservation is urgently needed." Investigative teams visited Veracruz and Ensenada to (1) document oceanographic conditions; (2) survey marine flora and fauna; (3) classify species for the Museum of Natural History; (4) ascertain the commercial and industrial value and appropriate closed seasons for species; (5) determine the capacity, conditions, and size of the fishing zone; and (6) determine ways of repopulating or protecting commercial species that had been reduced considerably and propose reserves to protect endangered species.[12]

During this period, information about marine and terrestrial flora and fauna was acted upon by foreign whalers. Norwegian whalers sailed the coast of Baja California harpooning blue whales, sperm whales, gray whales, and humpback whales. The whalers provided Mexican authorities with a rough idea of the economic potential of such an industry. A report written in 1927 by an inspector with the Ministry of Agriculture discussed the "considerable quantity of whales" that surrounded the peninsula and the abundance of whales found between Cabo San Lucas and Magdalena Bay. Although the inspector overlooked gray whales, he listed sperm whales, blue whales, humpbacks, and finback whales. All were species, he argued, that should be protected from whaling ships during their breeding season.[13]

Surveys expressed the will of the government to engage in conservation for utilitarian motives. Attitudes in such reports and proclamations reveal the notion of protecting natural resources for the good of the nation and a preoccupation with the state of the "natural riches" of a country subjected to a long period of intensive exploitation. Conservation was a by-product of the need to catalog resources, to "protect" these resources from foreigners and, for the first time in Mexican history, put them to use for the good of the Mexican people. This utilitarian attitude still permeates resource policies and agencies and has led to a conflict between officials interested in biodiversity preservation and resource exploitation.

Early Efforts to Protect Marine Mammals

Similar to the United States, early conservation efforts in Mexico were aimed at forest management, especially in the area of Mexico City, where industrialization and population growth increased demands for fuel wood.

The first national park, Desierto de los Leones, established in 1876 outside of Mexico City (an area now completely enveloped by the city), protected an important aquifer. Miguel Angel de Quevedo, the Gifford Pinchot of Mexico, pioneered early efforts to implement a national resource management policy.[14]

In 1901 Quevedo founded the first agency to deal with resource issues: the Central Assembly of Forestry. Illustrating the continuity in many agencies despite revolutionary upheaval in Mexico, Quevedo continued in the employ of the federal government, moving through the bureaucratic ranks of the Ministry of Agriculture and Development. He helped create the Forest Service in 1910 and the Department of Forests, Hunting and Fishing in 1914. From 1934 to 1940, Quevedo pushed Lázaro Cárdenas to create thirty-six national parks throughout the country, an accomplishment not matched by any of his successors.[15]

Early mammal conservation laws protected species subject to indiscriminate hunting, mostly by Americans, off the coast of Baja California. Little attention was paid to the plight of gray whales and other large cetaceans. The first law prohibited the hunting of sea lions on the Coronado Islands near the Mexico–U.S. border.[16] President Álvaro Obregón enacted legislation banning the hunting of manatees in 1921.[17] Laws passed in 1934, 1945, and 1981 placed manatees off-limits to hunters.[18]

In the early 1920s, members of the California Academy of Sciences undertook an expedition to Guadalupe Island to survey wildlife. After the visit they requested that President Obregón protect the few remaining elephant seals and Guadalupe fur seals on the island. Obregón passed legislation that outlawed hunting on Guadalupe Island in 1922.[19] Legislation prohibiting the hunting of elephant seals and Guadalupe fur seals throughout Mexico was passed in 1933.[20]

Although the federal government enacted decrees protecting nearly extinct marine mammals such as the elephant seal and the Guadalupe fur seal, it permitted whaling off Baja California for the endangered but commercially valuable gray whale. The federal government viewed whaling as an industrial activity in which Mexico could participate in the future and permitted foreign companies to harpoon throughout the 1920s. A condition of the whaling permit was that Mexican observers be placed on whaling vessels.[21]

Early legislative efforts to protect the nation's resources laid the foundation for future resource management programs in Mexico. Early marine mammal laws imparted a sense of obligation on the part of environmental policy makers, bureaucrats, and politicians. They encouraged policy makers to protect species considered uniquely Mexican and part of the national patrimony.

For policy makers, marine mammals such as gray whales point to the need to continue a tradition of protecting Mexican resources from foreign exploitation. Marine mammal protection is a small part of the foundation of the principles that the Mexican Revolution stood for—Mexico for Mexicans. These principles have been abandoned in practice by the ruling elite but are important symbols of the revolutionary legacy.

Internationalizing the Gray Whale

An important element in the history of gray whale conservation in Mexico is the country's participation in international regulatory bodies. This international dimension of whale conservation and research also provided Mexico with a forum to demonstrate its responsibility vis-à-vis conservation. This compares favorably with the whaling records of First World countries such as the United States, Russia, Japan, and Norway. Mexico earned international prestige by participating in these forums. Because the country did not have a whaling industry, it risked very little and gained a great deal from its efforts to protect the animals from whalers at home and abroad and reinforced its decision to protect the gray whale.

Mexico first participated in international forums to protect whales in 1933, when the federal government recognized the Geneva Convention for the Protection of Whales. The convention was the first international effort to regulate the whaling industry, whose activities threatened to drastically reduce the population of the world's large whales. Originally adopted by twenty-six countries in September 1931, the convention provided guidelines for the whaling industry by banning the harvest of calves, sexually immature whales, and lactating mothers. It also required the licensing of whalers and the submission of statistics on harvest yields by whaling companies to the Committee for Whaling Statistics.[22]

The International Agreement for the Regulation of Whaling, approved by nine whaling nations in 1937, provided a limited amount of protection to gray whales.[23] Article 4 of the agreement forbids the killing of gray whales and right whales. Nations that signed the agreement that had previously harvested gray whales included the United States and Norway. Canada signed the agreement in 1938.[24] At the 1946 meeting of the International Whaling Convention, also known as the "Washington Convention," the gray whale was again declared off-limits to commercial whalers. Oddly enough, Mexico was the only country invited to the first postwar conference regarding whaling (attended by nineteen countries) that did not attend.[25] Mexico joined the International Whaling Convention in 1949.[26]

While environmentalists criticize the IWC for its thinly veiled attempts to "scientifically" justify the indiscriminate slaughter of the world's whales, imposing an international ban on the commercial harvest of gray whales in 1946 was the most effective action it has ever taken. The ban offered an opportunity for the species to return to its probable preexisting population, a miraculous recovery for a critically threatened species.

In 1951, Japan became the last whaling nation to sign the agreement providing the gray whale with protection from countries along its migratory route.[27] Gray whales have not been legally harvested off the coast of Mexico since the Norwegian-Mexican factory ship *Esperanza* sailed the coast of Baja California in 1935.

However, a major problem with the ban is that some countries invoked Article 10 of the 1937 agreement, which grants permits for the scientific harvest of all whales, including "protected" gray whales. This allowed them to bypass the prohibition on the commercial harvest of the species. The announcement by Alexey Yablokov, a Russian researcher, that the Soviets drastically underreported whaling data during the 1950s and 1960s places the validity of data derived from all scientific and commercial whaling in doubt. Although Yablokov did not mention the harvest of gray whales, he argued for a comprehensive review of past commercial whaling operations to determine the extent to which whales have been overexploited.[28]

By the late 1980s, Mexico occupied an important position in the IWC when its delegate and gray whale researcher, Luis Fleischer, became cochairman. However, rather than encouraging actions that followed Mexico's historical legacy of marine mammal protection, Fleischer encouraged Mexico to adopt more policies favorable to commercial whaling and fishing interests, for which he was severely criticized. Conservationists repeatedly admonished Fleischer for taking what they perceived as a pro-whaling stance and for obstructing protection programs for small cetaceans. Fleischer's tenure at the IWC earned him the enmity of the entire Mexican marine mammal research establishment.[29]

Rethinking the Ban

As the population of gray whales slowly rebounded, pressure from the whaling industry to re-open the harvest of the species intensified. The fact that they migrate so closely to the west coasts of the United States, Canada, and Mexico makes killing them easy. Whaling companies eagerly looked south toward the calving and mating lagoons, with thousands of whales that are easy prey, and assumed that Mexico would eventually re-open its waters to commercial whaling.

Carl Hubbs of the Scripps Institution of Oceanography, a pioneer of gray whale research, recommended that whaling be permitted just outside the Mexican calving/breeding lagoons as "it would not do the species great harm to remove some of the excess males."[30] Julio Berdegue, a Mexican government fisheries biologist who worked closely with American gray whale researchers Raymond Gilmore and Gifford Ewing, argued that Mexico should be provided with an annual harvest quota for gray whales, "that along with a margin of protection, would allow this source of wealth to be reintegrated into the economy of the country."[31]

By the mid-1960s, it was apparent that the gray whale population, estimated at around twelve thousand, was growing. Biologists expected it to stabilize somewhere close to fifteen thousand. With these figures in mind, whaling companies pressured the Mexican government to re-open the Baja California coastline to whaling. In June 1965, Rodolfo Ramírez Granado of the Mexican Bureau of Fisheries proposed opening a whaling station to harvest gray whales off the Baja California coast.[32] Whalers would have been limited to a total catch of two hundred gray whales per year. Raymond Gilmore, a gray whale researcher affiliated with the San Diego Natural History Museum, criticized the plan, arguing that "the commercial value of the gray whale for dog meat and whale steaks is only a fraction of its value as a tourist attraction for both Mexicans and Americans."[33]

The day after that announcement was made, Ian Moore of the San

Diego Natural History Museum wrote to Mexican President Gustavo Díaz Ordaz asking that whaling be prohibited.[34] Carl Hubbs traveled to Mexico City to discuss this proposal. Government officials assured him that only a limited number of whales would be killed.[35] An international outcry by conservation groups in the United States and Europe quickly caused the Mexican government to reverse itself and deny its whaling plans. Jorge Echaniz, director of the Mexican Bureau of Fisheries, argued that if a season for gray whales was opened again, "Mexico wants its rightful share."[36] He later wrote a letter to influential Mexican environmental policy maker Enrique Beltrán, affirming his commitment to ensuring the continued growth of the population.[37]

Whaling for Grays in the United States

Although American scientists seemed outraged at the prospect of Mexico permitting the renewed harvest of gray whales, they raised only mild objections over whaling in U.S. and Canadian waters. From 1959 to 1969, 316 gray whales were killed for scientific purposes.[38] The director of the California Academy of Sciences, George Lindsay, raised the issue of the use of scientifically harvested whales for commercial purposes in a letter to the Bureau of Commercial Fisheries. He argued that it was a conflict of interest for the government agency involved in promoting commercial fisheries to promote the scientific harvest of cetaceans for commercial purposes.[39] The data collected from animals harvested from 1959 to 1969 provided Dale Rice and Allan Wolman with data for their monograph, *The Life History and Ecology of the Gray Whale (Eschrichtius robustus).*

The contradictory nature of the American scientific community's response to proposals to harvest gray whales was particularly evident when Rice and Wolman argued that between four and five hundred animals should be taken annually for commercial purposes. Raymond Gilmore, who had so vehemently opposed the harvest of gray whales by Mexicans in 1965, seemed unwilling to contradict Rice, who worked at the Fish and Wildlife Service's Marine Mammal Lab in Seattle. According to Gilmore, keeping the population near ten thousand would provide, "whales for the whalers and the public and science."[40] Killing between four hundred and five hundred whales annually was acceptable because commercial whaling would help the local economy. "I know conservationists say 'but they are used for dog food,'" Gilmore told a reporter. "Conservationists have dogs and they have to be fed. I regret there are so many dogs and cats."[41] From the perspective of Mexican policy makers, these statements were consistent with the overall U.S. relationship toward Mexico — paternalistic, hypocritical, and contradictory.

During the administration of President Luis Echeverría (1970–1976), plans for whaling in Mexico were shelved and the first gray whale reserve was established. The Mexican delegate to the IWC argued in 1974 that the commission would be remembered as "a small body of men who failed to act responsibly in terms of their very large commitment to the world, and who protected the interests of the few whalers and not the future of thousands of whales."[42]

Considering the utilitarian tradition of resource management in Mexico, it is surprising that Mexico did not permit whaling off the coast of Baja California. However, the federal government placed a higher priority on developing a national fishing industry than the establishment of a capital-intensive, technology-dependent whaling fleet. During the Echeverría period, a considerable federal investment was made in maintaining a large subsidized system of lobster and abalone fishing cooperatives throughout the Baja California coast. The opening of Mexico to whaling would have meant the loss of control over its coastal zone to large factory ships from whaling nations. In terms of national development, harvesting gray whales, even in a manner similar to that practiced in the United States, would have required providing concessions to foreign companies. Little would have been gained economically, and much would have been lost in terms of international prestige. The symbolic profits to be realized from conservation were much more valuable than earnings from the slaughter of whales.

Research and Conservation

The international dimension of gray whale conservation in Mexico expanded during the 1940s with the participation of American biologists in gray whale research and conservation in Baja California. These scientists used their knowledge of the demography and behavior of the whales in their winter habitat to work with their Mexican colleagues to lobby government officials in Mexico City for long-term habitat protection. This collaborative effort created a formidable partnership for gray whale conservation that still exists.

The first trip by an American scientist to study the whales of Baja California occurred on February 12, 1947. On that day, Carl Hubbs hitched a ride aboard a plane piloted by Ira McMullan. From San Diego they flew down the Baja California coast to pick up a sick sailor south of Magdalena Bay. For Hubbs, this was a chance to see the gray whales he had counted from his seaside observatory on top of Ritter Hall at Scripps two months earlier, in December 1946. A census of migrating whales could easily be taken in San Diego. The crucial issue was gray whale demography and behavior inside the lagoons of Baja California.

As the plane approached Cedros Island, northwest of the entrance to Scammon's Lagoon, Hubbs saw the first whale on the ocean's surface. The plane quickly descended and turned southeast as it neared the giant lagoon. Whales were in abundance — 55 outside the entrance, 11 just inside, and 35 scattered around the interior of the lagoon. These 101 gray whales were more than Hubbs had ever seen in one location. Heading south, the spotter plane skirted San Ignacio Lagoon, where Hubbs noted only a few whales, and continued down the coastline toward Magdalena Bay. They skirted the Pacific side of Magdalena Bay en route to Cabo Tosca, the southernmost point on Margarita Island. The immensity of the bay made it difficult for Hubbs to see whales.

After picking up the sailor 36 miles south of Cabo Tosca, the party looped back and hugged the coastline. As the plane reached the entrance to the Boca de Soledad, Hubbs quickly grabbed a pair of 7 × 50 binoculars to see how many whales he could count. He jotted, "If many [whales] had been present, some surely would have been seen. Obviously Magdalena Bay is not a major breeding ground, comparable to Scammon's and San Ignacio Lagoons." Later that day, on the return trip, Hubbs counted 69 whales at San Ignacio Lagoon and a total of 94 in and outside of Scammon's Lagoon.[43]

Early Research Efforts

With this initial flight, Hubbs began a program of gray whale research and conservation that scientists and resource policy makers carried out in both Mexico and the United States. This program still exists. Because Scripps is so close to the border, it was easier for American scientists from Scripps to visit gray whale lagoons in Baja California than scientists and researchers from Mexico City. There were no universities in La Paz during the 1940s, making it very difficult for Mexico City–based researchers to travel to the isolated lagoons on the Pacific coast of Baja California. Scientists such as Hubbs, Gifford Ewing, Raymond Gilmore, and Theodore Walker established a research program that involved collaboration with Mexican researchers and policy makers such as Julio Berdegue, a young fisheries biologist, and Enrique Beltrán, the influential director of the Mexican Society of Renewable Resources. For American researchers, the gray whale lagoons in Baja California formed part of a new frontier. Researchers traveled to the lagoons by boat or airplane. Traveling over land required a long, difficult journey over a rough dirt road. For researchers such as Ewing and Hubbs, busy with their duties at Scripps, overland travel made for long trips. Aerial surveys were more efficient. The first survey conducted by Hubbs would have taken over a month by car.

During the postwar period, scientists could not easily obtain funding for whale research. Financial support came from a variety of sources, including wealthy Hollywood actors and industrialists who were interested in the cetaceans. Erle Stanley Gardner, author of the Perry Mason books, became an acquaintance of Hubbs. Gardner wrote a number of popular accounts of his adventures by land and helicopter in the peninsula. Raymond Gilmore corresponded with film director John Huston, who reported on whales he sighted from his home in Puerto Vallarta.

Several wealthy industrialists supported research in Baja California. Kenneth Bechtel, of the Bechtel Corporation, funded gray whale studies through his Belvedere Scientific Fund. The Los Angeles–based Richfield Oil Corporation promoted early research efforts. David Day, the vice president of Richfield, was a friend of Raymond Gilmore and underwrote the cost of an air charter ($1,000) for aerial census work conducted in 1957. Richfield was also able to arrange logistical support for Gilmore at a salt mining venture around Guerrero Negro Lagoon operated by Daniel K. Ludwig.[44] The Disney Corporation also supported a combined research and documentary-film expedition to Scammon's Lagoon.[45]

Always on the lookout for funding and ways to earn publicity for Scripps, Hubbs became acquainted with Errol Flynn, the wealthy Hollywood actor, whose father was a marine biologist. Hubbs and Flynn devised a plan that would get Hubbs into Baja California and provide Flynn with a potentially profitable documentary film on gray whales. Hubbs offered to act as the project advisor, and Flynn agreed to provide money for a plane to transport the crew and a helicopter to film the whales. They also hoped to generate publicity as the first scientific expedition to use a helicopter.

Choosing the most appropriate location for the film was a tough choice between Scammon's and San Ignacio Lagoon, but Hubbs wrote to Flynn that "I regard San Ignacio Lagoon as more favorable in general for the work than Scammon's Lagoon. It is much smaller, and there is a closer concentration of the whales."[46]

The expedition departed for San Ignacio Lagoon in February 1948. Once there, the helicopter herded whales around the lagoon to obtain desired camera footage. Whales became so enraged by the helicopter noise that the behemoths churned the water of the lagoon into foam. Subsequently an adult whale rammed a boat filled with local fishermen.[47] Severe winds caused the well-planned and financed trip to end in disaster. An expedition airplane crashed on Pelican Island.

José Aguilar Villavicencio, a retired fisherman who lives in a tiny ranching settlement midway between San Ignacio and San Ignacio Lagoon, remembers the trip well. "We were out there in our pangas and this helicopter flew over the lagoon. There were quite a few whales around, and they started going crazy and created quite a commotion. I didn't want to get our boat rammed by a whale, so we went into shore. But some friends didn't leave, and their panga was rammed by a whale. There was a plane with them, and it crashed in the lagoon. We rescued the pilot and the crew and gave them some dry clothes and food until somebody came and got them."

A 1956 expedition to Scammon's Lagoon featured in *National Geographic* was sponsored by Douglass Aircraft, whose chairman, Donald Douglass, was the expedition host and skipper. During the expedition, Dr. Paul White, President Eisenhower's personal heart consultant, attempted to monitor the heartbeat of a whale but succeeded only in losing expensive electronic equipment. Protecting her calf, an angry female rammed an expedition skiff. The expedition ended in failure.[48]

Other incidents involving scientists and whales that turned sour include the killing of two adult female gray whales in Scammon's Lagoon during the testing of tranquilizer drugs in 1967, and the killing of a gray whale calf by Ken Norris in 1974.[49] In 1971, Sea World of San Diego captured Gigi, a female gray whale calf, inside Scammon's Lagoon for "scientific purposes." Sea World later returned Gigi to the sea as an adult.[50]

Early annual censuses of the gray whales in their winter grounds in Baja California were initiated in 1952. These censuses provided a rough but fairly reliable idea of the increase in the population and demography of whales in their three main habitats: Scammon's Lagoon, San Ignacio Lagoon, and Magdalena Bay. The publication of census data provided evidence that gray whale numbers were increasing. Early surveys also illustrated how critical each of the three main winter habitats in the peninsula were, especially Scammon's Lagoon, where scientists focused their attention. In February 1954, flights by Gilmore and Ewing and then Hubbs and Ewing also revealed mother-calf pairs of gray whales in the Sea of Cortez, near Yavaros, Sonora.[51]

Americans carrying out research in Baja California had to seek permission and help from the Mexican government. Researchers received letters of support and information regarding refueling and supply locations. The Consul of Mexico in San Diego, Santiago Campbell, aided Carl Hubbs, who reported the findings of his 1952 aerial surveys to the Mexican government.[52] In February 1956, Raymond Gilmore, who at the time was working for the U.S. Fish and Wildlife Service, invited Julio Berdegue along on an aerial census expedition, which resulted in the publication of the first scientific paper on the gray whale by a Mexican researcher.[53] Berdegue, whom Gilmore described as "a credit to his country as well as an unequaled representative to other countries," had what appeared to be a promising career ahead of him as a researcher. But he was dissatisfied with his government job and went to work for a fishing company in Sinaloa.[54]

The legacy of American whale research in Mexico did not create ideal conditions for Mexican marine biologists. Mexican scientists believed that foreign researchers marginalized them.[55] When Luis Fleischer became the head of the National Program for Marine Mammal Research and Conservation in the 1980s, permits for research that had once been easy to obtain were no longer available. Many American scientists blamed Fleischer. They argued that he was interested in fostering his own agenda by the exclusion of outside researchers. However, the denial of permits also became tied up in matters unrelated to whale research. The U.S. embargo against Mexican tuna enraged officials at the Ministry of Fisheries. Denying permits to American researchers became an unofficial payback for what they perceived as a hypocritical and unfair policy.

Ironically, in addition to stymieing much-needed marine mammal research in Mexico, the embargo also had a deleterious effect on gray whales and other sensitive marine life in Magdalena Bay. Workers who lost their jobs due to the closure of tuna canneries turned to whalewatching and sea turtle and lobster poaching to make up their lost income—proof that zero-sum battles in the environmental arena create losses on all sides.

The permit situation for American scientists has been rectified. American biologists have made a greater effort to promote coordinated science and research projects and have supported their Mexican colleagues. Research permits are now available to American scientists.

Conservation

In addition to their research agenda, American marine biologists actively lobbied the Mexican government to enact protective measures for gray whales in Baja California. In 1952, Hubbs recommended to the Mexican government that because of existing and planned human activities in and around calving lagoons, reserve designation was needed to provide gray whales with a safe refuge. He argued that all gray whale habitats, from Guerrero Negro to the Boca de Soledad, could be made into whale sanctuaries.[56] Later, in a 1956 letter to Enrique Beltrán, Hubbs discussed the potential impact from salt mining operations at Guerrero Negro Lagoon and planned phosphorite mining in Magdalena Bay.[57] Hubbs noted that the failure of gray whales to return to Magdalena Bay—once their preferred wintering ground—indicated that increased human activities deterred the animals from returning.

Proposals for gray whale conservation programs and policies were first discussed in Mexico in the 1950s. The 1956 research flight of Julio Berdegue over the gray whale lagoons of Baja California provided insight into habitat needs. Berdegue recognized that human activities and habitat activities within the lagoons would limit the future growth of the gray whale population. He argued that it was "indispensable and necessary for the Mexican government to closely monitor activities that could disturb gray whale reproductive areas, in order to avoid a decrease in their population."[58]

In 1957 Enrique Beltrán met with Carl Hubbs and Gifford Ewing in Mexico City to discuss potential impacts on gray whale habitat and possible conservation policies. Upon his return to San Diego, Hubbs remarked that the Mexican government "expressed concern over threats to gray whales from industrial activities and population growth" and was "considering conservation measures for the whale, including provision for sanctuary during the breeding season."[59]

Salt operations in Guerrero Negro Lagoon alerted the government to the economic development potential of the Vizcaíno Bay region, which includes Scammon's, Guerrero Negro, and Manuela Lagoons. The Mexican Navy announced plans to develop a large port in Guerrero Negro Lagoon in 1958.[60] Although that proposal was never implemented, in the mid-1960s the salt company announced plans to expand around Scammon's Lagoon. Ken Norris, a pioneer marine mammal researcher, argued that the project could have a negative impact on whales and that the lagoon should be declared a national park.[61] The company went ahead with its plans.

The General Office of Wildlife of the Ministry of Agriculture and Livestock proposed to establish a migratory bird refuge at Scammon's Lagoon in 1969.[62] Wildlife biologists Richard and Sylvia Gard, who worked under A. Starker Leopold at the University of California, prepared a feasibility study for a wildlife sanctuary there. In a letter to Leopold, Hubbs argued that the Gards should emphasize the importance of the lagoon for shorebirds and sea turtles as well as its importance to gray whales.[63]

When Scammon's Lagoon was declared a wildlife reserve, an official at the Mexican Fisheries office in San Diego noted that international wildlife organizations had played a role in pressuring the Mexican government.[64] American scientists such as Carl Hubbs, Gifford Ewing, and Raymond Gilmore interacted with policy makers and researchers in Mexico through the exchange of data and ideas on conservation and promoted the protection of whale lagoons in Baja California.

The efforts of American scientists to foster cordial relations with their Mexican colleagues played a large role in their success promoting gray whale conservation. Mexican policy makers and scientists reacted positively to an unofficial campaign that supported their ongoing lobbying efforts to protect gray whale habitat in Mexico.

The Echeverría Legacy

Gray whale conservation fit into the larger context of reclaiming Mexico's coastal and marine resources. The election of President Luis Echeverría in 1970 signified a shift toward environmental protection at the top echelons of government. Echeverría's predecessor, Gustavo Díaz Ordaz, paid little attention to natural resource issues and conservation.[65] However, Echeverría, a nationalist, was fully aware of the historical, economic, and cultural legacy of foreign control over national resources.

Echeverría, who had led Mexico into economic and political disaster by the end of his six-year term, was a complicated figure. He was not very well known prior to his ascendancy to the presidency. After observing Ordaz's subservience to the United States, Echeverría quickly made plans for Mexico to take a prominent role internationally. Promoting environmental and conservation policies was a way of earning positive political capital for Mexico.

Three years after declaring Scammon's Lagoon a whale sanctuary, he stated at the Third United Nations Conference on Rights of the Sea in Caracas, Venezuela, that "efforts by coastal nations to control and protect coastal resources for themselves is an example of the long and difficult fight to ensure sovereignty over natural resources."[66] At the time Echeverría was embroiled in efforts to establish a 12-mile exclusive economic zone to prevent foreign fishing boats from exploiting Mexican fisheries. Echeverría's philosophy was, "Conservation is the preservation of natural resources for the people."[67] The 1973 Club of Rome meetings on the limits to growth helped him understand the long-term effects of environmental destabilization. According to Echeverría, "The lack of arable land, control over sea territory—everything was connected. We realized that international forums were important and that we could only solve our problems by working with other countries. The old conservationist philosophy of 'don't touch' had changed to one of knowing how to touch in the right way."

The First Reserves

Seven months after establishing Scammon's Lagoon as a whale refuge in 1972, Echeverría declared Scammon's and San Ignacio Lagoons to be migratory bird and wildlife refuges.[68] The reserve decree required scientists studying flora and fauna to obtain permits and prohibited hunting or the destruction of vegetation within reserve boundaries.

Although the establishment of the first gray whale reserve was mostly a symbolic gesture that led to little on-the-ground conservation, it did provide the legislative framework for subsequent actions. Without that first and most important conservation action, it would have been more difficult for policy makers to prod future presidents to establish and implement a gray whale conservation agenda.

In 1979, President José López Portillo declared San Ignacio Lagoon a whale refuge and maritime tourist attraction zone. This decree established a permitting mechanism for scientific research and tourism in the area. The gray whale calving area of El Remate and the bird breeding islands in the northeast corner of the lagoon were placed off-limits to tourism. The no-tourism zone was included in a map that accompanied the publication of the decree. The vague wording of the original Scammon's Lagoon whale refuge decree prompted López Portillo to revise it in 1980 to include reserve status for Manuela and Guerrero Negro Lagoons.

The Ministry of Urban Development and Ecology (SEDUE) established a National System of Protected Areas in 1984. Protected areas were divided into four categories: national parks, natural monuments, ecological reserves, and biosphere reserves. Biosphere reserves were to be areas containing important representations of ecosystems needing government protection to ensure the survival of endangered flora and fauna.

A 1.5-million-hectare biosphere reserve west of Transpeninsular Highway 1 throughout the Vizcaíno Peninsula, including Scammon's and San Ignacio Lagoons, was proposed by SEDUE.[69] The idea behind the proposal was to incorporate terrestrial, coastal, and marine habitats into one protected area so that the entire ecological region would be managed as one entity.

The reserve proposal initiated funding to conduct monitoring studies and administrative activities throughout the proposed reserve.[70] From 1976 to 1982, the northern portion of the proposed reserve was under the administration of the staff of the Bahía de Sebastian Vizcaíno Migratory and Aquatic Bird Refuge, based in Guerrero Negro.[71]

Manuel Camacho Solís, the director of SEDUE, took a trip to Scammon's Lagoon in February 1988 and announced that President de la Madrid would sign legislation to create the biosphere reserve, which would be the largest protected area in Mexico.[72] The reserve proposed by Camacho had been amplified in 1986 to include bighorn sheep habitat east of Highway 1, the extensive pre-Columbian cave paintings of the Sierra de San Francisco, and portions of the western Gulf of California shoreline (see map 4.1).[73] Government officials viewed the reserve as a way of facilitating the management of an ecologically unique region with a small rural population.

Finally, on the last day of his administration in 1988, de la Madrid signed legislation creating the Vizcaíno Biosphere Reserve to encourage the conservation of endangered plant and animal species and permit compatible human activities throughout its boundaries.[74] The creation of the reserve was due in large part to the advocacy of SEDUE staff and the research and administrative staff of the Center for Biological Research (CIB) in La Paz. But it was the lobbying efforts of the Group of 100—a distinguished group of intellectuals and artists active in environmental affairs in Mexico—and especially its president Homero Aridjis, that gave the reserve proposal the final push it needed to get de la Madrid to sign it into law.[75]

The establishment of the biosphere reserve tacitly recognized that the health of gray whales depended on the protection of the terrestrial resources around Scammon's and San Ignacio Lagoons. The original decrees did not mandate conservation programs that included local people. By calling for ecologically compatible economic development, the biosphere reserve decree recognized that gray whales are directly linked to the people and land around them in Baja California Sur.

The establishment of gray whale reserves from 1971 to 1988 shows

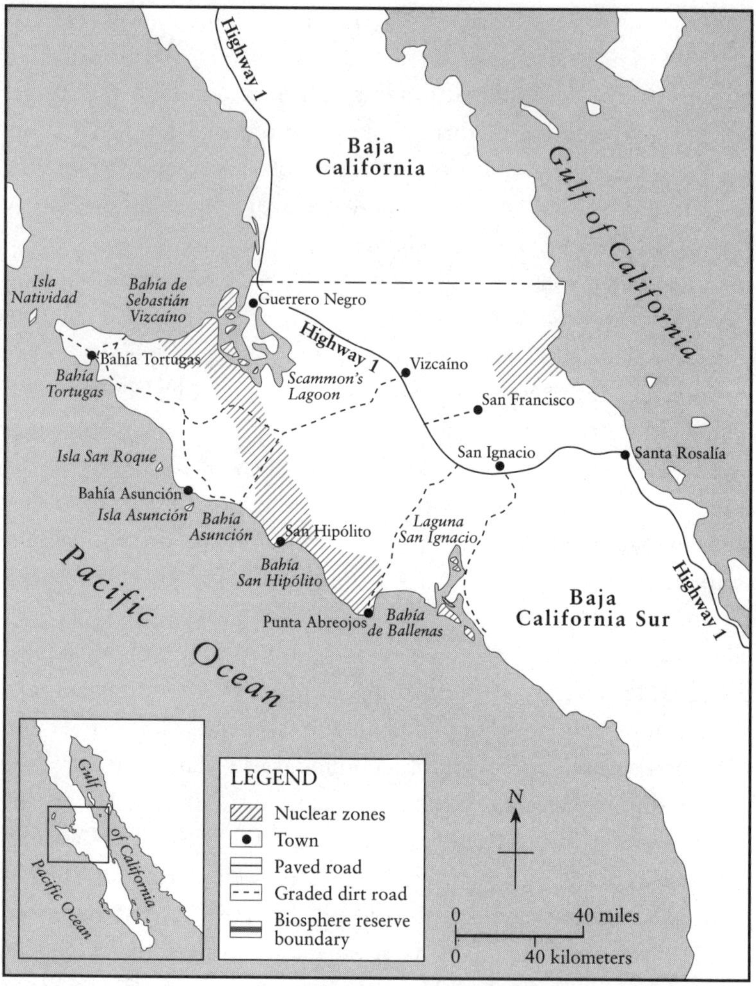

Map 4.1. The Vizcaíno Biosphere Reserve (Source: Ortega and Arriaga 1991)

how people inside and outside the Mexican government worked together to push proposals to the desks of Presidents Echeverría, López Portillo, and de la Madrid. However, unlike in the United States, where legislative proposals wind their way through Congress, in Mexico, proposals had to find a path to the chief of state.

International Cooperation

International cooperation played a major role in efforts to protect gray whale habitat. This involved sharing information regarding gray whale behavior, migratory patterns, habitat, and potential conservation needs. In 1974 the Scripps Institution of Oceanography sponsored a meeting between Mexican and U.S. scientists and government officials regarding marine and coastal management in Baja California. The meeting involved a wide range of high-level Mexican policy makers, including officials from the Office of the Presidency.[76]

Three years later, in 1977, the Mexican government sponsored the First International Symposium on the Gray Whale in Guerrero Negro. At that meeting, researchers and policy makers from both Mexico and the United States discussed the most effective methods of assuring the continued growth of the gray whale population and the successful conservation of the Scammon's Lagoon complex. In anticipation of the biosphere reserve concept, conference attendees recommended that Scammon's Lagoon be upgraded to a national park with buffer zones that would permit strict preservation, tourism, and other sustainable economic activities. A biological committee associated with the meeting and composed of Carl Hubbs, Douglas Chapman, and Richard Gard was formed. The committee reached the conclusion that potential impact on the gray whale population could occur as a result of "increased human activity and from mineral exploitation," and that whale conservation should be integrated with the protection of "other wild and resident species."[77]

The U.S. Marine Mammal Act of 1972 created a new context for bilateral efforts between the United States and Mexico to protect marine mammals and their habitats. The National Oceanographic and Atmospheric Administration (NOAA) sponsored meetings in Seattle between Mexican and American gray whale researchers in October 1978. At the meeting researchers discussed methods of comparing the results of field data and planned joint gray whale research projects.[78] Researchers met again in 1979 and 1980, but project funding was canceled in 1981.

The meetings sponsored by NOAA were the last time that American and Mexican researchers worked collaboratively under federal sponsorship to define a common gray whale agenda. During the 1980s gray whale conservation in Mexico left the international arena behind and moved into the world of program implementation, a process tied to Mexican politics rather than historical issues of sovereignty and nationalism.

5 Gray Whales and Mexican Politics

Todo es la política. Pura política.
— A WOMAN FROM MAGDALENA BAY

Mexico City is a world away from the gray whale lagoons of Baja California Sur. The most populated city on earth is an endless union of concrete, pavement, cars, and people—not mangroves, dunes, and desert. One Mexico City rush-hour subway train holds more people than the entire population of San Ignacio Lagoon. More federal money is spent on the city's Chapultepec Park than on the Vizcaíno Biosphere Reserve. On a Sunday afternoon more people visit the park than live in Baja California Sur. Yet it is in this megalopolis that the final decisions regarding the fate of gray whales are made.

I had an interview with the biologist responsible for approving whale-watching permits for Baja California Sur at ten o'clock on a Wednesday morning in Mexico City. As I turned the corner onto the narrow street where the Instituto Nacional de Ecología (INE) office is located, I found myself among hundreds of office workers. Pushing through the crowd, I asked a forty-something man wearing a worn corduroy jacket what was happening. "INE employees are on strike today," he said. "We haven't been paid in months."

Given the overwhelming political and economic problems of Mexico and the complex task of managing the country's natural resources—including its vast system of protected areas—gray whales and their habitat should not matter that much. But a niche has been carved out for this species within the complicated maze of the Mexican political system. The gray whales are, in effect, clients of the corporate state, serving a political machine that reinvents itself every six years.

Although gray whales are no longer killed for their oil, they are exploited for political and economic purposes. Their perceived importance and occupation of political space means that, like other clients of the corporate state, they have been provided with an entourage of managers, technicians, and politicians to tend to their needs. It is within this system—in which political capital is assigned to members of the corporate state—that gray whales are assigned a symbolic role within society.

For example, in 1994 the Ministry of Fisheries (Pesca) aired public service commercials on national television that displayed frolicking gray whales at the Boca de Soledad in Magdalena Bay. At the end of the announcement a message was flashed: "In Mexico we protect you—Pesca."

It is not surprising that gray whales have become part of the political system. In Mexico, the ruling party manages the political life of the country. Benefits to key sectors of society are distributed for ensuring the electoral victory of the ruling Institutional Revolutionary Party (Partido Revolucionario Institucional, or PRI). This makes it difficult for individuals or groups to work outside the system. Co-optation is essential for survival. Although gray whales are obviously incapable of participating in the system, the political space they occupy guarantees them a place in the same process. Like *campesinos* (peasants) and workers, they are depicted as symbols of the "revolutionary and progressive" Mexican State. The needs of gray whales, like the poverty of campesinos and workers, are irrelevant to the ruling elite. What is important is the political capital they bring to the ruling party empire based in Mexico City.

Environmental Legislation and Agencies

The protection of gray whales and their habitat in Mexico was achieved gradually through popular efforts to enhance the protection of the environment. Legislation used to protect gray whales fits within the trajectory of evolving national legislation for the environment. This inclusion of gray whales in the trajectory began in the 1970s under the administration of President Luis Echeverría.[1] Through various statutes, agencies are granted the legislative authority to provide general management guidelines for human activities near gray whales. While early federal environmental laws addressed pollution and were not specifically targeted toward wildlife, they established a precedent for future laws to protect gray whales.

In 1988, efforts to protect the environment merged with the enactment of the General Law of Ecological Balance and Environmental Protection. This law was the most significant environmental legislation in Mexican history and meant that gray whale conservation would be carried out under the jurisdiction and control of a single agency: SEDUE.[2] The agency was responsible for the development and implementation of gray whale conservation programs through its mandate of protecting biodiversity.

(The agency now responsible for the environment and gray whale protection is the Ministry for the Environment, Natural Resources, and Fisheries [SEMARNAP]). Although it is often vague, the General Ecology Law regulates protected areas (which include the Vizcaíno Biosphere Reserve), natural resource use, sanctions against polluters, and environmental impact assessments. Another law, a 1991 addition to the Mexican Penal Code, Article 254 (bis), prohibits the unauthorized capture of or injury to marine mammals. Violations can bring a prison term of three to six years.

Although environmental legislation provides a legal foundation for the protection of gray whales, it is difficult to implement. Six-year presidential terms disrupt the implementation of government policies, and result in a short-term approach to resolving problems. Further, a lack of sufficient funds for enforcement limits effectiveness, and the ambiguity of legislation results in uncertainty among government officials about how to implement environmental regulations.[3]

In general, regulatory laws are enforced through persuasion and bargaining rather than through strict enforcement. Local officials responsible for enforcing regulations rarely have the political power to carry out actions that might harm the interests of state clients, such as members of ejidos or unions.

During the first year of the Zedillo administration, in 1995, political appointees held over from the Salinas administration began a campaign to weaken federal environmental legislation. The campaign was similar to one initiated during the same period by former House Speaker Newt Gingrich and his corporate allies in the United States. During the April 1995 public hearing on the Zedillo administration's National Development Plan, Antonio Azuela de la Cueva, director of the Federal Attorney General's Office for Environmental Protection (PROFEPA), argued that Mexico needed an ecological law that was more "realistic" and that did not prohibit economic development. The director of INE, Gabriel Quadri de la Torre, argued that environmental legislation should reflect the economic and social needs of the country.[4] The most significant legislative victory for anti-environment crusaders was a revised General Ecology Law in 1996 that lessened restrictions on development in protected areas. The new law also includes a regulation requiring proof that protected areas do not restrict economic development.[5]

Defining the Agenda in Mexico City and La Paz

The INE strike illustrates the fundamental problem with centralized management—spinning on its own axis, it is responsible for, but oblivious toward, the rest of the country. Decisions, programs, policies, and plans percolate through state governments, then into *municipios,* and finally into rural areas, where they may or may not resemble their original features. Bureaucrats, technocrats, and politicians in the capital decide the fate of gray whales.

This is a problem not just in Mexico; it is the principal feature of centralized political systems. In Mexico, however, centralization is compounded by a closed political system controlled by the PRI. Every six years, new leaders emerge from the system (or are handpicked by the current players) and replace the previous cast of players. The new players blame their predecessors for creating whatever economic and political crises the republic is going through. These politicians and technocrats promise a government that will help campesinos, workers, and the middle class. Ultimately, they make the same mistakes as their predecessors and lead the country into a new spiral of economic and political crises.

The Mexican political system places roadblocks at every turn to the many dedicated and professional bureaucrats interested in making a difference. Contrary to the stereotype prevalent in the United States of corrupt Mexican government officials, most Mexican resource agency staffers are very dedicated to their jobs. While corruption at very high levels is a major problem in Mexico, the majority of federal resource agency staffers work long hours and receive paychecks infrequently. Park directors often pay the salaries of their employees out of their own pockets. For example, in 1997 the director of the Pinacate Biosphere Reserve in Sonora—home to endangered pronghorn antelope and bighorn sheep—paid the salaries of his staff when federal funds failed to arrive.

With the obstacles federal environmental agencies confront, it is amazing that anything is ever accomplished. Salaries arrive late or not at all. Office supplies and travel expenses are barely covered by the budget. One morning, while I was waiting for an appointment at a federal agency, I observed a woman arrive at her empty desk. Slowly emptying her purse, she pulled out family photos, pens, and finally a stapler. The 1994 pre-

Christmas peso devaluation eventually reduced purchasing power in Mexico enormously. Protecting gray whales or any other animals was secondary to surviving the crisis. To make ends meet—while waiting eight months for his paycheck to arrive—one Vizcaíno Biosphere Reserve employee sold his car and computer to pay his rent. His supervisor paid his rent by catering parties. Both of them contemplated contracting "born-again" ex-cons to make eco-jewelry to raise funds for the reserve.

A visit to any federal agency headquarters in Mexico City quickly dispels illusions of power and control. While upper-level managers occupy fancy offices, the people that do all the work labor with minimal access to computers and little staff support. The constant reassigning of administrators for political reasons increases the difficulty of obtaining records of agency actions and plans. During one government transition, federal officials showed up at the house of Francisco Mayoral, a longtime San Ignacio Lagoon resident and whalewatching guide, asking permission to borrow and photocopy his collection of bibliographic material on the lagoon (probably the best in Mexico).

The difficulties faced by government agencies result in a frenzied and haphazard approach to conservation. When paychecks and project funding arrive, Mexico City staffers work around-the-clock before the money runs out. They hastily address the environmental needs of multiple projects for the entire country. There is no time for strategic planning and prioritization. This limits their ability to build effective and long-term national, regional, and local partnerships both outside and inside the government. Despite good intentions, the result is that little effective action is accomplished. When the government changes leadership, a new cast of players enters the game and begins the process all over again.

The decision-making process involving conservation reflects the Mexico political system: it is centralized and hierarchical. Within environmental agencies, decisions are the domain of an administrative chief and his or her political allies and employees. Some refer to this type of group as a *camarilla*. Others call them a *grupo de amigos*. When issues become politically controversial, allies outside the government are often invited to help develop key policies and justify controversial decisions. These individuals are often former high-level agency employees who can help develop and lobby for political strategies palatable to key individuals inside the government.

SEMARNAP

The primary agency responsible for almost all matters related to the environment and gray whale conservation in Mexico is the Ministry for the Environment, Natural Resources, and Fisheries (SEMARNAP). The agency is the administrative umbrella for three agencies that deal with gray whale issues: the National Institute of Ecology (INE); the Federal Attorney General's Office for Environmental Protection (PROFEPA), and the Fisheries Agency (Pesca). Prior to the creation of SEMARNAP in 1994, both INE and PROFEPA were under the administrative umbrella of the Ministry of Social Development (SEDESOL). Luis Donaldo Colosio, assassinated during his bid for president in 1994, ran the agency.

During the Salinas administration (1988–1994), the main function of SEDESOL was to increase support for the ruling party by distributing public works and social development monies to at-risk counties and states. Political leaders virtually ignored INE and PROFEPA. President Zedillo established SEMARNAP immediately after his election in 1994. He assigned Julia Carabias, a respected biologist and the former INE chief, the task of leading the new agency. Her primary responsibility was to integrate resource management policies and programs spread between different agencies during the Salinas administration. A month prior to starting in her new post, Carabias told a reporter that the biggest obstacle to reducing environmental degradation was not the lack of environmental legislation but the inability to implement existing laws.[6]

As the director of SEMARNAP, Carabias has had her work cut out for her. Carabias is the only nonpartisan member of the Zedillo cabinet. She is also considered its most honest and competent member. Carabias is a true Clinton-style environmental policy wonk—capable of delivering long monologues on needed national park improvements or the history of fire management policy in Mexico. When Pesca—one of the most corrupt government agencies in Mexico—was downgraded from cabinet status to a subunit of SEMARNAP, Pesca bureaucrats were shocked to find themselves under the control of a "hippie environmentalist"—Julia Carabias. They happily predicted that her tenure would last only a few months. Even Carabias constantly prepared her staff for her eminent departure.

Why has President Zedillo left Carabias in office so long? Because she runs the one cabinet-level ministry that makes his government look good. Under her leadership, SEMARNAP helped to improve Mexico's environmental record. However, the other explanation for her long tenure is that it is partially due to the protection of her husband, José Woldenburg, the director of the Federal Election Commission. Woldenburg officially sanctioned the "clean" electoral victory of Zedillo in 1994.

Rising above the political fray and projecting an image of competence, Carabias has earned the respect and loyalty of SEMARNAP staff (with the exception of Pesca), the Mexican public, and a wide array of international agencies and organizations.

What will be Carabias' legacy? Will she leave behind an effective and decentralized resource management agency capable of building the public and private sector partnerships necessary to protect and manage Mexico's natural resources? The Mexico City SEMARNAP office does not appear to be relinquishing control over decision making, the budget, or political power. Few people reach the top and give everything away. In that respect, Carabias is no different from her cabinet-level colleagues. Although she has made some tough decisions—such as halting the proposed saltworks at San Ignacio Lagoon—without her presence SEMARNAP would have floundered.

The National Institute of Ecology

The National Institute of Ecology is the operational arm of SEMARNAP and is the agency charged with gray whale conservation. Its responsibilities also include conserving and utilizing natural resources, managing protected areas, overseeing environmental impact assessments, and issuing whalewatching permits. Due to the leadership of Julia Carabias, INE emerged from the disaster of the Salinas years with the reputation of an agency that tried to make a difference in the environmental arena. However, the appointment of Gabriel Quadri de la Torre as agency director caused the entire agency to slide into a state of institutional paralysis. Quadri, a committed anti-environmentalist, was appointed as a counterweight to Carabias. His biggest institutional goal: selling protected areas in Mexico to the highest bidder. After failing to sell Cacahuamilpas Caves National Park in the state of Guerrero (the Carlsbad Caverns of Mexico) to Barry Sendel, a Canadian developer with plans to build a Jurassic Park–style theme park inside the caves, Quadri publicly toned down his efforts to sell Mexico's natural heritage.

The vast improvement in protected area management in Mexico during the Zedillo administration is due to the efforts of Carabias to develop a fully functioning national park system. During her tenure at INE, Carabias embarked on an ambitious effort to provide long-term support for ten of Mexico's most ecologically significant protected areas. Support for the program came from a $25 million grant from the Global Environmental Facilities (GEF) program of the World Bank and $6.9 million from the Mexican government.

In theory, the World Bank's GEF program should have been a global Marshall Plan for the 1990s. The program was an attempt by the World Bank and the international development lending community to mitigate years of neglect and abuse of the environment. The World Bank, the United Nations Development Program, and the United Nations Environmental Program jointly administer the program.

Beginning in 1991, First World nations provided $1.5 billion for a three-year GEF pilot program. In March 1994, the initial pilot program was terminated and an additional three-year program was authorized with over $2 billion in funding. Mexico received GEF funding in two categories: biodiversity and climate change. The purpose of the $25 million grant was to build protected area infrastructure, integrate protected areas into the society, and create financial mechanisms to promote the long-term management of the areas. Two key components of the program involved integrating local people into conservation and promoting the sustainable development of traditional economic activities.[7]

An administrative unit was established within the National Institute of Ecology to manage the project. In the case of the Vizcaíno Biosphere Reserve, GEF funding secured park staff, some equipment, and a draft management plan. The World Bank required that all reserves in the program be "supervised" and "guided" by a Technical Advisory Committee (TAC) "composed of representatives of local communities, nongovernmental organizations, and local governments."[8]

After the program began, GEF-Mexico staff quickly learned it was not working. Because World Bank funding traveled through Banobras (the Public Works Bank), the Ministry of Finance, the Ministry of Social Development (and later SEMARNAP), the INE, and finally to the various state offices that worked with the selected reserves, funding almost never reached the field. According to one INE employee, "You join that many bureaucracies together and we get murdered."

An independent analysis of the program conducted by Pronatura, a Mexican conservation organization, and The Nature Conservancy revealed that by 1995, although the World Bank had approved $3.9 million for disbursement, only $1.5 million fell into the hands of SEMARNAP. According to the report, "GEF project funds are not flowing to the projected areas in an efficient manner."[9] The solution involved bypassing the Mexican government altogether. With the support of the World Bank, the U.S. Agency for International Development, and the lobbying efforts of The Nature Conservancy and the World Wildlife Fund, the nonprofit Mexican Conservation Fund was established. The organization acts as manager for World Bank funding for protected areas. The establishment of the organization is a positive step in the decentralization of conservation and protected area management in Mexico.

PROFEPA

In the early 1990s, with debate over the North American Free Trade Agreement raging throughout the United States, Canada, and Mexico, the Salinas administration needed to demonstrate to its critics at home and abroad that it was serious about environmental protection. The establishment of the Federal Attorney General's Office for Environmental Protection (PROFEPA) proved that Mexico was committed to resolving serious high-profile issues such as industrial pollution and toxic waste disposal. The watchdog agency insures that the private sector and government agencies comply with federal environmental regulations, permits, and environmental impact assessments. The ability of PROFEPA to levy fines and send environmental polluters to jail gave the impression, at least on paper, that Mexico was improving its environmental record. Between 1992 and 1995, PROFEPA fined 4,000 companies a total of $8 million.[10]

The separation of INE and PROFEPA was meant to reduce the potential for corruption so that the people who write environmental rules, hand out permits, or review environmental impact assessments are not responsible for enforcing them. In the words of one agency employee, the task of

PROFEPA is to "inspect the inspectors." For example, while INE issues whalewatching permits, PROFEPA checks the permits in the field and makes sure outfitters follow regulations. INE is charged with reviewing development plans that could harm gray whale habitat. If a project is approved, it is up to PROFEPA to make developers implement required mitigation measures.

The initial focus of PROFEPA on environmental pollution left its field inspectors with little understanding of how to oversee wildlife conservation programs. However, park rangers throughout Mexico now receive PROFEPA training and certification, so they have the legal authority to halt poaching and other activities that threaten Mexico's endangered wildlife.

Because PROFEPA is not involved in creating gray whale management plans, managing protected areas, or issuing whalewatching permits, the agency does not actively participate in gray whale protection at the central level. However, in 1998 the agency made a small but politically significant contribution to gray whale conservation efforts. In the case of the 1997 deaths of approximately ninety-four sea turtles and the three hundred batteries that were found in the channels of Scammon's Lagoon, PROFEPA fined Exportadora de Sal approximately $100,000. This groundbreaking case is the first example of a federal agency taking action against the most powerful corporation in Baja California Sur for degrading gray whale habitat and killing endangered species that reside there.

Making the System Go Round: La Paz

Although bureaucrats in Mexico City make the final decisions about gray whale conservation in Baja California Sur, La Paz is where the political forces opposed to and in favor of gray whale conservation converge. The capital of Baja California Sur is where policies are disputed, discussed, and finally implemented. The fact that the city is hundreds of miles from gray whale lagoons is irrelevant.

La Paz is where overworked, underpaid, and out-of-the-loop bureaucrats present the policies of distant colleagues to the people who have to live with them. Unlike in La Paz, there are rarely any constituents in Mexico City who make ugly scenes about gray whale–related policies that do not work. The people who have a stake in gray whales and San Ignacio

Lagoon and Magdalena Bay make demands in person in La Paz. The field comes to La Paz. La Paz rarely goes to the field.

Federal bureaucrats in La Paz broker decisions, mediate disputes, and keep things running smoothly for their counterparts in Mexico City. La Paz is where all three levels of government—municipal, state, and federal—meet. Within this process, the concept of management is replaced by the need to keep the system moving forward. Management plans create the illusion of purpose, decentralization, order, and democracy. They are acknowledged and quickly forgotten—much like protected areas themselves. Management plans interfere with a system that follows a set of unwritten rules (known to all actors in the political system) rather than bylaws or the Mexican constitution.

If bureaucrats in Mexico City are plagued by difficulties due to lack of funding and information, along with recurrent national economic crises, then in La Paz, distant from the purse strings of the capital, problems are only magnified. But working in La Paz is easier than being stuck at an outpost in the desert, far from telephones, water, food, and the type of life that most middle-class, college-educated federal officials take for granted. In addition, working in the field takes officials away from the state capital and is not a wise strategy for moving up the career ladder. Nobody moves up the career ladder by solving the problems of San Ignacio Lagoon.

Federal environmental officials in La Paz are a step closer to gray whale lagoons than colleagues in Mexico City—but not that much. Traveling to San Ignacio Lagoon, for example, requires a rugged vehicle to negotiate treacherous roads and a boat with a reliable outboard motor to get close to gray whales. Even with all these things, people with families do not want to camp for months at a time without salaries and supplies. The nearest hospital to San Ignacio Lagoon is a two-hour drive down a rutted dirt road and then another two-hour drive on the main highway to Guerrero Negro. Better to stay in La Paz close to a boss, grocery stores, schools, and medical care. By establishing a residence in La Paz, officials enable their family members to pursue their own careers rather than be dependent on federal paychecks that often arrive months late or not at all.

On any given day in the La Paz office of SEMARNAP, someone who has traveled a great distance waits patiently for an *audiencia* with an official. It is an expected and fundamental part of government life in Baja California

Sur. In that respect, the system is democratic. The offices are open to everyone, and a meeting can always be arranged. Personalizing politics opens the system to the powerless.

Despite the lack of funding, supplies, and personnel, the La Paz office of SEMARNAP is charged with regulating and monitoring whalewatching through the issuance of permits and field inspection visits. The office also reviews environmental impact assessments for development projects in and around gray whale habitat.

Although Mexico City assumes final responsibility for gray whale conservation, local agencies take advantage of the positive symbolism of the gray whale to bolster their own image. For example, in 1994 and 1995, the La Paz PROFEPA office placed two almost identical articles regarding its whale protection program in the *Sudcaliforniano,* the state's daily newspaper.[11] This was despite the limited involvement of PROFEPA in gray whale conservation.

In the 1994 article, Jorge Jiménez López, the state PROFEPA director, argued that the increased growth of whalewatching could harm gray whales. To assure local outfitters that his agency would be flexible in the enforcement of whalewatching regulations, he recognized the need for economic activities that were compatible with conservation. The article published the following year argued in favor of limiting whalewatching but affirmed the need to balance environmental protection with economic development.

The messages depict how government agencies must continually balance the need to refrain from alienating allies of the ruling party with the need to demonstrate their political power. A well-placed message in the newspaper is both a subtle management tool designed to open the process of negotiation over whalewatching access and a political tool designed to show representatives of the system that the agency is protecting the state's most important animal.

Changing the Rules of the Game

Until the 1980s, gray whale conservation was a process involving a limited number of scientists, policy makers, and international organizations (primarily from the United States) working through the established political system in Mexico to specific conservation objectives (e.g., establishing protected-area decrees and stopping whaling plans). However, by the late

1980s and into the 1990s, issues emerged around the use of gray whale habitat by local communities and multinational corporations. The paradigm of state development has changed from defending natural resources against foreign interests to selling natural resources to the highest bidder. The entire political context of gray whale conservation has changed.

The future of gray whale conservation lies in a more decentralized and democratic system in which a plurality of groups—stakeholders in gray whale protection—are able to articulate a conservation agenda without running the risk of violating the unwritten rules that forbid independent and nonaligned voices. As shown in the next two chapters, the more recent issues of gray whale conservation involve numerous organizations in Baja California Sur with strong ties to groups in Mexico City and abroad that can help them articulate a gray whale conservation agenda independent of the state. The symbolic political capital of the gray whale provides groups and individuals fighting to be heard the extra weight they need to be seen by technocrats and politicians in La Paz and Mexico City. Whether organizations are involved in stopping multinational development in San Ignacio Lagoon or fighting over access to gray whale habitat in Magdalena Bay, these new groups are defining the gray whale conservation agenda themselves rather than empowering the Mexican state to solve problems. The political system in Mexico is often a fortress. Gray whales are helping open the doors to democracy.

6 The Battle over San Ignacio Lagoon

I would be troubled also if I felt that either Mitsubishi Corporation or the Mexican Government, our majority partner in Exportadora de Sal S.A. (ESSA), would do anything to endanger these magnificent animals.

—JAMES BRAUM, EXECUTIVE VICE PRESIDENT,
MITSUBISHI INTERNATIONAL COMPANY

The first impression of San Ignacio Lagoon—the last undisturbed place on earth that gray whales swim to each winter to give birth, raise their calves, play in the surf, and mate—is overwhelming. A forest of elephant trees and cactus blends into vast and impenetrable salt flats. The salt flats blend into the shallow waters of the lagoon, where black turtles feed on eelgrass. Bottlenose dolphins cruise the shoreline searching for a corvina supper. Osprey swoop over the lagoon like F-16's with mullet payloads on their way to hungry chicks hidden in fortress nests made of driftwood, plastic, and dead cactus. On a windless winter afternoon, the whoosh and splash of gray whales breathing and breaching can be heard from miles away.

San Ignacio Lagoon is unique. If Exportadora de Sal and the Mitsubishi Corporation of Japan have their way, the natural beauty and wildlife of the lagoon could disappear.

It is over the fate of this lagoon and its surrounding landscape and wildlife—the heart of the Vizcaíno Biosphere Reserve—that the biggest battle over conservation and development in the history of Mexico is taking place. Exportadora de Sal plans to build the largest industrial salt harvesting facility in the world on the shore of San Ignacio Lagoon—even bigger than the one they already operate at Scammon's Lagoon, which is currently the largest in the world. The Mexican government owns 51 percent of Exportadora de Sal. The Mitsubishi Corporation, one of the largest and most environmentally destructive corporations on the planet, owns the remaining 49 percent.

The predatory acts by Mitsubishi against the environment are so extensive that the San Francisco–based Rainforest Action Network is conducting an international boycott against the company. CorpWatch, an environmental watchdog group also based in San Francisco, damned the Japanese conglomerate in 1998 with a Greenwash Award for "its ceaseless efforts to portray its various businesses — some of the most destructive on earth — as environmentally friendly."[1]

Given Mexico's history of gray whale conservation and public rhetoric about its commitment to the protection of the species, it will be hard for President Ernesto Zedillo to justify selling the last undisturbed gray whale breeding and calving lagoon to a foreign corporation. The development of the saltworks will determine whether the Zedillo administration will continue Mexico's history of gray whale conservation.

The fight over the project pits the Mexican government against itself. On February 27, 1995, the INE rejected a project environmental impact assessment. The primary reason was that an industrial saltworks in the middle of a biosphere reserve is "incompatible with the goals of conservation."[2] Given the severity of the economic crisis, the decision to halt the project is the most important defense of the environment taken by a government agency in Mexican history. However, Exportadora de Sal contested the decision. The INE agreed to reevaluate the saltworks after the completion of a new environmental impact assessment in the fall of 1999.

Battle lines regarding the saltworks have been drawn in the salt flats surrounding the lagoon. The most powerful ally of the project is Herminio Blanco, the head of the Ministry of Commerce and Industrial Development and the president of the Exportadora de Sal board of directors. Former Baja California Sur governor Guillermo Mercado, who governed Baja California Sur from 1992 to 1998, waged an all-out attack against the INE and environmental organizations opposed to the project. Almost every politician in Baja California Sur publicly supported the governor and the saltworks.

The battle over salt and San Ignacio Lagoon illuminates a political system able either to marshal all of its power to protect gray whales or — at the snap of a finger — to destroy their habitat. Controversy over the saltworks resulted in a convergence of political forces in La Paz with one goal: to co-opt all individuals and all groups opposed to, or ambivalent about, saltworks construction. No individual, group, company, or government agency was too small or unimportant to matter. Even destitute ranchers living in the most remote desert in Baja California Sur were recruited to speak in favor of the San Ignacio Lagoon saltworks.

The debate between politicians and environmentalists over the saltworks illustrates how gray whales create conservation space in the political system. To understand the tension between gray whale conservation and the development of gray whale habitat, it is important to follow the roles of scientists, politicians, the press, and environmentalists in the controversy. All of these groups played a part in the protection of gray whales and San Ignacio Lagoon. Now they are locked in a fight to determine whether Mexico will continue its policy of gray whale conservation. If the saltworks is approved, a precedent will be established for Mexico and other developing countries to pretend that industrialization is the same as nature protection. The San Ignacio Lagoon saltworks will transform the Vizcaíno Biosphere Reserve—the largest nature reserve in Mexico—into the world's largest industrial park.

The History of the Saltworks

Salt has been commercially harvested from Scammon's Lagoon since the late 1800s. Exportadora de Sal, originally owned by American Daniel K. Ludwig, began salt operations in and around Scammon's Lagoon in 1954. The company received a concession to produce salt in the San Ignacio Lagoon area in 1953.[3] Ludwig sold the company to Mitsubishi in April 1973. Six months later the Mexican government acquired 25 percent of the company and in 1976 the Mexican National Mining Commission purchased another 26 percent. Due to changes in the national mining law and the ownership of Exportadora de Sal, a new concession was granted to the company in 1992.[4]

Scammon's Lagoon, about 120 miles north of San Ignacio Lagoon, is currently the location of the world's largest solar salt-harvesting facility. Much of the shoreline and desert surrounding the lagoon is off-limits to the public despite its status as a protected area. Industrial salt evaporating and crystallization ponds cover thousands of acres. Giant tractors hauling 120-ton trailers ply the desert, loading salt day and night, seven days a week. Barges that hold up to 6,500 tons of salt transport it about 54 miles from Scammon's Lagoon to Cedros Island, where the company stores up to a million tons of salt at a time. The salt is held until it is finally offloaded to industrial cargo ships headed for Japan, New Zealand, Canada, and the United States.

When I asked one longtime Guerrero Negro resident about the validity of Exportadora de Sal's argument that the new saltworks would improve

San Ignacio Lagoon, he responded, "Who does the company think it is fooling? After thirty years, Guerrero Negro doesn't have paved streets. The entire town becomes a mud pit after it rains." Guerrero Negro—a town bordering Mexico's largest wildlife reserve—is the company town that serves as Exportadora de Sal headquarters. Set among the windswept and mosquito-infested salt flats of Scammon's Lagoon, the town is a collection of plywood and cement-block houses and unpaved streets.

The director of Exportadora de Sal, Juan Ignacio Bremer, is the head of an empire of salt. He is the most powerful man in Baja California Sur and the political boss of Guerrero Negro. As the director of one of Mexico's most profitable state-owned enterprises, Bremer is used to courting Mexico's political elite, including President Zedillo. Short and stout, with a passion for collecting antique watches, Bremer draws his power from his partners: Mitsubishi and Herminio Blanco.[5]

The $120-million San Ignacio Lagoon saltworks proposed by Bremer would include 124,000 acres of evaporative and crystallization solar salt ponds surrounded by earthen dikes and a hazardous waste disposal site (see map 6.1). About 6,000 gallons of saltwater per second would be pumped out of the lagoon by seventeen diesel engines operating around the clock. The pumping operation would be located just northeast of two bird nesting islands and a gray whale calving area.[6]

A new town adjacent to the existing fishing village of Punta Abreojos, with a present population of seven hundred, would house more than fourteen hundred temporary and two hundred permanent workers and their families. A 1.2-mile-long loading pier would be built north of the lagoon entrance near Punta Abreojos in the middle of valuable lobster, abalone, and pismo clam grounds. Approximately eight large cargo ships would haul away salt each month. Project roads would crisscross half a million acres of the Vizcaíno Biosphere Reserve. Project construction would be phased in over six to eight years.[7]

Exportadora de Sal and Mitsubishi hope to earn over $100 million in annual gross revenues and $25 million in net revenues from a project that will double Mexico's annual salt production from around 7.5 million tons to 15 million tons. With annual worldwide salt production at an estimated 180 million tons, the project would increase total global salt production by more than 4 percent.[8] Mexico is currently the seventh largest producer of salt in the world.

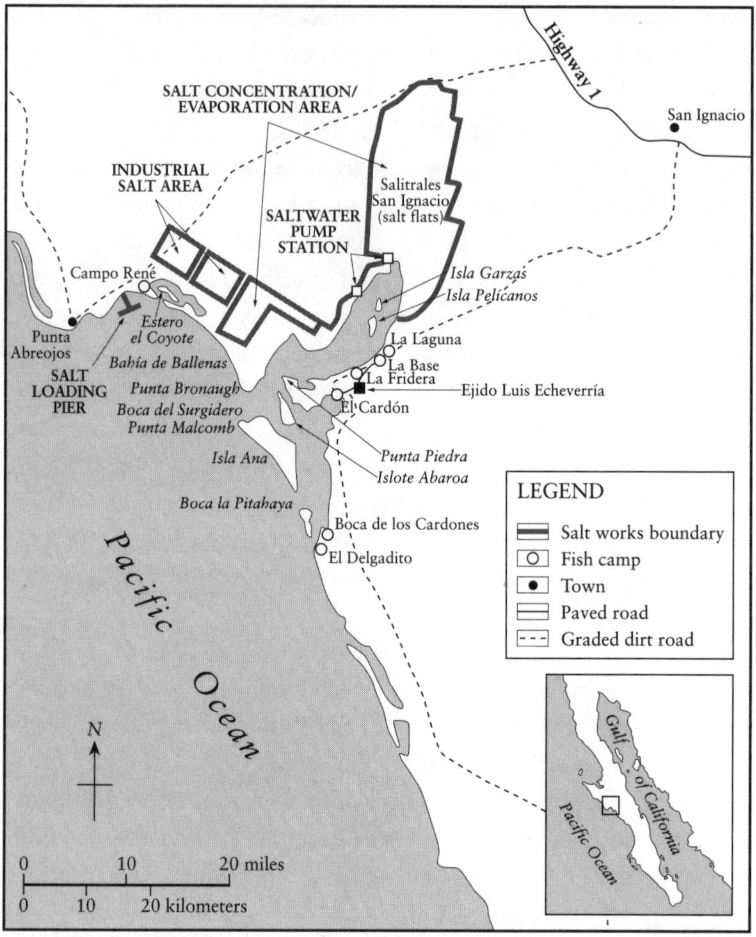

Map 6.1. The proposed San Ignacio Lagoon saltworks. Project plans are preliminary and are subject to revision. Approximations are based on Bremer 1994 and Exportadora de Sal 1992.

According to Juan Bremer, the original justification for the San Ignacio Lagoon saltworks was to increase Exportadora de Sal's long-term profits by decreasing production costs. The difficulty in docking and loading operations at Cedros Island increases Exportadora de Sal costs and decreases its competitiveness. By building another plant, the company could reduce the costs of double-handling salt loading and shipping at the Guerrero Negro facility by shipping out all salt from both facilities through Punta Abreojos.

Eliminating the barge operations in Scammon's Lagoon would require Exportadora de Sal to send salt to the pier at Punta Abreojos via a rail line extending across the only remaining habitat for the nearly extinct peninsular pronghorn antelope (see maps 2.1 and 6.1). However, building and maintaining a rail line to transport salt from Scammon's Lagoon to Punta Abreojos would be even more difficult than shipping it to Cedros Island. Barge operations at Cedros Island will continue.

With Exportadora de Sal's main justification for the project eliminated, why spend $120 million to increase global production of salt and risk a worldwide decrease in salt prices? According to Mark Spalding, a San Diego–based environmental attorney who investigated the economics of the saltworks for the Natural Resources Defense Council NRDC, Exportadora de Sal currently provides Japan with half its salt, and the Scammon's Lagoon operations can no longer expand.[9] Spalding argues that there appears to be little existing demand for the saltworks project. However, that could change, says Spalding, especially if Mitsubishi "has inside information regarding the salt industry, or if it has calculated that there is a reasonable expectation for growth in the salt market."[10] The industrial salt produced by Exportadora de Sal will be a fundamental component for chemical production, food processing, and water treatment for many years to come. However, it is too soon to tell whether the combination of the collapse of Asian economies and a severe global recession could hamper the development of the San Ignacio Lagoon saltworks.

Many company employees and residents of Guerrero Negro believe the real reason Exportadora de Sal is pushing for the new project is so that it can eventually close the Scammon's Lagoon facility. This would allow the company to increase its profitability by getting rid of its militant unionized labor force of approximately one thousand people and eliminate the expensive Cedros Island shipping operations. Exportadora de Sal denies this. However, because only two hundred jobs would be created by the new project (with only half available to Mexican nationals), closing the Scammon's Lagoon facility would permit labor savings of 80 percent.[11] To build support for the project, however, Bremer told one reporter he would employ "everyone" in the region.[12]

The biggest mystery is who is bankrolling the project. It seems unlikely that the Mexican government, in the middle of a severe economic crisis, can afford the $120 million price tag. Indeed, the Mexican National Mining Trust (Fideicomiso de Fomento Minero), the federal agency that controls Exportadora de Sal, denied any role in providing project funding.[13] This only leaves Mitsubishi as the main source of funding. However, Juan Bremer told me that Exportadora de Sal is funding the saltworks. He vehemently denied that Mitsubishi is a source of capital.[14] Ironically, while Bremer bragged about the excellent financial state of Exportadora de Sal, in 1998 he informed his employees that the company was nearly broke.[15]

There are three explanations for this contradiction. The first is that Bremer is eager to avoid the political fallout from acknowledging the dominant role Mitsubishi plays in the state-owned company. It is more than likely that the conglomerate will provide the technology, capital, and market for the San Ignacio Lagoon saltworks.

The second explanation is that the scheme could be a way for the Mexican government to privatize Exportadora de Sal and sell it to Mitsubishi. According to Guzmán Lazo, former general manager for Exportadora de Sal, if the Mexican government permits Mitsubishi to fund the San Ignacio saltworks, the Japanese conglomerate would then have to become the majority owner of the salt company.[16]

The third explanation is that project funding would originate from a third "silent" partner. By providing project funding, the silent partner would own a portion of Exportadora de Sal. That partner, or consortium of individuals, would then be in a position to purchase the company if it is privatized.

In 1996, Homero Aridjis, president of the Group of 100, speculated that Raul Salinas, brother of ex-president Carlos Salinas and currently a Mexican federal prison inmate, might be that third "silent" partner in the San Ignacio saltworks. In October 1995, the newsmagazine *Actual* published photos of Salinas and his third wife, Paulina Castañon, at the Scammon's Lagoon facility wearing company jackets and caps.[17] One month later, Swiss police arrested Castañon as she retrieved fake passports containing the photo of Raul. The fact that police found $130 million in Raul's account made him appear to be the perfect "silent" partner in the saltworks deal.

The saltworks may have been one of many shady dealings in which Raul Salinas was involved. Swiss police investigators released a report in September 1998 alleging that Raul earned hundreds of millions of dollars facilitating the transport of drug shipments belonging to Latin America's biggest *narcotraficantes* through Mexico.[18] Salinas could have used the San Ignacio Lagoon saltworks to launder money. Others could do the same.

Many San Ignacio Lagoon residents believe that a network of state *caciques,* or political bosses, who control the economy of Baja California Sur stand to profit handsomely from the San Ignacio saltworks. Guerrero Negro and the surrounding desert is a narcotics transshipment center. The development of the project will lead to a vast new network of roads, landing fields, warehouses, and boats that could be used in the drug trade by rogue company employees and their narcotics-related partners. A large illegal seafood trade (in abalone, scallops, lobsters, clams, and sea turtles) worth millions of dollars is also centered in Guerrero Negro. The development of roads around San Ignacio Lagoon would facilitate the taking of marine species by well-connected seafood pirates.

From the moment Exportadora de Sal went public with its plans for the San Ignacio saltworks, the company argued that the project would benefit San Ignacio Lagoon and its wildlife. The slogan developed by the public relations machine of Exportadora de Sal and Mitsubishi for the project is "Expanding Our Partnership with Nature."[19] However, the expansion of the Exportadora de Sal empire into San Ignacio Lagoon could mean the loss of the only lagoon where gray whales can mate and mother their calves without being bothered by commercial ship traffic or be at risk from industrial pollution. Salt company dredging and barge operations caused gray whales to abandon Guerrero Negro Lagoon (just north of Scammon's Lagoon) from 1957 to 1967.[20] More recently, in 1998, the Mexican Federal Attorney General's Office for Environmental Protection found extensive evidence that toxic salt brine and other hazardous waste discharged into Scammon's Lagoon by Exportadora de Sal resulted in the deaths of ninety-four endangered sea turtles. Farther south in Magdalena

Bay, commercial tankers and fishing boats pass through the middle of gray whale habitat. San Ignacio Lagoon is the only remaining undeveloped winter refuge for the gray whale.

The saltworks could also ruin the ecological features—high salinity and lack of development—that make the lagoon such an ideal place for gray whale birthing and calving. Exportadora de Sal ship and vehicle traffic, road building, and urbanization would indirectly impact more than 4 million acres inside the biosphere reserve, or more than 60 percent of the largest protected area in Mexico.[21] The project would cover more than 525,000 acres, or 8.3 percent of the Vizcaíno Biosphere Reserve, an area that is larger than 89 percent of all the wildlife reserves in Mexico.

Exportadora de Sal argues that the majority of the areas that will be developed consist of "biologically dead" salt flats. However, San Ignacio Lagoon is a drainage for three mountain ranges. During high tides and after rains, salt flats become flooded wetlands for months at a time. During the five months I lived along the shore of San Ignacio Lagoon, I observed coyotes, osprey, and even bobcats wandering the salt flats. Other species that could be harmed by the project include peregrine falcons, pronghorn antelope, and black and green turtles.

What is most worrisome is the effect the project could have on the people who live in the region. Prior to the development of the existing saltworks at Scammon's Lagoon in the 1950s, there was only one family living in an area now occupied by a town of 7,000. The project will add a new town to the existing fishing village of Punta Abreojos, a tightly knit community where the only source of employment is fishing.

What local fishermen fear most is that the new town at Punta Abreojos will put even more pressure on the federal government to privatize lucrative abalone and lobster fisheries. Caciques affiliated with the saltworks empire could stand to gain control of the most lucrative fishery in Mexico. According to a study prepared by the World Wildlife Fund–Mexico, fisheries production in the region is worth $60 million annually.[22] If the government can prove that the cooperatives are not able to adequately manage the abalone and lobster fisheries, government officials could justify the sale of the concessions to their political cronies.

Fisheries resource piracy is epidemic in the region. Resource poachers from Guerrero Negro and San Ignacio carry out night raids on the lobster and abalone grounds of Punta Abreojos and La Bocana. But many residents and local government officials avoid confrontations with poachers for fear they may be narcotraficantes in disguise. According to Ignacia Pacheco, a longtime inhabitant of San Ignacio Lagoon, "Fishermen don't know if the pangas they see out in the ocean belong to pirates or *narcos,* so they leave them alone. Nobody wants to risk getting killed." To compound the problem, many poachers also work for narcos.

Some cooperatives are so concerned about poaching that they use radar dishes to detect pirate skiffs. In 1997, co-op members from La Bocana, north of Punta Abreojos, opened fire on a skiff stealing lobsters, killing one of the most notorious poachers in Baja California Sur.

According to the World Wildlife Fund–Mexico study, the saltworks would result in serious harm to fishing in the region. As a result of the increase in the population of the region, the subsequent rise in the number of fishermen would disrupt the social cohesiveness of Punta Abreojos. This would also lead to greater resource piracy.[23] The fear of being invaded by resource pirates and losing its valuable lobster and abalone concessions is the reason the Punta Abreojos fishing cooperative is vehemently opposed to the San Ignacio Lagoon saltworks.[24] One lifelong Punta Abreojos resident and member of the local fishing cooperative told me, "Nobody wants the project. We have nothing to gain and everything to lose." Exportadora de Sal employees will earn less than a third what locals make from fishing and ecotourism.

Because the San Ignacio saltworks has been in the planning stages since 1953, the discussion of the project in the Vizcaíno Biosphere Reserve management plan should have received a top priority. A well-prepared management plan could also have served to define the critical issues surrounding the development of the saltworks project. After all, doubling an industrial activity that already occurs within the reserve will alter the physical landscape as well as transforming the socioeconomic conditions of the region.

Oddly enough, the original 127-page management plan prepared by the Northwest Center for Biological Research (CIBNOR) in La Paz failed to mention the saltworks. A revised management plan prepared by reserve director Victor Sanchez devotes only one line in fifty-two pages to the proposed project.[25] Given Sanchez's lack of concern over the saltworks, it was not surprising to find him prominently displayed in the Exportadora de Sal web site, downplaying the potential impact of the project.[26]

The primary problem with the San Ignacio Lagoon saltworks is that, according to the Vizcaíno Biosphere Reserve decree, it is completely prohibited. The decree (Article 10, Section 1) clearly states that new population centers within the reserve are not permitted.[27] And according to Victor Sanchez—headquartered in the trash-covered wasteland of Guerrero Negro—urbanization is one of the gravest threats to the Vizcaíno Biosphere Reserve.[28]

The Government Places the Saltworks on Hold

On February 27, 1995, National Institute of Ecology director Gabriel Quadri de la Torre rejected the Exportadora de Sal proposal to build the San Ignacio Lagoon saltworks on the grounds that the project was "incompatible with the goals of conservation" of the Vizcaíno Biosphere Reserve and that "there are no valid opinions to justify the loss of the natural environment in such an extensive area and within a biosphere reserve." Quadri justified the decision by citing the potentially adverse impact on fourteen plant species and seventy-two animal species.[29] Although Quadri signed the document, INE insiders assured me that he received orders to halt the project directly from his boss, Julia Carabias.

Juan Bremer was floored by the decision. In 1993 he had bragged to *Sudcaliforniano,* Baja California Sur's pro–ruling-party daily, that the project would be operational by 1997.[30] Bremer, surrounded by his coterie of political cronies, misread the international landscape of gray whale conservation. The emperor of salt forgot that gray whales have a lot of friends.

Bremer has nobody but himself to blame for failing to persuade environmental authorities the project was viable. The Northwest Center for Biological Research, the same academic institution that prepared the original reserve management plan, also wrote the first saltworks environmental impact assessment. The document was so poorly prepared and so biased in favor of its client, Exportadora de Sal, that Julia Carabias had no choice but to veto the project.

The 465-page document released in 1995 is a model of how not to write an environmental impact assessment. The report contains only twenty-one pages of impact analysis. Five pages are devoted to potential mitigation measures. The gray whale receives a mere twenty-four lines. None of the studies carried out over the years in San Ignacio Lagoon is cited. According to the CIBNOR report, the pronghorn antelope is the only species that might be adversely affected by the project.[31] Clearly, the academic institution was ill-prepared to carry out a study on a project of such magnitude and complexity.

The lack of impact analysis in the first environmental impact assessment is ironic, considering that CIBNOR staffer Aradít Castellanos is probably the world's leading authority on the impact of the Scammon's Lagoon saltworks operation on local wildlife. In a 1985 report on the pronghorn antelope, he and his colleagues argued that loss of habitat caused by Exportadora de Sal development was the primary cause of the decrease in the pronghorn antelope population.[32] Today the species is near extinction.

At the same time that CIBNOR was preparing the saltworks environmental impact assessment, it was also preparing the Vizcaíno Biosphere management plan and lobbying the INE to grant the institution a contract to administer reserve funding. It is unclear why the federal government permitted such an obvious conflict of interest.

Rather than helping the public and the government to understand the issues surrounding the San Ignacio Lagoon saltworks, CIBNOR director Alfredo Ortega Rubio became a project advocate. After the environmental impact assessment was made public, he declared that the Group of 100, the main opponent of the project, was really a puppet of the California salt industry.[33]

Prior to its involvement with the saltworks environmental impact assessment, CIBNOR was Baja California Sur's premier advocate of protected areas and biodiversity conservation and a devoted friend of the gray whale.[34] Ortega and his staff collaborated with Homero Aridjis in lobbying President Miguel de la Madrid to create the Vizcaíno Biosphere Reserve. Ortega also coedited a book on the reserve that argues that due to the history of exploitation of natural resources at the hands of foreigners, "The conservation of natural resources of Baja California Sur and their legal protection is an act of the purest form of nationalism."[35] The book, published by CIBNOR, includes a prologue by Homero Aridjis in which he declares his "moral commitment" to gray whale conservation.[36]

In June 1995, Exportadora de Sal placed an advertisement in the *New York Times* announcing its plans to prepare a new environmental impact assessment that would be subject to the review of distinguished scientists.[37]

The whale moans, "All of us, including whales, want to make love and give birth in private," while the man in the boat waves and calls "Come back soon. We're going to miss you." The signs read "Tourist Attraction," "XXX — Adults Only," and "Come and see how whales do it." The stake in the whale's back is labeled "lancheros" for the whalewatching guides, and the knife is labeled UABCS for the Autonomous University of Baja California Sur.

At the same time, Julia Carabias requested that the IWC assist in reviewing project plans and assessing the potential environmental impact.[38]

Part of Exportadora de Sal's willingness to prepare a new environmental impact assessment and open the project up to scrutiny probably derives from a three-page "Informative Note" published by the Mexican government on May 29, 1995. In the document, the INE affirms its willingness to accept the saltworks if Exportadora de Sal mitigates potentially adverse impacts.[39]

Julia Carabias has made a concerted effort to open up the review process to guarantee that a subsequent environmental impact assessment would be more objective than the document prepared by CIBNOR. She also revolutionized the environmental impact review in Mexico. The project was the first in Mexico to be posted on the Internet. In contrast, federal authorities never released the first environmental impact assessment to the public.[40]

Carabias convened a scientific advisory committee to oversee the new environmental impact process. Composed of seven distinguished scientists, the panel developed the terms of reference for the new environmental impact assessment and will evaluate the final report. The committee also held a six-hour hearing in La Paz on February 29, 1996, to receive public input.[41] The meeting was the first time that federal officials in Baja California Sur bothered to solicit public input about a development project. By establishing a public review process for environmental impact assessments, Julia Carabias contributed in a small but important way to the democratization of Mexico. Opening any government process to the public is a significant achievement for a country where information is guarded more fiercely than the public treasury.

Exportadora de Sal contracted the Autonomous University of Baja California Sur (UABCS) to prepare the second environmental impact assessment, hoping to have the report completed by the fall of 1999. Two scientists from the Scripps Institution of Oceanography are assisting the university in assessing the impact of the project on the lagoon's physical processes and benthic communities. Exportadora de Sal officials proclaimed that if the Mexican federal government rejected the San Ignacio Lagoon saltworks after reviewing the new environmental impact assessment, the company would shelve expansion plans.[42]

Carabias made a grave error by allowing Exportadora de Sal to give a million-dollar contract to UABCS to prepare the study. The university has neither the capacity nor the independence to carry out an objective evaluation of the saltworks. The feeling among university staff is that former governor Mercado and Jesús Druk, the university's former chancellor, forced the project on them. According to one member of the environmental impact assessment team, the conclusion of the report has already been "preordained" in favor of saltworks development. The university stands to gain lucrative future research contracts from Exportadora de Sal. Hopefully, the scientific advisory committee can mitigate the pro-project biases of the environmental impact assessment team.

The Governor Plays Politics with Whales

Although the saltworks is in a holding pattern while the new environmental impact assessment is completed, a political campaign in its favor was organized by former governor Guillermo Mercado, who staked his political career on the saltworks. The decision by Julia Carabias to halt the project did little to weaken his campaign. The governor became the designated point man to shore up support for the San Ignacio Lagoon saltworks. Immediately after Carabias stopped the project, Mercado made sure that the ruling party establishment, including candidates for upcoming legislative and municipal president seats, jumped aboard the saltworks bandwagon to prove to party leaders they were loyal team players.

The campaign orchestrated by the governor quickly attracted the support of the entire political establishment of Baja California Sur. Past declarations of concern for gray whales were forgotten as the governor and his cronies proclaimed the project to be desperately needed economic development. Mercado framed the saltworks controversy as a battle against elitist and international interests using gray whale conservation to stop Mexican workers from securing decent jobs.

The salient feature of Mercado's campaign was his avoidance of mentioning Mitsubishi's association with the project. The governor never mentioned the opposition of local fishing cooperatives and *ejidatarios* (members of communal landholding associations). As Mercado pointed the finger at environmentalists, the economy of Baja California Sur crumbled around him. The collapse of the agricultural economy of the Santo Domingo Valley, the state's premier agricultural region, resulted in the loss of thousands of jobs.

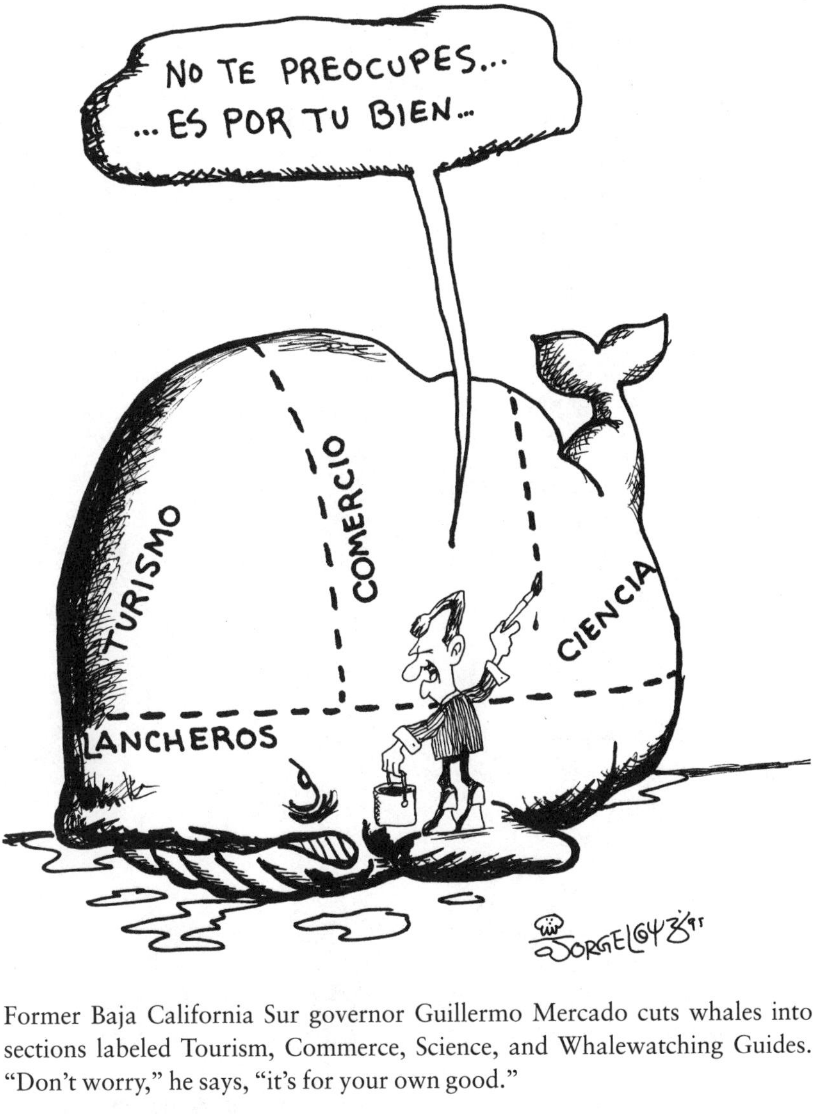

Former Baja California Sur governor Guillermo Mercado cuts whales into sections labeled Tourism, Commerce, Science, and Whalewatching Guides. "Don't worry," he says, "it's for your own good."

The victory in February 1998 of Leonel Cota, a member of the opposition Revolutionary Democratic Party, is evidence that state residents rejected the PRI's development model, which has destroyed the economy of the state. It remains to be seen if Cota, a former PRIísta, will continue the pro-saltworks campaign.

The old man declares, "The Group of 100 is opposed to the expansion of Exportadora de Sal, maybe due to their possible loyalty to transnational interests." The young man, holding a sign that reads "I'm looking for work," answers, "Wow." The old man adds, "Four hundred direct jobs lost," and the young man asks, "Who did you say was against it?" The old man replies, "The only group of 100 who haven't lost their jobs." The young concludes, "They even act like PRIistas."

Local Press and the Saltworks

Governor Mercado used the *Sudcaliforniano* to highlight "popular" support for the saltworks. Except for a handful of independent newspapers in Mexico (there are none in Baja California Sur), the press in Mexico serves the interests of ruling party politicians and the small and all-important class of technocrats. Freedom of the press in Mexico often means the freedom of the government to control the press. Reporters often receive payoffs for the stories they write for politicians and bureaucrats. They rarely rely on first-hand reporting but instead print the entire text of a press release as a legitimate news story. Newspapers have a small circulation and are generally more expensive than their U.S. counterparts. Many pro-government dailies receive direct subsidies from local, state, and federal governments.

Although the *Sudcaliforniano* is avidly pro-PRI, it publishes anyone who purchases print space. The newspaper is part of the Hearst-style Organización Editorial Mexicana, owned by Mario Vázquez Raña, which publishes pro-government newspapers throughout Mexico. A shameless self-promoter, Vázquez uses his newspapers to promote himself *and* the ruling party.

The governor orchestrated his campaign to ensure that all coverage of the saltworks benefited Exportadora de Sal. As a result, the newspaper manipulated "objective" information such as the date the INE rejected the project. For example, *Excelsior,* the pro-government Mexico City daily, carried news of the government's rejection of the saltworks on March 1, 1995.[43] On the same day, the *Sudcaliforniano* headlined Mercado's declaration that the saltworks would not harm the environment. He conveniently forgot to mention the INE decision.[44] Three days later, in a front-page headline, the *Sudcaliforniano* finally announced that federal environmental authorities had rejected the saltworks. However, in a subheadline the newspaper quoted the Baja California Sur INE director, Alfredo Bermúdez, as saying that the project could still be developed.[45]

Soon after the INE rejected the saltworks, ruling party allies throughout Baja California Sur voiced their support for the project. This initial phase of rounding up support for the project began with Mercado's March 7 comment that the saltworks had not been canceled.[46] The following day, Mulege County Supervisor Gilberto Flores Yee declared that Baja

California Sur supported "Governor Mercado with the ultimate objective of ensuring that the project [the saltworks] be developed."[47] The National Federation of Fishing Cooperatives announced its support for the saltworks on March 9, 1995, even though the fishing cooperatives of San Ignacio Lagoon and Punta Abreojos are opposed to the project.[48]

The political roundup by Mercado culminated in the declaration by Herminio Blanco that the saltworks would make Mexico a global leader in salt production.[49] By manufacturing a wave of political support for Exportadora de Sal, Mercado assured Blanco that the ruling party was firmly behind the project. Blanco visited Guerrero Negro and declared his support for the project one day after the company appealed the INE's decision to halt the saltworks.

Although the *Sudcaliforniano* printed misinformation about the saltworks, an independent columnist for the paper managed to criticize the government for its pro-saltworks campaign. Between April 21 and July 10, 1995, José Soto Molina published twenty columns on the saltworks, providing opponents of the project, including many government insiders, with a forum to cite details of the venture ignored in the environmental impact assessment.

The most important point made by Soto Molina was how the project fits into a state development trend in which state and federal agencies sell large portions of the coastline to foreign multinationals with little benefit for surrounding communities. The obvious case is Guerrero Negro, where the presence of Exportadora de Sal for forty years has not resulted in any noticeable improvement in the region. The other is the Los Cabos region, an excellent example of overdevelopment and poor planning. In both areas, Soto Molina argued, state and federal officials sanction destructive development that provides low-wage jobs with almost no tax benefits for local governments. Soto Molina no longer works for the *Sudcaliforniano*.

Diputados Take a Field Trip

For ruling party politicians, especially future candidates in state and federal elections, demonstrating support for Exportadora de Sal was secondary to using Mercado's saltworks campaign to promote their own political careers. The project became a perfect opportunity for politicians to position themselves favorably with the governor and PRI officials prior to the selection of candidates for seats in the state and federal legislatures and county governments.

A team of federal legislators traveled to Guerrero Negro from Mexico City in early May 1995 to "investigate" the saltworks for themselves. Included in the delegation were the presidents of the Commission of Ecology and the Environment, the Commission of Fisheries, the Commission of the Navy, and the Commission of Tourism. In addition, a legislator from Comondú County, Rodimirio Amaya Tellez, was also present. Amaya, better known as "Rody" in his Comondú County district, was thinking of running for the office of Comondú County Supervisor. Needing as much outside political support as possible to ensure that he would be selected as the PRI candidate, Rody declared that the saltworks would not harm marine mammals.[50] The *Sudcaliforniano* complied by running photos of Rody at the project site for the following two days.

As part of the roundup of support, legislators located two campesinos to pose for photos and declare their support for the saltworks. Reacting to the comment by Group of 100 president Homero Aridjis that the children of Mexico would cry if Exportadora de Sal destroyed part of their natural heritage, the campesinos responded that the children of the Vizcaíno Desert were so hungry they did not have time to cry.[51]

Based on their two-day evaluation of saltworks operations in Guerrero Negro and their visit to the salt flats of San Ignacio Lagoon, the twenty-three legislators who made the field visit along with twenty-four congressional colleagues urged Julia Carabias to reconsider her decision to halt the saltworks. Of the forty-seven legislators who signed the letter, forty-one were members of the PRI. Four were members of the right-wing National Action Party (PAN). The Worker's Party and the Democratic Revolutionary Party each were represented by one deputy.[52]

Now that opposition parties control the federal legislature by a slight majority, Mercado and Exportadora de Sal can no longer be sure of the support of a once-important ally. The current head of the Ecology Commission is a member of the Partido Ecologísta Verde (the Green Party). The Mexican Green Party pushed the Mexican Congress to form a new commission to investigate all aspects of the San Ignacio saltworks.[53] They did this on June 25, 1998. This new commission, with twelve members from five political parties, is another example of how the saltworks debate and the political capital of gray whales are slowly pushing open the door of a political system often described as the "perfect dictatorship."

The Opposition Steps Up to the Plate

Maria Elena Sanchez of the Group of 100 was astounded when she received a telephone call on January 13, 1995, informing her of Exportadora de Sal's plans to build a new saltworks around San Ignacio Lagoon. Why would the Mexican government risk losing the last undeveloped refuge of Mexico's environmental superstar?

The Group of 100 is Mexico's most influential environmental group. Members include Carlos Fuentes, Homero Aridjis, Günter Grass, Peter Matthiessen, Roger Payne, David Brower, Lester Brown, Gary Snyder, and Tom Hayden, among others. (Nobel laureate Octavio Paz was also a member.) The Mexican government does not like having the names of intellectuals such as Homero Aridjis and Carlos Fuentes used against its pet projects.

Homero Aridjis is one of Mexico's most well respected writers. A poet and novelist, Aridjis is the president of PEN International, a writer's lobbying group. He is also Mexico's fiercest defender of endangered wildlife. Aridjis played a major role in pushing the Mexican federal government to enact laws to protect Monarch butterflies and sea turtles. However, the poet is most passionately involved with the protection of Mexico's gray whales. In 1988, he lobbied President Miguel de la Madrid to create the Vizcaíno Biosphere Reserve. That same year in a letter to Manuel Camacho Solís, then chief of the federal environment agency, Aridjis accused Exportadora de Sal of spilling 4 million gallons of diesel fuel into Scammon's Lagoon.[54]

After Sanchez received the January 13 phone call, Aridjis and the Group of 100 international coordinator, Betty Ferber (an American who is married to Aridjis), sprang into action. A week later, on January 21, the Mexico City independent daily *Reforma* published an op-ed piece written by Aridjis, "Mexico Sells Whale Sanctuary." Despite national turmoil over the collapse of the economy and Zedillo's last-minute push to capture revolutionary leader Subcomandante Marcos, the article was widely read. After Aridjis outlined how the San Ignacio saltworks threatened gray whales, he asked, "Where are the environmental authorities? Are they authorizing its [the Vizcaíno Biosphere Reserve's] destruction?"[55]

One month later *Reforma* published another Aridjis article that provided a detailed description of the saltworks along with a discussion of the inadequacy of the first environmental impact assessment.[56] Six days later on February 27, 1995, INE director Gabriel Quadri de la Torre halted the project.

The primary goal of the Group of 100's campaign, besides killing the saltworks, was to turn the project into an international issue. Articles on the project soon appeared in the *Los Angeles Times,* the *San Diego Union-Tribune,* and the *New York Times*. The Mexican government hates negative press attention, especially during periods of economic and political upheaval. The focus of the international press on the issue was a particularly effective way of convincing federal environmental authorities, especially Julia Carabias, to maintain a cautious distance from Exportadora de Sal.

The Group of 100's use of the press culminated with the May 10, 1995, publication of an advertisement in the *New York Times* accusing Mitsubishi of planning to suck San Ignacio Lagoon dry. With the publication of the ad, Exportadora de Sal, Mitsubishi, Herminio Blanco, and Guillermo Mercado lost the propaganda war. In response, Exportadora de Sal and Mitsubishi ran consecutive full-page ads in the *New York Times* on June 26 and 27 announcing their intention to revise the project's environmental impact assessment and permit international experts to review the plans.

By using the press to focus worldwide attention on the saltworks, the Group of 100 was at least able to delay its development. The efforts of the environmental group ensured that a panel of scientific experts, rather than just harried technocrats under the glare of Herminio Blanco, would be able to review project plans. This was an extraordinary victory in a country where secrecy regarding state matters is official policy. The pressure of the Rainforest Action Network's international boycott against Mitsubishi also likely contributed to Exportadora de Sal's decision to prepare a new environmental impact assessment. Prior to its ad in the *New York Times,* Mitsubishi avoided acknowledging its role in the saltworks.

While the Group of 100 successfully used the power of the international press to make the saltworks an international issue, the environmental group actively pursued the project in the equally important legal arena.

Gray whales rock their newborns to sleep in this warm Mexican lagoon. Their only enemy? Mitsubishi, a giant Japanese conglomerate with plans to suck it dry.

The United Nations and the government of Mexico recognize it as the Vizcaino Desert Biosphere Reserve, one of the most precious places on Earth and the largest protected area in Latin America.

But that hasn't stopped Japanese giant Mitsubishi and Mexico's own government from planning a huge salt factory right in its heart.

In jeopardy? Creatures on the brink of extinction: Peregrine falcons, Pronghorn antelope, sea turtles...

And the single most spectacular recovery made by an endangered species in the last half century: the gray whale.

One of the World's great success stories...in danger again.

The gray whale migrates down from Alaska each year to Baja's warm and buoyant salt lagoons, protected by the Mexican government since the 1970s.

There the whales mate and calve, largely undisturbed. So successfully, in fact, that only last year they were finally taken off the Endangered Species List.

Yet suddenly, danger has returned.

Exportadora de Sal (ESA), an industrial salt producer co-owned by the Mexican government and Japan's Mitsubishi (see box) plan a seventy square mile salt operation at Laguna San Ignacio.

Honored as a UNESCO World Heritage Site, Laguna San Ignacio is the most pristine gray whale nursery.

But what will it look like after operations doubling ESA's output begin? Plans call for:

▲ Pumping 462 million metric tons of water a year out of the lagoon. This will reduce its salinity and the buoyancy prized by the whales.

▲ Building a mile-long concrete pier directly in the whale's path.

▲ Dredging the lagoon itself for barge traffic if the pier is damaged by the area's frequent hurricanes.

▲ Shipping salt out and bringing diesel fuel in, ship traffic—and chances of pollution—will increase tremendously. Another Baja lagoon once frequented by the whales has been all but abandoned since commercial traffic increased.

Is Mitsubishi at war with the world?

Mitsubishi has a history of exploiting the environment:

- **Alaska**—Convicted of anti-trust and collusion; cuts in Tongass National Forest, the largest intact temperate rainforest in the world.
- **Oregon & Washington**— Huge purchaser of whole logs for export; costs US mill jobs.
- **Chile**—Promotes cutting of ancient forests for export as wood chips to Japan.
- **Brazil**—Largest timber mill in the Amazon rainforest, buys most of its wood from loggers operating without permits.
- **Malaysia**—Owns Daiya Malaysia, country's largest wood exporter; buys from other companies logging in territory of native groups.

Also at risk: $1 million given by the World Bank to administer the Biosphere Reserve, *based on a 1995 management plan that omits any mention of the $120 million commercial salt operation.*

This is a world-class nature refuge, not an industrial wasteland.

Despite the obvious damage such a huge industrial operation would do to Latin America's largest nature reserve, the salt company calls it a "wasteland" and completely ignores any possible harm to the lagoon itself.

In fact, its 465-page Environmental Impact Assessment devotes just 23 lines to the gray whale.

Not surprisingly, the Assessment was rejected by the National Ecology Institute, Mexico's equivalent of the Environmental Protection Agency.

With millions in export earnings at stake, the government, which owns 51% of ESA, has appealed the decision of its own environmental agency.

This is not a case of nature vs. jobs. The balanced development of the Biosphere Reserve includes the fishermen and their families who live there. The salt operation will devastate fishing— and destroy the increasing number of jobs based on "eco-tourism" attracted to the area's rich natural diversity.

Salt, on the other hand, will mean a false economy: just 200 permanent jobs, with fenced compounds for Mitsubishi's staff and near-poverty conditions for the Mexican workers.

The first test of Mexico's resolve after NAFTA and the peso's collapse

NAFTA raised many environmental warning flags in North America. Now we will see if those concerns were justified.

Gray whales summer in U.S., Canadian and Russian waters. If the Mexican government ruins their winter refuge, the effect will be felt throughout the NAFTA region.

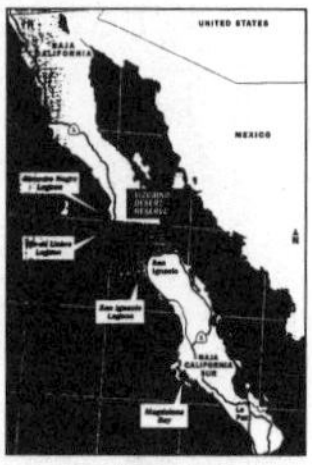

Grupo de los Cien (The Group of 100), Mexico's leading environmental organization, is concerned about the human and natural consequences of Mexico's economic crisis.

We know that such times place the environment in greatest peril, as myopic decision-makers rush to sacrifice ecology for cash. The Mexican people have paid the terrible price for this sort of thinking many times before in their history.

That's why we ask you to join with us in solidarity with nature, which knows no human boundaries, and in hope of a sustainable future—the foundation for which can already be found in the Vizcaino Desert and Laguna San Ignacio.

Please mail the coupon to the President of Mexico. Time is short. We need your support. Thank you.

The following are just a few of those endorsing protection of this globally significant area.

Homero Aridjis	Octavio Paz
Sir James Goldsmith	Lester Brown
Günter Grass	Roger Payne
Margaret Atwood	David Brower
Kjell Espmark	J.M.G. LeClezio
Yves Bonnefoy	W.S. Merwin
Allen Ginsberg	Anne Ehrlich
A.S. Byatt	Peter Matthiessen

Grupo de los Cien International
International Fund for Animal Welfare
Greenpeace
Animal Welfare Institute
Whale and Dolphin Conservation Society
Cetacean Society International
World Wide Fund for Nature International
International Wildlife Coalition
Earth Island Institute
Humane Society International
Sierra Club
Rainforest Action Network
Friends of Animals
Save the Whales
Consejo para la Defensa de la Costa Pacifico
Japan Whale Conservation Network

President Ernesto Zedillo
c/o The Embassy of Mexico
1911 Pennsylvania Avenue NW, Washington, DC 20006

Mitsubishi's proposed salt operation at Laguna San Ignacio, in the Zicaino Desert Biosphere Reserve, is a test of Mexico's environmental laws. The whole world is watching, including your partners in NAFTA, who were assured of Mexico's good faith during negotiations. Don't endanger the gray whale. Help build a sustainable future.

NAME

ADDRESS

Save the Baja gray whale nursery. Stop Mitsubishi and Mexico's government.

Grupo de los Cien Internacional
Homero Aridjis, President
466 Green Street , San Francisco, CA 94133

No government, however troubled, and no corporation, however strong, has the right to threaten the gray whale nursery in Baja. I support your domestic and international efforts to protect the integrity of the Vizcaino Desert Biosphere Reserve. ☐ I enclose my contribution of __$20 __$35 __$50 __$75 __$100 __$500 __Other.

NAME

ADDRESS

Grupo de los Cien (The Group of 100) was founded in Mexico by prominent artists and intellectuals in 1985 to raise public awareness of Mexico's severe environmental problems and prod the government to respond. Grupo activists have scored significant victories on species and habitat protection, air pollution, river preservation, and other issues. They were the first Mexican recipients of the UN's Global 500 environmental award.

The Group of 100's advertisement in the *New York Times* of May 10, 1995, which rocketed the saltworks controversy to the top of the international "eco-battle" charts. (Courtesy of the Grupo de los Cien 1995)

Under the Mexican Law of Ecological Balance and Environmental Protection (the General Ecology Law), any nongovernmental organization or individual has the right to contest an environmental impact assessment and request that the government halt the project. In practice this almost never occurs. Government technocrats are highly suspicious and resistant to any public participation in the decision-making process.

The Group of 100 and the Mexican Green Party filed a petition on August 21, 1995, with the INE claiming that Exportadora de Sal did not have the legal authority to harvest salt at its existing facility at Scammon's Lagoon. In 1992, the federal government granted Exportadora de Sal a new mining concession. According to Article 41 of the General Ecology Law, Exportadora de Sal should have prepared an environmental impact assessment when it received the new concession. Both groups also requested that the federal attorney general's Office for Environmental Protection formally investigate existing Exportadora de Sal activities in Guerrero Negro to determine the extent of company-related environmental damage.[57]

The work of the Group of 100 against the saltworks provided Julia Carabias with the political support to justify her decision to halt the pet project of Herminio Blanco. Without the national and international press attention that the Group of 100 directed toward the project, the saltworks might not have been stopped. The Group of 100 had enough ammunition to impede the advance of Exportadora de Sal. However, it required the additional support of a wide coalition of national and international environmental groups to ensure that Carabias would establish a transparent environmental review process. This also ensured that she would have political support to withstand increasing political pressure to approve the saltworks.

The Washington, D.C.–based Natural Resources Defense Council (NRDC), one of North America's most influential environmental groups, entered the saltworks fray on February 27, 1996, by sending a joint letter with the Group of 100 to Julia Carabias requesting "an open and participatory" environmental review process. Mark Spalding represented NRDC at the February 29, 1996, public hearing in La Paz. At the meeting, Spalding chastised the INE for failing to establish a participatory public review process, using the public hearing as a prime example. Environmental authorities had announced the meeting date only a few days before it was held.[58]

A large public outcry against the saltworks was generated by the NRDC campaign. An effective direct mail campaign urged respondents to send letters to President Zedillo and Mitsubishi. So far, Mitsubishi, the government of Japan, and the Mexican government have received more than 650,000 letters asking them to halt the project. According to Jacob Scherr, international director of the NRDC, the objective of the anti-saltworks campaign is to "attack it from every single angle."[59]

The NRDC campaign has helped to maintain the important press attention on the issue. A media and VIP whalewatching trip organized in collaboration with the International Fund for Animal Welfare (IFAW) in March 1997, featured Jean Michel Cousteau, Robert Kennedy Jr., Pierce Brosnan, Glen Close, Homero Aridjis, and a diverse group of international reporters. The trip generated media coverage of the saltworks in *Newsweek,* the *Los Angeles Times,* and other outlets in the United States and Mexico. NRDC followed up the trip with another in January 1998. By including Hollywood stars on its campaign, the anti-saltworks message reached the ears of a segment of the population that is usually not concerned with whales. Articles about the San Ignacio trip appeared in the gossip magazine *Hello!* and the society pages of *Reforma.*[60]

One of the most critical components of the NRDC campaign is its partnership with local and regional environmental groups in Baja California and Baja California Sur. With the help of Pro Esteros, an environmental group based in Ensenada, NRDC organized a Baja California coalition of nongovernmental organizations to share information about the project. The coalition, Pro Peninsula, includes local fishermen, a San Ignacio Lagoon whalewatching business, and regional environmental groups. The support of heavyweights such as NRDC and IFAW provided coalition members with the political support they needed to speak out against the saltworks. The creation of Pro Peninsula was the first step in building a solid base of local and regional organizations that can carry out the task of long-term gray whale conservation on their own.

The World Wildlife Fund–Mexico entered the saltworks battle in February 1997 and is working behind the scenes with Julia Carabias to provide her with the science-based information she needs to kill the project. The Mexico City–based organization prepared a study documenting the great economic value of local fisheries for Carabias to help counter Juan Bremer's claims that the saltworks will boost the local economy. Holly

Payne, the coordinator of the World Wildlife Fund–Mexico effort, is the daughter of Roger Payne, a pioneer in whale conservation. Holly grew up in Argentina, where her parents studied the right whales of the Patagonian coast. She is right at home fighting to save the gray whales of San Ignacio Lagoon.

Although politicians and the media portrayed opposition to the salt facility as the work of a Mexico City poet, two ejidos from the Vizcaíno Biosphere Reserve declared their opposition to the saltworks at the same time as the Group of 100. Ejidatarios around Scammon's Lagoon have fought for years to receive just compensation for lands expropriated or rented by Exportadora de Sal.[61] In a letter to President Zedillo, leaders of the San Ignacio and the Luis Echeverría ejidos, both of which control land adjoining the shore of San Ignacio Lagoon, argued that the project could harm their ability to earn a living from aquaculture and fishing inside the Vizcaíno Biosphere Reserve.[62] Ignored by the media and the political establishment, the letter provided Julia Carabias with evidence that the agency's rejection of the project had local support.

Jorge Peón, the president of the San Ignacio Lagoon–based Luis Echeverría ejido, wrote a detailed letter to the federal government on April 20, 1995, detailing resource piracy in the region and the potential impact on local fisheries from the saltworks. In the letter he asked, "When will the interests of the residents of the region [around San Ignacio Lagoon] be a priority for the government? Do you expect that after the resource piracy that we have seen [in San Ignacio Lagoon], that when plans are announced to build an industrial project that will take millions of gallons of water out of our lagoon that we will hold a party and welcome the project even though we know it will destroy the resources we depend on?"

Frightened of continuing their opposition, leaders of the San Ignacio ejido declined to sign the letter. Ironically, an article was planted in the *Sudcaliforniano* citing the willingness of the Luis Echeverría ejido to accept the saltworks if they were given support for aquaculture projects.[63] According to ejido leaders, the article was a fabrication.

Julia Carabias Lays Down the Law

When Julia Carabias sat down at the VIP table in the Autonomous University of Baja California Sur auditorium in La Paz on April 19, 1995, to inaugurate a marine mammal conference, she was seated between Governor Guillermo Mercado and University Chancellor Jesús Druk—a symbolic seating arrangement between the foremost political authority of the state and the foremost representative of science. Carabias traveled to La Paz to bolster her decision to halt the saltworks. While Carabias occupied the seat of honor, Gabriel Quadri de la Torre, the director of the INE, was placed at the extreme right end of the VIP table, next to a representative from the city of La Paz. I have no doubt that Mercado's failure to greet Quadri during his opening remarks and salutations to the VIPs on the dais was deliberate.

While the governor professed his concern for environmental protection and the conservation of the Vizcaíno Biosphere Reserve, Carabias declared, "Science and not politics will determine whether or not the saltworks is built."

That Exportadora de Sal feigned surprise at the depth of the international opposition to the San Ignacio Lagoon saltworks is astonishing. The declaration by Carabias that science is more important than politics is proof that gray whales are as valuable as the future profits of Exportadora de Sal. If environmental groups can continue to pressure the Mexican government and support Carabias, gray whales have a slight chance of surviving the saltworks.

But if the PRI and its economic allies consider Guerrero Negro and Los Cabos to be models of sustainable development, then the people, whales, and wildlife of the Vizcaíno Biosphere Reserve have much to fear. In the battle over salt and San Ignacio Lagoon, politics, *not* science, will determine how much Mexico values the gray whale.

7 Fishing Communities and Gray Whale Conservation

Conservation was made up by politicians who drive big cars and have never experienced hunger.

—A RETIRED FISHERMAN, SAN IGNACIO LAGOON

The gray whale lagoons of Baja California Sur are at the periphery of the political system in Mexico. For bureaucrats in Mexico City, the reality of gray whales and the people that interact with them is almost irrelevant. Mexico City reacts to events and issues filtered through the politics of La Paz. At times officials in La Paz and Mexico City create policies that reflect the reality of the gray whale lagoons of Baja California Sur. But that is rare.

The inhabitants of San Ignacio Lagoon and Magdalena Bay are now at the center of issues involving the control of, and access to, gray whales and their habitat in Mexico. Understanding the human dimension of gray whale conservation at the local level requires delving into the geography of San Ignacio Lagoon and Magdalena Bay, the lifeways of the people who live there, and their interactions with government officials responsible for implementing policies created in distant capitals. In the gray whale lagoons of Baja California Sur, the past shaped the present. The future of gray whale conservation is in the hands of people whose livelihoods are linked to the long-term survival of these marine mammals and the lagoons of Baja California Sur.

The *Zona Abandonada*: San Ignacio Lagoon

Atardecer. Sunset. The upper part of San Ignacio Lagoon and the Sierra de San Francisco are bathed in pink twilight. Thousands of cormorants fly over my trailer near the beach at La Fridera on their way to Isla Garzas. They passed the day feeding in tidal flats ten miles to the south. One group moves across the setting sun, wings flapping hard. Stragglers try to catch up. Flying in a V formation, undulating, they move toward the mountains and disappear in the fading twilight. I hear tiny squeaks and flapping noises as they pass overhead.

As the sun falls into the Pacific, I listen for the first sounds of the evening symphony. Whale spouts are barely audible. A chorus of black brant honks begins, with intermittent whale spouts for added bass. Finally, the finale: honks, spouts, and at last the whoosh of a whale breach and splash in the darkness.

Only by traveling overland to San Ignacio Lagoon do you begin to appreciate the scale of the landscape that surrounds it. The car-killing dirt road from the town of San Ignacio to the lagoon rambles past cactus-covered desert hills that descend into impenetrable salt flats. The first view of the lagoon on the slow descent from the hills and mesas west of Rancho El Alamo is overwhelming. To the west are the humpback peaks of the Sierra de Santa Clara. Spreading out to the north is the clay-colored Sierra de San Francisco. The jutting escarpments, layered peaks, and hidden canyons of the Sierra de Guadalupe now seem even closer than before. It is easy to understand why San Ignacio Lagoon is such a desirable place for whales. It is surrounded by a fortress of desert and mountains that make it a safe haven from the onslaught of civilization. A bad road is a good way of ensuring the long-term survival of gray whales.

Traveling the roads to the southernmost settlements of the lagoon requires a local guide to navigate the treacherous sand dunes, salt flats, and mud of a no-man's-land. Take the wrong turn and you end up on a twenty-mile detour that leads to a salt flat crossing filled with water and mud so thick that even walking is difficult. Every few hundred yards, isolated tire tracks head out into the flats and nowhere.

Located in the county of Mulege, San Ignacio Lagoon is approximately 700 miles south of the U.S.–Mexico border (see map 2.1). The 200,000-acre lagoon forms the southern boundary of the Vizcaíno Desert. It receives little rainfall and is located within a desolate, windswept landscape of tidal mudflats, mangroves, salt flats, sand dunes, and a sparsely vegetated desert plain intersected by more densely vegetated arroyos. Three mountain ranges surround the landward edge of the lagoon: Sierra de Santa Clara to the north; Sierra de San Francisco to the northeast; and Sierra de Guadalupe to the southeast.

Divided into northern and southern sections, or "arms," the lagoon has three outlets to the Pacific Ocean (see map 2.2). Two barrier islands protect it from the open ocean. The majority of the lagoon is composed of large intertidal flats and deep, narrow channels.

At low tide, the water recedes hundreds of yards, revealing pockmarked tide pools inhabited by sea horses, octopus, and juvenile grouper. Two small islands, Isla Garzas and Isla Pelícanos, are located in the upper portion of the northern arm. A third, Islote Abaroa, is located west of the northern entrance.

The nearest town, San Ignacio, is approximately forty miles to the northeast. A dirt road connects the lagoon to San Ignacio and Highway 1, the main north–south arterial in the peninsula. A series of tracks pass southward through salt flats and sand dunes, connecting the lagoon to San Juanico and Ciudad Insurgentes via a paved road a hundred miles to the south.

With the exception of gray whales, most of San Ignacio Lagoon's wildlife is not easy to spot. Shorebirds blend into the tidal flats. Octopus hide in empty fan scallop shells. Great blue herons hide among mangroves. Bobcats sneak across the road and disappear into a cactus thicket. Green sea turtles pop their heads out of the water for an instant. Coyotes, however, are not shy. Paddle a kayak around Punta Piedra and you'll see a coyote on the shoreline checking on the crab life.

San Ignacio is an important hatchery for commercially valuable fish and shellfish species. Lobster is the most valuable species harvested inside the lagoon. Bay and fan scallops, close to commercial collapse, are also lucrative. Fish caught inside the lagoon include corvina, snook, halibut, and sierra. Patient and knowledgeable fishermen still earn a living hand-lining for halibut, bass, and grouper near Punta Piedra. Some risk their lives rounding up thick schools of corvina and snook with nets in the surf line at the main entrance to the lagoon. Others set gill nets over the entrance to mangrove inlets and haul in mullet, stingray, guitarfish, and small halibut.

The shallow waters and mangroves of San Ignacio Lagoon are critical habitat for the shorebirds and waterfowl of the Pacific flyway. In early October, the first arrivals fill the tidal flats during low-tide feeding sessions. White pelicans bob their heads in the water for a quick meal as they float out of mangrove inlets with the tide. Yellow-crowned night herons, exhausted from their long migration, hide in the rocks of Punta Piedra. In November, flocks of skittish black brant conceal themselves near the mangroves at high tide. At low tide they move out into the expanding tidal flat where they feed, bottoms in the air. Surf scoters are the last birds to settle in for the winter. With their wide orange beaks and black bodies, they are easy to spot bobbing among brown pelicans and cormorants feeding on baitfish.

People of the Lagoon

Conceptualizing San Ignacio Lagoon as only a body of water ignores its importance in infusing the Vizcaíno Desert with life. Originally named Bahía de San Cristóval by Spanish explorers, San Ignacio Lagoon historically has had few permanent residents. This was most likely due to the lack of any freshwater in the area. After the demise of indigenous people from disease, residents from the town of San Ignacio and the ranches of the Sierra de Guadalupe occasionally visited the lagoon to fish and extract salt at the Salina el Cuarenta, a few miles south. They carried water by burro from the foothills of the Sierra de Guadalupe.

The parents of many longtime area inhabitants moved to the coast in the 1920s from nearby mountain ranches. Other residents are relatives of people who occasionally lived at the lagoon throughout this century. They fished for sea turtles and sharks. These original settlers are part of the Californio culture, descendants of the European and mestizo immigrants from mainland Mexico who worked on ranches near mission sites during the colonial and postcolonial periods of the eighteenth and nineteenth centuries. Semipermanent fish camps along the southern shores of the lagoon were established in the 1920s. These camps still exist. The families that live there survive on income from fishing and whalewatching.

Long-established lagoon inhabitants retain close ties with relatives in the town of San Ignacio and throughout the Sierra de Guadalupe. For those who set up camp along the shoreline, finding water was a two-day affair and required filling wooden barrels from water holes in the Sierra de Guadalupe foothills. According to Tatito Aguilar, the brother of Antonio Aguilar, a lagoon whalewatching guide, "It was a two-day trip by burro to San Ignacio. But we mostly walked. We were so poor back then that my nine brothers and sisters and I used to fight over dates we found." Tatito and his family still struggle to make a living from a ranch at the end of an unmarked sandy track tucked away in a hidden canyon about an hour east of the lagoon. He survives by trading and selling meat and firewood to lagoon fishermen and occasionally selling a cow to buyers who roam the backcountry in dilapidated Ford pickups.

Prior to fanning out to the rocky, lobster- and abalone-filled shoreline of the Vizcaíno peninsula sixty years ago, fishermen rarely ventured outside San Ignacio Lagoon to fish. It was safer to handle handmade pangas inside the lagoon than to brave the surf outside. Using white cotton sails to catch the morning and afternoon winds, a pair of oars when the wind died, and a harpoon, early-twentieth-century fishermen from the Sierra de Guadalupe and San Ignacio made the lagoon the first fishing ground of the central Pacific coast.

José Camacho, an 83-year-old retired fisherman, lives with his wife at Rancho Agua Verde, about 30 miles east of the lagoon. He has the broad shoulders and muscular arms of someone who spent much of his life rowing a boat and hauling up lobster traps. While sitting on a handmade wooden bench under the *palapa* of his plywood ranchhouse, he tells me about the early days of fishing. "We used to sail up toward the *bocana* [entrance] in the morning, to harpoon sharks and sea turtles. If there was no wind to push us home in the afternoons, we'd row back to camp. Sometimes we'd spend the night on one of the islands. There was a lot of life in the lagoon back then."

Until the 1930s, the fish camp of La Fridera, where the Aguilar family now lives, was a port for the loading of salt obtained at the El Cuarenta salt flat. In 1935, eighteen-year-old Ricardo Aguilar walked 60 miles north to El Cuarenta on foot from his father's ranch in Cadeje to ask for a job. He landed the job but earned only 15 *centavos* for every 220-pound sack of salt he filled. A day's labor earned him about a peso and a half in wages but not in cash. Wages were paid in frijoles. After a week of back-breaking work, Ricardo quit and walked back to the ranch. The remains of a pier used to load salt can still be seen at La Fridera.

In a region where wildlife is difficult to hunt, San Ignacio Lagoon has always meant life. It required a lot of effort to chase and shoot a white-tailed deer through rocky canyons and hillsides. But sea turtles, sharks, and shrimp were abundant. Sea turtles were the main staple for the ranchers who descended from the Sierra de Guadalupe and the residents of San Ignacio who trudged forty miles with their burros. Sea turtle oil and cow brains were used to cure tanned hides. The oil is also considered to an excellent cure-all and many lagoon inhabitants ingested a few tablespoons of oil daily. According to Josefina Cota, who has lived at the lagoon for more than forty years, "A lot of the older fisherman would slit the throat of a turtle and collect the blood in a cup and drink it. They said there was nothing better for living a long, healthy life." Given the remarkable physical condition of many senior residents of the region, they may have been right.

Other lagoon wildlife occasionally hunted by local residents includes the white pelican, noted for its tasty breast meat, and black brant, which, although valued as a game bird, is difficult to shoot. Coyotes, a hated pest along the coast, are always fair game. Coyote meat is used as a traditional folk remedy for arthritis and lower back pain. Raw coyote is applied directly to the afflicted area in question, or the fat is rendered and rubbed directly on the skin. Some lagoon residents told me that fishermen occasionally use pitchforks to spear bottlenose dolphins. However, no one I talked to had actually witnessed this. The meat is not prized as it is in Chile.[1]

San Ignacio Lagoon became part of the twentieth century with the arrival of American scientists who studied gray whales. Due to the pioneering visits to San Ignacio Lagoon by Scripps researcher Carl Hubbs (see chapter 4), San Ignacio Lagoon became the subject of documentary films and feature articles in publications such as *National Geographic*. In 1977, gray whale researchers Mary Lou Jones and Steven Swartz initiated their six-year study of gray whale behavior and demography in San Ignacio Lagoon. In subsequent years Marilyn Dalheim, Bruce Mate, and Jim Sumich joined them. These researchers interacted with local people and inadvertently promoted the lagoon as the foremost place on the planet to touch, hug, pet, and kiss wild whales.

Today, although there are six fishing communities with a population of approximately three hundred permanent residents, San Ignacio Lagoon is barely connected to the twentieth century. Lagoon inhabitants live without any of the amenities of modern life—access to potable water, grocery stores, health care, electricity, or decent roads. Their children study at a boarding school in San Ignacio after the sixth grade if they continue their education beyond primary school. Because the lagoon is so isolated, area residents must travel to the town of San Ignacio and surrounding ranches to obtain water, gasoline, propane, and basic foodstuffs. There are no services. The closest source of potable water is located twenty-five miles from the lagoon at Rancho El Alamo.

Three communities—La Laguna, La Base, and La Fridera—are on the southern shore of the lagoon's northern arm. Longtime lagoon residents inhabit them. Another settlement, Ejido Luis Echeverría, is approximately a mile southeast of La Fridera. It has a plywood evangelical church, a few scattered houses, and the area's only elementary school. El Cardón is two miles south of La Fridera and is a classic shoreline migrant fish camp. The inhabitants of this tidal-flat community live in makeshift shoreline houses that flood when it rains or during high tides. Sea turtle and shellfish pirates often camp at El Cardón, hiring their cash-starved neighbors.

During the 1980s, immigrants from impoverished areas of mainland Mexico arrived at El Cardón, seeking work in local fisheries. Some came to escape political and drug-related violence. Many worked in the Pacific bay scallop industry, which involved up to one thousand people scattered around the lagoon working three shifts. The presence of a large, mobile population combined with the lack of civil authority contributes to a climate of lawlessness. Consequently, local residents refer to San Ignacio Lagoon as a *zona abandonada*.

Two additional communities, La Boca de los Cardones and El Delgadito, are at the extreme southern end of the lagoon. La Boca de los Cardones is a ragtag collection of dilapidated shacks inhabited by migrants who work as day laborers in the pismo clam industry at the edge of a small channel. The camp is almost impossible to reach by land. Getting there requires crossing treacherous dunes and mudflats that are impassible during rains or high tides. Then the camp can only be reached by boat. El Delgadito (The Skinny Place) is on a sand peninsula that separates the lagoon from the southern ocean entrance. About fifty plywood homes are crammed together. A cooperative harvests pismo clams about a mile offshore.

Lagoon houses are constructed from plywood, cardboard, plastic tarps, and driftwood. Old truck freezer compartments make convenient and watertight dwellings. A few of the longtime residents have cement floors, screened-in windows, and satellite dishes powered by solar panels and wind generators.

The seasons in San Ignacio Lagoon are determined more by the migrations of fish than by the weather. With the exception of occasional thundershowers during late-summer *chubascos,* local weather is a constant dose of biting northeasterly winds and cloudless, sunny skies. Around

November and December, storms from the north bring in drizzle that locals call *equipatas* and that makes driving through mudflats an ordeal but does not fill empty water holes or satisfy thirsty livestock in the mountains.

During the summer and early fall, lagoon and ocean temperatures are warm and fishermen chase schools of sierra and corvina through the surf. By late fall, when water temperatures cool down, both species are hard to catch. Gill nets are then set outside the lagoon for blue shark, stingray, Pacific angel shark, and halibut. In October, the lobster season opens, and although only a few people set traps inside the lagoon, many more illegally dive for them. By December, preparations for Christmas visits to Sierra ranches and the decrease in the availability of fish coincide with the migration of gray whales.

During the January to April gray whale season, some residents work as whalewatching guides. Others continue to collect pismo clams. Some find work with seafood pirates from La Paz and Ciudad Constitución. Corvina and sierra, both high-priced fish, slowly return with the arrival of summer and warm water.

Outside the Lagoon

Because fishing is so difficult and whales are so friendly, it is no surprise that more and more fishermen from San Ignacio Lagoon view working as whalewatching guides as a safer and more economically secure way of earning a living than fishing. One day, I asked my neighbor Angel Ruelas to let me accompany him on one of his fishing forays into the ocean outside the lagoon. I wanted to witness firsthand the rigors of lagoon fishing and understand why locals eagerly embrace work in the whalewatching industry.

As I walked from my trailer to Angel's house on a mid-December morning, the red sun rising over the Sierra de Guadalupe sharply outlined the mesa that fronts the lagoon *salitrales* (salt flats). Fortunately, the wind was not blowing very hard. Angel had a cup of strong coffee waiting. No *pata rajada*,[2] or choyero fisherman, travels anywhere after waking up without first turning on the radio and slowly sipping a cup of strong, sweet, black coffee. Baja fishermen wake up with a strong pot of coffee and retire to bed after sipping a last cup.

Chuy, Angel's dark, serious, stuttering four-year-old son, was standing next to his dad in the doorway as I entered the whitewashed, two-room plywood shack Angel shares with his wife, Pola, and four young children. I gladly accepted the steaming cup that Angel handed me. Varo, a strong, quiet, bull-like thirty-year-old from San Ignacio who also works as a whalewatching guide, walked over from the little, blue plywood house next to my trailer at La Fridera. Antonio Aguilar, who also owns the panga we went out in, owns both houses. Angel and Varo each get a third of the catch, and Antonio gets the other third.

We sat down at the tiny table in Angel's front room, which serves as a kitchen, living room, and dining room. The only bedroom in the house was behind us. Angel's young wife was asleep with her six-week-old baby, Conchita, and her two other children: two-year-old Ulysses and five-year-old Antonio. Angel is always the first one up.

Grinning, Angel held Chuy on his knee. He looked at me and said in his San Lucas accent, "I know that you're used to being out on the water, but there is a difference between being on a little surfboard near the beach and traveling twenty miles out into the open ocean in a panga. You're gonna get seasick." I assured him I'd be okay. Angel and Varo looked at each other knowingly.

In his mid-forties, Angel is handsome, with sparkling brown eyes and almost-shoulder-length, graying hair. He's been waking up early for work since the day his mother sent him to work on an uncle's ranch outside of Cabo San Lucas when he was nine years old. When he was seven, his father drowned when a fishing line attached to a shark snagged him out of a wooden skiff. Angel rarely attended school and spent most of his childhood wandering the dry, rugged Sierra de la Laguna foothills, chasing cattle in his *huaraches* and torn pants, always hungry, wondering what he did to deserve being sent away from his family when his friends were in school.

Angel dresses in old, stained pants (a sign of a real fisherman) and is never without his huaraches, the distinguishing characteristic of the pata rajada. After a life of working on tuna boats and traveling between Pacific fish camps, Angel landed in San Ignacio Lagoon working scallops. He met Pola in El Cardón. Pola, who is plump, pretty, and twenty years younger than Angel, spent most of her life working rice fields with her family in Michoacán. Angel moved into an empty house a few years ago at La Fridera when he started working for Antonio. An excellent *panguero*,

Angel intuitively knows the lagoon and the ocean. He is well regarded for his boat handling skills around whales.

Angel enjoyed teaching me skills that anyone raised around the ocean should know: the proper way to fillet halibut and bay bass (sharp knife with flowing, even movements), the correct way to grill mullet (butterfly-style with hot, bright mesquite coals), and the right attitude and tire pressure when driving through dunes and wet salitrales (calm, smooth, never stopping, straight through the water, with tires between 15 and 20 psi).

After sipping our coffee, Angel, Varo, and I loaded up the panga with about twenty gallons of gas, water, and lobster burritos made that morning by Antonio Aguilar's wife, María Luisa. The three of us donned yellow foul-weather gear in anticipation of the surf and spray we were likely to encounter.

An hour later we were heading west through the main channel of the lagoon. Angel held the throttle of the 125-horsepower Mariner engine, which was covered with an old blue T-shirt. I admired the flock of black brant near the shoreline a few hundred yards away. Scared by the engine noise, a group of about two hundred suddenly took off, forming a giant arc. Their wings flapping hard, they headed west. When the tide drops, they feed in the tidal flats between Punta Piedra and Islote Abaroa, near the main lagoon entrance. Varo, next to me in the middle of the boat, looked starboard and pointed at a bottlenose dolphin. The dolphin dove and then reappeared next to the bow. Diving, surfacing, bow surfing.

Another panga was behind us. It held two fishermen from Bahía Kino, Sonora, dressed in old coats and torn polyester pants, and a twenty-year-old from the border town of Mexicali who looked like he wished he was anywhere else on the planet. They worked for Roberto Gutiérrez, a balding, thirty-something fish dealer from Ensenada who had promised them they would earn lots of money in Baja California Sur catching shark and halibut. Their panga looked as if it was ready to break apart. The two Sonorans had driven the panga 70 miles across the Sea of Cortez from Bahía Kino to Bahía Los Angeles, where Roberto had loaded it up in his Ford F-350 freezer truck and driven it to the lagoon. Their 65-hp Yamaha outboard was dangerously underpowered for fishing outside the lagoon.

Rounding Punta Piedra, Angel gunned the engine and we headed toward the bocana and the open sea. In theory, because the tide was dropping and midmorning was approaching, the nightly brisk northeasterly should have been decreasing. But as we rounded Punta Bronaugh, the sandy northern point that juts out into the bocana, the wind at our backs was picking up strength. Boils in the middle of the channel indicated reefs filled with lobster. Due to the currents it is impossible to leave a trap there. The entire lagoon was emptying as the tide turned. White-capped breakers revealed sandbars. Twenty minutes outside the lagoon we passed the marker flag buoy that marks the channel. Turning to the southwest, we headed out into the open ocean. The other panga was behind us. Between the swells I saw the bow, high in the air.

Varo scanned the ocean and pointed starboard. "Ballena," he said matter-of-factly. A gray whale surfaced and dove slowly about 200 yards west. Angel turned the panga to the southwest. The whale disappeared. Forty-five minutes later we were ten miles outside the buoy. The northeast wind was increasing in velocity, creating rough conditions. Angel battled four- to five-foot wind chop. Down one swell, coasting a short distance, then rolling up, and then down another. Angel looked worried. He turned the boat 180 degrees to face the swell. With our bow to the wind, Varo pitched the anchor overboard.

Above the roar of the wind, Angel yelled, "We have to wait for the wind to drop. It is impossible to pull up the nets when she's blowing like this." As he finished talking, a coffee-colored bull sea lion swam up to the boat. The longer the nets are out without being tended, the more first-class fish—halibut, corvina, and cabrilla—the pinnipeds are able to eat. And sea lions only like the expensive stuff. No one had a shotgun to scare it away. Sea lions are no friends of fishermen.

The other panga finally arrived. The Sonorans looked worried and cold. The *mexicalense* looked miserable. They didn't have an anchor. Their boat was turned around, and they kept the engine running, bow into the wind, while Angel and Varo pondered what to do. The wind was not tapering off, and the waves were getting bigger. Gusts were hitting about thirty to thirty-five miles per hour. We hung on for about ten minutes, and then Angel told Varo to pull up the anchor. He cranked the outboard and we were off. I held on to the bowline, standing up, and my back and coffee-filled kidneys absorbed the shock of breaching through the chop. The ride out was fast and comparatively easy. Behind us, the bow of the other boat was barely visible through the spray as we took the chop head on. A hairline crack in the fiberglass hull seemed to expand each time the boat slapped the water. I could only imagine what was happening to the other, older panga.

Three hours later we arrived at La Fridera. My body hurt. We had used over fifty dollars' worth of gasoline and oil with nothing to show for it. Angel said, "I just hope that the whales and tourists arrive early this year. I don't want to go through that again."

The wind blew all day and through the night, finally calming down at daybreak the next day, when we went out again and pulled in 400 pounds — $350 dollars' worth — of halibut, Pacific Angel shark, stingrays, and blue shark. A good *marea*.

Angel and Varo's day is typical of the hardships the inhabitants of San Ignacio Lagoon deal with to make a living and obtain food, water, and shelter. It is a struggle to drive the forty miles to the town of San Ignacio to purchase groceries or see a doctor. It is hell on the truck suspension to drive the 50-mile round-trip to fill water barrels at Rancho El Alamo. If an outboard breaks down outside the lagoon, there is no Coast Guard to save anyone. Taking tourists to see whales is considerably easier than battling the ocean for fish.

A good day of fishing might bring in what an average factory worker in Mexico City earns in a month. But money earned fishing is immediately invested in a new outboard or pickup, or to fill up on gasoline and motor oil, or to pay for bus fare to Santa Rosalía and La Paz to obtain permits. While some fishermen at the lagoon drive what appear to be well-maintained four-by-four pickups, close inspection reveals milk-carton gaskets, tires with no tread, and brakes that barely function.

My neighbor, Antonio Aguilar, is far from destitute, with two pangas and three plywood houses at La Fridera and another cement-block house in San Ignacio. But he is always on the edge of economic disaster. A good season of whalewatching might be followed by an illness in the family that requires selling a few head of cattle at his brother's ranch. A severe drought means using extra money or trading new calves for expensive alfalfa from Vizcaíno. An unexpected late summer chubasco can result in the loss of $10,000 worth of boats, nets, and motors.

Fishermen receive credit from corrupt fish buyers who charge outrageous prices for equipment. They take a hundred-percent payback in the catch, leaving fishermen without money to buy food. Families in El Cardón that fled rural violence and debt peonage in Sinaloa and Michoacán arrive at the lagoon to fish and immediately become indebted to the Castro family from Ensenada, who reportedly sell fishing supplies at high prices and buy fish at below market prices.

Compared to urban life, life in the lagoon is difficult. But compared to the years before automobiles and outboard engines, life today is actually easier than it used to be. For El Gringo, the fishing master of the central Pacific coast, the forty-mile drive to San Ignacio is nothing compared to rowing a panga around the lagoon harpooning sea turtles and sharks.

To most Americans, the life of Angel's in-laws in El Cardón would seem unendurable. However, they are much better off than they were living in semifeudal conditions in Michoacán. I asked Don Chon, Angel's father-in-law, a proud, wiry man in his late fifties, what he would do if the federal government evicted his family from the flood-prone house pieced together out of an old fish trailer and plywood on the shore of El Cardón. "I'd just move over to the other side of the lagoon," he said without hesitation.

For fishermen such as Antonio Aguilar and his cousin Maldo Fischer who grew up on ranches, prestige and identity are based on their good character, honor, and respect for their families. That is why Antonio and Maldo are highly esteemed in the eyes of lagoon residents. For those fishermen who descended from the mountains into the sea, in the absence of any form of government support, only family ties provide a safety net. Working as whalewatching guides decreases the dependence of Antonio and Maldo on decreasing fish and shellfish stocks.

At times the adversity people face at the lagoon overwhelmed me. One day at El Dátil, I met Don Pancho, a distinguished fisherman in his mid-seventies. El Dátil is a garbage-strewn fish camp fifteen miles south of El Delgadito, surrounded by salitrales and sand dunes. It is the home of the brooding, stocky Chepinos, natives of the Sierra de Guadalupe village of San José de Gracia. Don Pancho had recently lost his legs to diabetes and lived in an old, brown Ford Econoline van with four flat tires, next to the shack of his youngest son. His daughter-in-law, who had recently given birth to a baby girl, took care of the old man.

Don Pancho loved to watch children playing soccer. *Fayuqueros* (peddlers) stopped by to sell oranges and say hello. He waved to fish trucks that sped through El Dátil on their way to the fish market 200 miles south in Ciudad Constitución. Occasionally he navigated his wheelchair over the beach where he inspected the morning catch.

Don Pancho talked about his trip to California in the 1940s when he worked as a *bracero* (migrant worker). "I was in Bakersfield, and it was hot as hell in the summer. There was a public swimming pool near where I was staying. We wanted to go swimming, but the gringos wouldn't let us. There was a sign there that said 'No Dogs or Mexicans Allowed.' I'll never forget that. No dogs or Mexicans."

Later that day back at La Fridera, Antonio Aguilar told me that Don Pancho was one of the best fishermen around. Maybe only El Gringo and his partner, Doroteo Aguilar, knew the lagoon better. A couple of months later, I stopped in to say hello to Don Pancho and to drop off photos of his son and new granddaughter. The back doors of the van were open, and he was sitting in a bed built into the van. Don Pancho looked ill—disheveled hair, dirty clothes—but his face lit up when he saw the photos of his granddaughter and beaming son.

A few months later Don Pancho passed away in Ciudad Constitución. His van still sits empty at El Dátil.

Communication and Conservation

Whales are an important part of the past, present, and future of San Ignacio Lagoon. American whalers and gray whale researchers helped bring the outside world into the lagoon. The arrival of gray whales each January is a reminder to put nets away. Lagoon inhabitants who work as guides paint their pangas and overhaul their engines in anticipation of tourists.

Because gray whales are welcomed by San Ignacio Lagoon residents, future conservation programs have a good chance of success. However, without understanding the hardship the people of San Ignacio Lagoon deal with, government agencies devise conservation programs doomed to fail. Lagoon residents love gray whales but out of necessity will choose the jobs that will allow their children to survive. It is up to government officials, conservationists, and tourist outfitters to find ways to make gray whale conservation compatible with local livelihoods.

In 1990, the federal government decided to restrict fishing inside San Ignacio Lagoon during the whale season as a way of protecting gray whales from fishing nets, outboards, and pangas. During a meeting held to discuss the issue, local fishing cooperative leaders informed government officials that unless they were provided with fellowships to replace their lost incomes, they would continue fishing around whales despite restrictions. They did suggest an alternative. Instead of restricting fishing, the government could grant them exclusive access to whalewatching permits. Up until then, the majority of American outfitters used their own guides and skiffs and rarely employed locals. The Ministry of Urban Development and Ecology (SEDUE) agreed. Starting in 1991, residents of San Ignacio Lagoon received exclusive access to whalewatching permits.

Initially resentful at the federal government for making them hire locals who they felt were unqualified to work with their clients, American outfitters now feel that hiring locals was a solution to burdensome paperwork requirements for obtaining whalewatching permits. Giving locals exclusive access to the permits initiated a slow but growing relationship based on trust, friendship, and mutual respect between local fishermen-turned-guides and American outfitters.

Since then locals have contracted their services to American outfitters and formed their own companies, which provide food, lodging, and whalewatching tours to tourists who arrive at the lagoon on their own. This situation has resulted in increased communication between lagoon residents, outfitters, and government officials on how to manage the growing whalewatching industry. However, despite the success of government efforts to regulate whalewatching at San Ignacio Lagoon, local residents argue that attention is paid to the area only during a short period during the whale season. A whalewatching guide and fishing cooperative leader from San Ignacio Lagoon told me in 1994 that, "We haven't seen the government here since they held the meeting four years ago to discuss stopping fishing at the lagoon." That changed in 1994 when the Vizcaíno Biosphere Reserve sent out rangers to live at the lagoon during the winter whale season to monitor whalewatching and American tourist camps.

Gregorio Mendez, a serious, bearded inspector in his thirties, was dropped off at a tourist camp miles away from the fish camps of San Ignacio Lagoon in late January 1994. Not sure what he was expected to do and unhappy about being so far away from year-round residents of the lagoon, Gregorio told me, "The government went out and hired us, and it is not like we have specific training for this." An architect by training, Gregorio had spent the previous two years working with nonprofit conservation and social-welfare organizations in Morelos. Prior to that he ran a candy factory. The prospect of working in so isolated an area filled with wildlife sounded intriguing, and he signed on as a ranger for the Vizcaíno Biosphere Reserve.

Although he was hired in the summer of 1993, Gregorio soon realized that there was little prospect of receiving a paycheck for at least six months. He stuck around anyway and helped with the semiannual bighorn sheep count for the Vizcaíno Biosphere Reserve. Finally, in early January 1994, Gregorio was paid for the previous six months. He was told not to expect another paycheck until May.

An American company that operates a whalewatching camp at San Ignacio Lagoon offered room and board to the rangers, who arrived without field supplies, boats, or vehicles. While it made for a pleasant vacation, Gregorio was interested in getting to know the rest of the lagoon. He also wanted to avoid incidents like the one caused by his partner who, along with company employees, pulled out and confiscated the lobster traps of Celestino Garza, a longtime San Ignacio Lagoon fisherman. The Americans were angry about the traps, arguing that they were a threat to whales.

Lagoon residents were also outraged—but at the rangers and tourist camps. Francisco Murillo, a longtime lagoon resident, said, "Celestino is the owner of the lagoon—not them." According to Celestino, who has fished the lagoon for more than sixty years, "Nobody ever came and told me there was a problem. I have a permit to take lobster out of the lagoon. All they [the rangers] had to do was talk to me."

Gregorio was unhappy about the lobster-trap affair and was eager to meet year-round residents of San Ignacio Lagoon. He arranged to accompany Jorge Amaya, a longtime whalewatching guide who has assisted scientific expeditions to the lagoon since the 1970s, on a tour of the bird nesting islands in the northeast corner of the lagoon. Gregorio also wanted to talk to Jorge about why he had been denied a whalewatching permit for the season. Because Jorge was the first fisherman in the Baja California peninsula to work as a whalewatching guide, his inability to get a permit seemed particularly unjust. Even Jorge's local competitors recognized the unfairness of what had happened. Antonio Aguilar angrily asked me, "If he doesn't have the right to a permit, who does?"

A lifetime of backbreaking work and bad breaks had culminated in the public humiliation Jorge received when he had traveled to La Paz a month earlier to pick up his whalewatching permit. The trip was like any other in rural Baja California Sur—filled with unexpected pitfalls. All four local guides traveled to San Ignacio together to catch the night bus to La Paz. Disaster struck when the wheel of their 1978 Ford pickup fell off on the dusty, rocky road to San Ignacio. Luckily no one was hurt and the rest of the journey was uneventful. In La Paz, not only was Jorge humiliated but, to make matters worse, he returned home with three neighbors who had received their permits. (He later received his when an INE staffer visiting the lagoon from Mexico City learned of Jorge's predicament, telephoned her boss from San Ignacio, and obtained a permit the same day by fax.)

Jorge was waiting for Gregorio and me inside his front yard, which was adorned with potted plants and bleached whale bones. They had met each other a few weeks earlier at the INE office in La Paz and gave each other a big *abrazo* (hug). Jorge told Gregorio about his permit problems, then said, "Well, what are we waiting for?" We headed for the islands.

Isla Pelícano, the western and larger of the island pair, is about a mile offshore from the fish camp of La Laguna and rises out of the water like a cactus-covered battleship. Gray whale mothers and calves seek shelter in the channel of El Remate, east of the island. The thousands of cormorants usually present on the westernmost tip were out feeding. We jumped ashore to examine a large, round, waist-high osprey nest composed of dried-up cholla cactus, twigs, and bits of plastic. It was just above the shoreline on the edge of a cliff. We tiptoed over to the nest and spied on two large brown-speckled eggs. Jorge said they would soon be ready to hatch. The adult osprey circled above, calling angrily.

As we returned to the beach and the panga, Jorge told Gregorio about the problems of protecting the islands. About 150 osprey nests dot the two islands, along with the nests of great blue herons, western gulls, and brown pelicans. The absence of predators makes the sites especially suitable locations for nesting birds. Black sea turtle shells littering the beach are evidence that poachers camp on the island and get rid of the evidence of their activities there. A few days after we left the island, scallop poachers set up a camp on the same beach. Drug planes occasionally land on the rough, open area of the island that serves as an airstrip.

Skirting the northern shore of the lagoon, Jorge pointed out pairs of American Oystercatchers and flocks of Caspian Terns strolling along the shore. Crossing a short channel, we arrived at Isla Garzas. Its eastern shore is elevated forty feet above the shoreline. We disembarked on a tiny beach near the cliff guarded by brown pelicans and cormorants and scrambled up the rocks cluttered with fossilized seashells. The top commands a view of the northern end of the lagoon, an area continually in visual flux, depending on winds, tide, and rain. Gray whale spouts haunt the stillness. We did not spot any whales.

Gregorio walked to the edge of the cliff and pointed down to the whale bones stuck in the rocks. About thirty ospreys circled the air, angry with us for invading their space. Compared to the rest of the island, we were in an oasis of lush desert vegetation. Multibranched *garambullo,* or old-man cactus, and treelike cardón cactus were everywhere. Old osprey nests were stuck in the middle of garambullo patches. Jorge led us to a nest occupied by two eggs and a recently hatched sleeping chick. The parent circled above. We slowly backed away to the edge of the cliff. The mother dropped back into her nest. Jorge pointed out an abandoned great blue heron nest stuck amidst a cactus patch. Gregorio broached the subject of the whalewatching permit. Close to tears, Jorge said, "I just don't understand why I didn't get one. What else am I going to do this year? What are my sons going to do?" Gregorio said he would see what he could do. We headed back to Jorge's house.

Later that evening Gregorio said, "If anyone deserves a gray whale permit, Jorge does. But you know what INE told me about what is going on here? *Absolutamente nada*. The problems here are totally political. But what am I supposed to do? We have no power and don't really have much influence over what occurs. It would take at least a few months of just doing what we did today to figure out how to solve the problems here. Hanging around tourist camps all winter is not going to solve any problems."

Gregorio left San Ignacio Lagoon a few weeks later. He told me that he was going to try to get a job as an observer for the Inter-American Tropical Tuna Commission.

Learning the Rules of the Game

The great advantage that field agents from the Federal Attorney General's Office for Environmental Protection (PROFEPA) have over their counterparts from the Vizcaíno Biosphere Reserve is field experience in Baja California Sur. When the agency was formed in the fall of 1992, the majority of the staff were longtime federal agency employees and Baja California Sur natives who intimately knew the state.

Inspectors from PROFEPA enforce whalewatching regulations. Violations of permit conditions by outfitters may result in fines and even future loss of permits. Vizcaíno Biosphere Reserve rangers can only monitor illegal activities. They cannot actually stop anyone from breaking the law. However, when PROFEPA first sent its inspectors out into the field, their only enforcement tool was the ability to write a legal deposition. They then returned to their office, where other agents undertook an investigation. This process took several weeks. By the time the fine was issued, it was obviously too late to halt the original activity. Fortunately, some protected areas in Mexico now have rangers trained by PROFEPA on staff, who issue citations or can make arrests. Most rangers and park directors choose to use persuasion and bargaining to solve problems rather than making an arrest or issuing a fine. If locals are treated with respect and compassion, they can become cheerleaders for conservation.

Inspectors from PROFEPA rely on local people and tourism outfitters to provide information about potentially unlawful activities. Because of their experience in the state and their connections in whale lagoons, PROFEPA inspectors had an easier time integrating themselves into the communities of San Ignacio Lagoon and Magdalena Bay than their counterparts from the Vizcaíno Biosphere Reserve.

On a chilly, overcast afternoon in early February 1994, two PROFEPA inspectors arrived in San Ignacio Lagoon in a small pickup loaded with camping equipment They parked in front of Antonio Aguilar's house at the fish camp of La Fridera. Antonio's wife, María Luisa, is one of the best cooks in the state. Many official visitors to the San Ignacio Lagoon establish their base camp at La Fridera, and after a long day in the field, they are often treated to heaping portions of freshly caught halibut, homemade tortillas, and beans, with the possibility of lobster and scallop ceviche as side orders.

Antonio was away. His father-in-law, Antonio Camacho, greeted the inspectors as they emerged from a white Nissan twin-cab pickup. Retired from a life of fishing and managing his gas station in San Juanico, Don Antonio spent most of his time listening to the news on his portable radio next to the tiny camper shell he shares with his wife, Antonia. He loved to voice his opinion on his favorite subjects: government corruption and the incompetence of bureaucrats.

Emiliana Ortega, an attractive woman in her mid-thirties with hoop earrings and long brown hair, is in charge of the inspection. Her counterpart, Guillermo Cota, is tall and stocky with sparkling blue eyes and gray hair. He had spent the ten previous years working in various capacities for the federal government along the Pacific coast. Before that, Guillermo lived in Puerto Adolfo López Mateos, where he played for the cannery baseball team. Both Guillermo and Emiliana have a great sense of humor and like to laugh. A good sense of humor is probably the most important trait a government official can have when dealing with people in rural areas. Many make the mistake of being too serious.

Waving his hands, Don Antonio said to the inspectors, "The *gobierno* told us we couldn't take sea turtles out of the lagoon. There is plenty out there. What do they know? These people that sit behind a desk all day ruined it here for the working man. I don't need someone behind a desk to tell me what lives in the lagoon and what I can take out of the lagoon."

The following morning, Guillermo and Emiliana, with agency photo ID cards tagged to their shirts, met with Antonio Aguilar, his cousin and partner Maldo, and María Luisa. Emiliana was *levantando un acta,* or taking a legal deposition from Antonio.

"It isn't fair about Jorge," Antonio said. "He lives here and has taken people to see whales longer than anyone. Why can't he get a permit? Other people from outside the lagoon get permits, and Jorge can't."

Guillermo replied, "I used to work with the brother of Jorge at San Juanico. We'll see what we can do. And by the way, we heard about the inspectors who received money from outfitters last year. You guys aren't to give a dime to anyone who comes around asking for handouts. What happened in previous years, it is not going to happen again." Maldo, Antonio, and María Luisa looked pleased. Antonio signed his statement. The interview was officially over.

The next day I accompanied Guillermo and Emiliana during their inspection of American whalewatching camps. During our boat ride to the first camp, whales appeared in all directions.

We met with Michael Jorgensen and Beth Conway, employees of a San Diego–based outfitter, at a dining table under an old army surplus tent that serves as a dining room, kitchen, and recreation area. Guillermo and Emiliana were interested in hearing about payments made to inspectors in past years.

"The inspector was embarrassed about asking for money. He said it would cover his salary. As we understood it, he was under the orders of one of his bosses to do this," Beth informed the inspectors.

"If he was embarrassed, he wouldn't have asked for the money," replied Guillermo. Everyone has to live on the same salary, and there was no sympathy in his voice for someone who covers his expenses with extra income.

According to Beth, the inspector received two installments of $250 over a two-month period. The last installment was made at his office. What made the fee seem official was the fact that they asked for and received a handwritten receipt. In 1992 the company paid $400 to two inspectors, but no receipts were issued. Guillermo and Emiliana shook their heads in amazement. This was just one camp. There were two more camps plus large tourist boats. Each inspector must have earned thousands of dollars in "inspection" fees. The bribe takers no longer show up at the lagoon. Their boss was transferred to a post in another state.

During the return trip to La Fridera, we searched the lagoon for whales. After watching a few disappearing tails and distant spyhopping, Guillermo said, "Let's go home."

The Chesapeake of the Pacific

If San Ignacio Lagoon is a landscape of scale, defined by the overwhelming sea of land that almost absorbs it, Magdalena Bay is a mangrove kingdom. The bay is impenetrable and vast, a never-ending maze of waterways, islands, dunes, mangroves, sea turtles, bottlenose dolphins, sea lions, great blue herons, and gray whales whose breaching, spouting, and spyhopping echo throughout its waters each winter.

San Ignacio Lagoon has remained largely disconnected from the onslaught of modern civilization. In contrast, since 1539, when Spanish explorer Francisco de Ulloa first sailed into Magdalena Bay aboard the 120-ton *Santa Agueda,* outsiders have plundered its resources and gray whales, leaving a path of destruction in their wake.

The most centrally located vantage point to absorb Magdalena Bay is from the highest peak on Magdalena Island, a volcanic outcrop that slides into the Pacific Ocean, accessible via a steep, scarred canyon (see map 2.3). Scrambling up rocky, bare slopes, I reached the summit, where the bay and Pacific unfolded before me. From my precarious perch, a panorama of dunes, mangrove, *estero,* desert, and ocean encircled me.

It is easy to see why gray whales like this place, sometimes referred to as the "Chesapeake of the Pacific." The bay is more than big enough for gray whale mothers and their newborn calves. Juveniles and other adults swim, play, and surf in five openings to the ocean that separate the islands from each other and the mainland.

To the west, or straight down from the slippery volcanic ledge, is the Pacific Ocean—deep blue under clouds that move silently southward with the steady north wind. From December to April the ocean below me is filled with gray whales traveling south and then north again. During the month of May, when the winds and water turn cold and the coastal fog moves in across the dunes, loggerhead turtles swim north to feed on dense schools of *langostinos,* or pelagic red crabs, which swarm in the ocean and turn bay beaches bright red.

The endless sandscape of dunes and hidden mangroves of Magdalena Island lies to the north. Magdalena Island is one of five barrier islands that protect the bay—or a series of interconnected waterways, bays, and esteros—from the open ocean. To the east is the mangrove-lined channel that connects the main portion of Magdalena Bay to the channel eighty miles northward. The town of San Carlos lies at the entrance to the channel. The peaks of Margarita Island are to the south.

Commander George Dewey of the U.S.S. *Narragansett* referred to Magdalena Bay in 1880 as "one of the most spacious and safe harbors in the world."[3] From my vantage point I understood why. Bahía Almejas was barely visible through the clouds. The rest of the bay was lost—absorbed by the inland desert to the east and the faint peaks of the Sierra de la Giganta that divide the peninsula.

The inlets and esteros of Magdalena Bay are like the salitrales and mudflats of San Ignacio Lagoon—easy to get lost in and never-ending. Mangroves merge into dunes that appear one-dimensional as you hit the shoreline but open into a gauntlet of hidden moguls, sinking sand, once-a-year rain gullies, and a sea of dune vegetation waiting to flower when the once-a-year rain falls.

A short walk along the shoreline of Magdalena Bay reveals hidden treasures: an osprey perched on a cactus, bright yellow mangrove warblers chirping in the middle of a mangrove thicket, and a flock of white ibises feeding in the tidal flats. Wildlife is similar to that in San Ignacio Lagoon and includes one of the largest colonies of California sea lions on the peninsula, as well as a large bottlenose dolphin population. Black turtles feed outside and inside the bay, and loggerheads migrate past the outer shoreline of the bay during summer months. The largest colony of Magnificent Frigatebirds and the only known nesting pair of bald eagles on the peninsula inhabit the bay.

Magdalena Bay is also an important nursery for shellfish and fish, including sardines. Residents of the bay collect fan and bay scallops, chocolate clams, lobsters, blue crabs, and abalone. Fishermen travel outside the bay to haul in squid, sharks, giant sea bass, halibut, and sea turtles.

A glance at a map of Baja California Sur creates the impression that Magdalena Bay is a series of separate bays rather than one system. The different names for the southern and central portions of the bay (Bahía Almejas and Bahía Magdalena, respectively) add to the confusion. However, shoreline residents consider the bay to be one ecological and cultural region, with economic activities and social ties extending approximately 180 miles from north to south.

Although most of Magdalena Bay is accessible only by boat, two of its largest cities, San Carlos and Puerto Adolfo López Mateos, are connected to the rest of the peninsula and Highway 1 by paved roads. A paved highway connects the northern towns of La Poza Grande and Santo Domingo to Ciudad Insurgentes, an agricultural community twenty-four miles east of Puerto Adolfo López Mateos along Highway 1.

San Carlos, with a population of about 3,000, is the largest town along the bay and is a regional port. The town has two fish canneries, an electric-power plant, three small hotels, two whorehouses, and twenty liquor stores. Oil tankers dock at San Carlos and unload heavy fuel oil for the nearby power plant. Modern port facilities and storage containers are used to export corn, wheat, and garbanzo beans from the Santo Domingo Valley. Rusting hulks of shrimp boats sit next to the main pier, where boats from the Mexican tuna fleet dock. Out in the main part of the bay, sardine and shrimp boats trawl the main channel, competing with small pangas for whatever is left of a rapidly diminishing fishery. The bodies that frequently wash ashore on the edge of town prove that drug trafficking rather than tourism is the newest growth industry.

Magdalena Bay is divided into three zones: north, central, and south. The North Zone extends from the San Jorge fish camp to the Curva del Diablo, twelve miles south of the Boca de Soledad ocean entrance. This is the area most favored by gray whales. Between two hundred and three hundred animals congregate around the Boca de Soledad from January to March and swim south along the main channel to the gray whale calving area known as La Florida. When the tide is low, the whales swim out with the tide and out beyond the breaker line. This is the area that up to twenty-five thousand tourists visit each winter to catch a glimpse of gray whales. These tourists are only the latest in a series of outsiders who have descended upon the bay and disrupted the solitude of whales.

Since the first time that Francisco de Ulloa explored Magdalena Bay in 1539, a cycle of speculative ventures—including exploration, contact, colonization, resource exploitation, and finally failure—have occurred along its shores, involving two parallel worlds. One was the quiet subsistence world of the fishing and ranching families that settled the bay. Throughout its history, regardless of the state of capitalist ventures, Magdalena Bay's inhabitants have moved quietly through the mangroves, setting crab traps, harpooning sea turtles and sharks, collecting mangrove oysters, and running goats through the cactus forest of the desert shoreline. The other was the world of *conquistadores* and colonizers, whose visits produced a swath of destruction. Occasionally these two worlds met, especially when labor, goods, and knowledge were needed by the outsiders, who arrived at the bay with dreams of the treasure chests they would find there.

Learning about the worlds of the local inhabitants and the foreigners who descended upon Magdalena Bay is essential to understanding the conflicts that have emerged there over whalewatching and the future of Baja's mangrove kingdom. This cycle of boom and bust, colonization and exploitation still continues. Although the scale of destruction is not as great as it was, especially prior to the Mexican Revolution, when the bay and much of the peninsula belonged to foreign companies, capital intensive investment in resource extraction—mining, fishing, agriculture—has always been followed by failure and the beginning of a new cycle. In the 1800s and early 1900s, whaling was the most important enterprise in the bay. Gray whales were the first resource of the bay to be overexploited. Today, whalewatching is booming.

When Francisco de Ulloa sailed into Magdalena Bay, it is doubtful he expected to find such a large bay. He was probably more frustrated than surprised when he could not find a reliable source of fresh water. Juan

Cabrillo, who sailed into Magdalena Bay on July 18, 1542, wrote in his log that it was "a good port and it is sheltered from the west winds; but it has no water or wood."[4] When Sebastian Vizcaíno landed in the bay on July 21, 1602, he named the bay Bahía Santa María de Magdalena. Ulloa named the southern portion of the bay Bahía Almejas, or Clam Bay, due to the profusion of clams he and his crew found.[5]

The stories the people of Magdalena Bay tell about lost treasures — gold trinkets, Spanish swords, cannons, pirate skeletons — is the testament to the importance of the bay as an excellent anchorage for the galleons that sailed from New Spain on their way to the Philippines.

Spain was not the only nation interested in Magdalena Bay. Admiral Du Petit Thouars of France sailed there in 1839 in *La Venus*. That same year Sir Edward Belcher surveyed and mapped the bay. The lack of government presence in the peninsula, due especially to the declining mission system, enabled smugglers to carry on extensive trade with residents while anchored inside the bay.

Toward the end of the nineteenth century, Americans sought land south of the border. Unlike the Mexican-American War of the 1840s, when the United States invaded Mexico and seized two-thirds of its territory, Mexican presidents Benito Juárez and the dictator Porfirio Díaz, handed over Baja California without a fight. Consequently, Magdalena Bay and much of the peninsula became the property of American land speculators, confidence men, some of the richest capitalists in the nation, and the U.S. Navy. Like prerevolutionary Shanghai, Magdalena Bay was controlled by a foreign country — lock, stock, and barrel.

Whalers ushered in the first round of exploitation of the bay's natural riches, even though many of the whalers, with the exception of a few who settled permanently in inland mission towns, had little desire to live around the shores of what was then perceived as a barren bay. However, the presence of so many whalers inside the finest harbor on the Pacific coast aroused the curiosity of capitalists interested in luring potential investors to settle the area. From 1864 to 1933, five U.S. companies received concessions at Magdalena Bay and along much of the Pacific coast of the peninsula.

Benito Juárez granted a concession to a group of American speculators headed by Jacob P. Leese in 1864 that totaled 48,600 square miles from north of La Paz to Colonet, about a hundred miles south of the U.S.–

Mexico border. Leese failed to comply with the terms of the contract, so on August 4, 1866, the concession was transferred to a group of New York capitalists operating under the name of the Lower California Company.[6]

The occupation of Magdalena Bay had begun. That same year, J. Ross Browne was sent by the company to inspect the lands for which it had obtained a concession. Although Browne was not overly impressed with the peninsula, he grudgingly recognized that its "geographical position gives it a value, to which its intrinsic resource can never entitle it."[7]

In 1870, Captain J. S. Hawland sailed into Magdalena Bay on a Nantucket whaler on his way back from South America. Having been to the Galapagos Islands, Hawland recognized that the Spanish moss, or *orchilla,* growing in the desert around the bay was similar to the lichen harvested there to make dyes. Hawland quickly organized an orchilla venture with Ecuadorian Manuel Cobos, forming Cobos & Company.[8] In 1871, a Mexican government census of Magdalena Bay found 21 American families, 54 Mexican men, and 426 orchilla workers employed by the company.[9]

Under the terms of its concession, the Lower California Company agreed to settle a minimum of two hundred families. Its inability to organize a settlement led to the annulment of the concession by the Mexican government in September 1871. A month later, on October 28, Manuel Cobos, taking advantage of the government's enmity toward the company and its ventures at Magdalena Bay, led a party of seventy Mexican soldiers to the bay to oust the remaining settlers. He allegedly stole $150,000 worth of orchilla from Americans and Europeans associated with the company.[10] The annulment of its grant and the theft of company property by Cobos led the Lower California Company to file a $25 million claim against the Mexican government. In 1872, to avoid a costly settlement, the authorities provided the Lower California Company with a six-year concession to harvest orchilla along the Pacific coast from Cabo San Lucas to Bahía San Hipolito, north of Punta Abreojos.[11]

After the Lower California Company concession ended in 1878, three additional American companies obtained concessions to exploit Magdalena Bay. The extraction of orchilla was the most successful venture. Joseph P. Hale, an Irish businessman, established his dye business on Magdalena Island in 1873 and used the tiny port on Magdalena Island for ships to transport the lichen directly to England.[12] Hale's enterprise, Flores Hale and Company, extracted the lichen from 1873 until 1903, when he sold the business to the Chartered Company of Lower California. In 1874, when John F. Janes visited Magdalena Bay, he observed a "fine little village of about twenty houses . . . a splendid warehouse and fine dwellings."[13] The port was the home of up to five hundred people—mostly Mexican workers and their families—a customs house, a district court, and in 1887 a public school.

The inability of American companies to induce settlers and investors to take part in their Baja California ventures resulted in a foreign policy "crisis" in the United States. The U.S. Senate attempted to stop what members perceived to be a secret attempt by Japan to purchase Magdalena Bay and open a naval base on the west coast of North America.

The crisis had its origins when the Chartered Company of Lower California purchased the concession owned by Flores Hale and Company. However, due to the lack of a market for Spanish moss (synthetic dyes were found), Chartered could not persuade colonists to settle the bay. The company was reorganized into the Magdalena Bay Colonization Company in 1908, under the ownership of Delbert J. Haff.[14] Due to financial problems, Haff attempted to sell a portion of his concession to a Japanese company. The Japanese would not purchase any land without the approval of the U.S. government, and the State Department objected to the sale. Haff and the Japanese quickly ceased negotiations. However, Senator Henry Cabot Lodge of Massachusetts, sensing that behind the deal lurked the specter of future Japanese control over the eastern Pacific, asked President William Howard Taft to provide the Senate with information regarding the sale of the bay. Rumors regarding the Japanese presence in Magdalena Bay were probably fed by the establishment of Japanese fishing operations on the southern Pacific coast of the peninsula. Kondo M. K. Fisheries, a San Diego–based Japanese company, operated out of Margarita Island.[15] It probably did not help matters that on December 11, 1910, two Japanese warships on their way to Manzanillo—the *Asama,* under Admiral R. Yashiro, and the *Kasaki,* under Admiral Mihihide Tanaka—sailed into the bay.[16]

Despite a round of denials by the Japanese government that it had any intention of opening a military base in Magdalena Bay, on July 31, 1912, the U.S. Senate voted 51 to 4 to approve the Lodge Corollary to the Monroe Doctrine. The corollary stated the foreign occupation of any port or area in the North American continent for military purposes would be considered a threat to the security of the United States.[17]

Out of the Past

In 1904, eight-year-old Agustín Olivas left his house near the mission town of Comondú about fifty miles north of Magdalena Bay. He traveled with his father, John Oliver, a Scot who had jumped ship and settled in Comondú, in a small community of foreign whalers. The trip took two full days. They trudged through arroyos, over steep hillsides, and down into the vast, hot, thorny Santo Domingo Valley. Finally they arrived at the *embarcadero* (wharf) of San Jorge, a loading area for ranchers who sold their cheese, beef, vegetables, and fruit to foreign vessels in the bay.

Agustín was overwhelmed by what he saw. The ranch he had left two days before was hot and dusty. His life there consisted of herding cattle, chasing goats, and helping his family take care of their *huerta* (garden) and its mangos, figs, sugarcane, chiles, and orange trees. In the summer, the heat was terrible. Magdalena Bay was different. Here a breeze moved across the bay. There were plenty of fish and lots of sea turtles to be harpooned. One only had to be careful of the dangerous devil-fish that swam around the bay for a few months each year. Agustín promised himself that one day he would return and live here.

I met Don Agustín on a hot August afternoon. From his bench on the patio of the whitewashed adobe house he had built himself in La Poza Grande, a few miles east of San Jorge, Don Agustín told me about his life. At ninety-five, he was the oldest living fisherman in the region and a legend in an area where some people live for more than a century. With his smooth, dark skin, he did not look a day over seventy.

After a series of adventures, including walking to Scammon's Lagoon at the age of fourteen with his father and two American treasure seekers ("I cannot talk about it, I suffered too much," he told me) and fighting in the Mexican Revolution, Don Agustín moved his family to Magdalena Bay at the age of twenty-four. When he moved to the coast, there were few other fisherman and no towns. With sea life abundant, the Olivas family did not starve, but finding water was another problem. Don Agustín was lucky, however; water was discovered. The town he founded, La Poza Grande, means "the Big Well."

Today, the town sits a few miles west of San Jorge. In the early years, despite an ample supply of seafood, it was never easy to be a fisherman. Pangas were made by hand from wood dropped off by schooners or brought in by burro from La Paz. With his small panga Agustín never ventured into the open ocean. Why risk death? There was plenty of sea life inside the bay. The only trick was avoiding the whales in the narrow channels. Harpooning sea turtles and sharks was hard; selling them was nearly impossible. The nearest market was almost two days' journey inland by burro. Nevertheless, a load of fish and turtle meat might bring a few pesos, enough for a few bags of flour and sugar.

Don Agustín's daughter Ramona—whose son-in-law, Domingo Romero, had founded a whalewatching cooperative in Puerto Adolfo López Mateos—told me that although there was never much money, there was always enough food. One visit from a friend initiated a fiesta. "Then we would celebrate and eat every type of sea-turtle dish you can imagine. It was wonderful," she said.

For Don Agustín the life of a fisherman was a practical solution to an economic problem. He could have remained inland and worked for a pittance, but he preferred to fish. When I asked him if he was a good fisherman, Agustín replied with a smile and a shrug, and said, "They say I was."

As I listened to Don Agustín in his garden, family members stopped by to say hello. By the time I left, more than nineteen had gathered. I asked if it was unusual for so many people to visit. His daughter Nena replied, "We visit twice a day—every day of the week."

A year after I met Don Agustín, he died in his small adobe house, surrounded by friends and family who had come to his deathbed from all over the state. Just before he died, he visited Ramona in the town of Puerto Adolfo López Mateos, forty miles to the south. Ramona later told me with tears in her eyes, "Every day when the *muchachos* came in from fishing, he'd slowly walk over to the beach and watch them bring in the day's catch. He said they reminded him of his sons."

Into the Present

By the time Raymundo Lucero, one of the oldest living residents of Magdalena Bay, arrived in 1920 with his family where Puerto Adolfo López Mateos now stands, the island community of Bahía Magdalena was already in decline. The Luceros built their home on a beach called La Fridera, in recognition of the tryworks that nineteenth-century whalers had established there. In comparison to their life taking care of cattle in the Sierra de la Giganta, life by the bay was a relief. The Luceros became fishermen, as well as the founding family of Puerto Adolfo López Mateos.

Many of the residents of San Carlos and Puerto Adolfo López Mateos are migrants from the interior of Mexico who arrived in the Santo Domingo Valley in the 1950s and 1960s searching for work in agriculture and moved to the bay when canneries opened. Magdalena Bay entered the modern era with the construction of a fish cannery at Puerto López Mateos in the late 1950s and the subsequent inauguration of port and cannery facilities at San Carlos in the 1960s.[18] Today, bay inhabitants are employed primarily in the fishing industry, with some working as independent fishermen, others employed by fishing cooperatives, and still others working as wage laborers for seafood companies.

The privatization of the cannery in Puerto Adolfo López Mateos in 1988 resulted in the laying off of many of the plant's longtime workers. The plant workforce has been dramatically reduced, and the direct state subsidies of up to $200,000 per year that kept the plant competitive have been eliminated. Today, former cannery employees look wistfully toward their old workplace and wish for the good old days when the federal government provided free medical care, housing, work clothes, electricity, and water. The plant even had its own baseball team with semi-pro ringers imported from all over the country.

The good old days are gone in Puerto Adolfo López Mateos. Plant workers currently earn about $3 a day, and the company that purchased the plant is close to bankruptcy. Brightly colored plywood houses the federal government provided for cannery workers are boarded up. Many families have moved to La Paz in search of work and better opportunities for their children. Those who remain continue to fish. Others work as tourist guides.

Whalewatching has only recently become an important part of the local economy and is viewed by politicians and government planners as the only sector of the local economy with the potential to grow. In the last few years, agriculture and fishing have been dismal, which has resulted in widespread unemployment. Although tourism allows about fifty families to earn extra money for a brief six-week period from the last week of

January to the first week of March, it is not enough to keep the town from dying. One has only to visit in the summer to see how limited the income really is. The farmers' market is packed with shoppers during the whale season; it is almost empty during the months of July and August, and families have little money to spare.

The history of Magdalena Bay is like the history of the gray whale: subject to boom-and-bust cycles of exploitation and destruction. Both the whales and the community have bounced back from adversity and are mutually dependent. It remains to be seen how far tourist outfitters and government officials can push gray whale tourism. In the past, American and European whalers harpooned gray whales for their oil. Today, American and Mexican tourist outfitters hunt for the animals in skiffs so that tourists can videotape and photograph them. Hopefully, the growth of whalewatching will not lead to the same end as whaling: the absence of whale spouts from the bay. Gray whales have abandoned the bay in the past, and there is nothing to stop them from leaving in the future.

Conflict and Conservation

Although the management of whalewatching in San Ignacio Lagoon is far from perfect, the ability and willingness of locals, government officials, and outfitters to discuss problems and ways of resolving them is a vast improvement over the situation in Magdalena Bay. One INE official jokingly told me, "The only way to solve whalewatching problems in Puerto Adolfo López Mateos is to remove the whales from the bay."

Gray whale tourism is big business. In 1994, gross earnings for American outfitters in San Ignacio Lagoon and Magdalena Bay were approximately $8 million. Less than 1 percent was spent on local salaries and supplies.[19] Prior to 1988, with the exception of a few families, fishermen in Magdalena Bay had little interest in working as tourist guides. But decreasing fish harvests and the layoffs at the local fish cannery in Puerto Adolfo López Mateos in the early 1990s quickly changed local interest in whalewatching.

Gray whale tourism in Magdalena has been racked by conflict between American outfitters and local residents over rights to whalewatching permits. The result has been threats of violence and an excessive number of whalewatching pangas. To ameliorate what they considered an unequal distribution of tourism permits, residents of Puerto Adolfo López Mateos demanded that federal authorities make American outfitters hire them as whale guides and issue permits only to local residents.

The explosive situation in Puerto Adolfo López Mateos was exacerbated by the decline of the town's economy due to the struggling cannery and compounded by the national economic crisis and peso devaluation in 1994. This coincided with a dramatic increase in tourists traveling to Puerto Adolfo López Mateos to go whalewatching. Prior to the 1994 gray whale festival, only a few thousand people arrived per season. Now, about twenty-five thousand Mexicans and foreign tourists visit each season.

Tensions in Puerto Adolfo López Mateos over access to whalewatching permits reached a boiling point in January 1994. The thirty-four-member Acuendi Tourism Cooperative threatened to stop American companies from operating in the area around town. They were upset that foreign companies had received permits to use a total of seven whalewatching skiffs while locals had received permits to operate a total of only six.[20]

The message from locals was clear: If American outfitters do not hire locals, they should not receive permits. They were aware that San Ignacio Lagoon residents received exclusive access to tourism permits. The Acuendi cooperative demanded that the INE make permit regulations uniform throughout the peninsula.

Federal officials in La Paz agreed with them. In 1994 the INE was under the direction of the Ministry of Social Development (SEDESOL). Presidential candidate Luis Donaldo Colosio managed the agency. Members of the Acuendi cooperative were former cannery union leaders and ardent PRIístas. They boasted of having met Colosio during his visits to Baja California Sur. (Some even traveled to see him speak in La Paz on March 23, 1994, a few hours before he was killed in Tijuana.) Colosio and his agency could not afford to alienate hard-core party members prior to the upcoming elections, especially in a county under the control of the opposition National Action Party.

In an attempt to placate the whalewatching guides from Puerto Adolfo López Mateos, the INE sponsored a meeting during the last week of January 1994 in Puerto Adolfo López Mateos to discuss the permit issue. At the meeting local guides argued that the permit process was unfair and pointed out that foreign outfitters did little for the local economy. The owner of an American company did not win many friends when he declared that the issue of local economic impact was irrelevant since his firm spent millions of dollars annually in Mexico. According to Juan Rodríguez, an Acuendi member, the response from locals was, "Yeah, but he doesn't spend a peso here."

The permit situation was a result of the decision made in Mexico City to grant outsiders permits, and officials in La Paz were expected to resolve it unofficially. Bureaucrats in Mexico City had no interest in curtailing the business of American outfitters. To appease locals, Special Expeditions, a New York–based outfitter, agreed to hire two Acuendi members per whalewatching session as guides and to contract with a local restaurant for a once-per-tour beach barbecue. The INE orally agreed to allow the Acuendi Tourism Cooperative to operate without restrictions on the number of skiffs in the water at any one time. Unfortunately, while this agreement satisfied Acuendi demands, it set a precedent of not establishing a limit on the number of skiffs allowed in the water simultaneously. Scientists are still unsure about the number of boats that should be allowed around whales at any one time. They are sure, however, that thirty-four boats chasing whales in a confined area is probably too many. Outfitters also complain that the excessive numbers of skiffs leave little opportunity for tourists to enjoy a quality nature experience. Increasing the number of boats in the water also increases the potential for accidents.

Problems between local and foreign outfitters were compounded by the fact that many of the American companies working the area around Puerto Adolfo López Mateos in 1994 operated without any permits at all. For example, two American outfitters let their clients observe whales from kayaks—a dangerous and illegal activity. Some buried their trash and human waste in the dunes of Magdalena Island. Whereas in Scammon's and San Ignacio Lagoons large tour boats are prohibited from entering calving areas, in the North Zone of Magdalena Bay there are no such restrictions. Two American outfitters sailed large boats through the middle of the main gray whale calving area south of Puerto Adolfo López Mateos. Because of its status as a federal maritime shipping zone, prohibitions on commercial ship traffic in Magdalena Bay cannot be established without changing federal laws regulating maritime commerce in the bay.

In its ongoing campaign to monitor whalewatching in Baja California Sur, PROFEPA inspectors arrived in Puerto Adolfo López Mateos during the third week of February 1994. Guillermo, the ex–baseball player who had played for the local cannery, had just finished a tour of Scammon's Lagoon after he left San Ignacio Lagoon. He laughed when I saw him on the small beach next to the cannery at Puerto Adolfo López Mateos. "It was hard to leave Antonio's house at La Fridera," he said. "We don't eat like that anywhere else." His new partner, Rodolfo Gómez, was a longtime forestry inspector recently assigned to the whale detail.

Rodolfo was in a foul mood due to problems with an American outfitter the day before. He and Guillermo had checked the permit of the company's kayak camp that moves up and down Magdalena Island throughout the whale season. The camp manager did not have a permit for that particular operation. Instead, he had a copy of a permit for another company camp. Rodolfo confiscated the permit.

Later that afternoon, after returning to Puerto Adolfo López Mateos, Rodolfo called his boss and asked about the status of the company's permits. Meanwhile, the camp manager showed up in town, threatening to hold the PROFEPA outboard hostage until the inspectors returned his permit.

The following morning, Guillermo invited me to accompany him and Rodolfo on their visit to tourist camps strung along the dunes of the eastern shore of Magdalena Island.

We headed north across the narrow channel that fronts Puerto Adolfo López Mateos in the 25-foot PROFEPA panga. Guillermo and Rodolfo disembarked as soon as we arrived at the shoreline camp of the potential outboard kidnapper. The camp manager, who looked like a heavyweight boxer, walked out from the camp to meet them. He wanted to avoid troubling his clients, who are members of the Sierra Club.

Rodolfo angrily asked him, "What about yesterday? Do you have something to say to us? If you do, I'll write down any statement you want to make. All I know is that your permit is not the one that you should have." The stocky manager backed down and told Rodolfo how sorry he was. He hoped Rodolfo understood that the whole affair was the fault of the company owner, an American who resides in La Paz.

Rodolfo relaxed and said, "You're not in trouble. Don't worry." Rodolfo and Guillermo shook hands with the manager and boarded the panga. The next destination was a tour boat leased by the same company.

The 65-foot *Aguila del Mar* was anchored near the middle of the main channel less than a mile south of the Boca de Soledad. Tourists were observing a pod of frolicking gray whales from the top deck. Pulling up behind the stern, Guillermo tied off the skiff and asked permission to climb aboard. The captain, who was in his late fifties and had a thick gray beard, peered over the deck and approved the request. Rodolfo climbed aboard and wandered off with the captain. They were immediately engaged in a heated discussion. Ten minutes later they returned and shook hands before we departed.

As Guillermo untied the panga from the *Aguila del Mar,* Rodolfo was angry. "Who is the owner of this company anyway?" he asked. "Why does he have a monopoly on whalewatching here? Is he the owner of the entire bay?"

In his dark aviator sunglasses Guillermo said quietly, "People in town who need a job should be able to work as guides. Tourism shouldn't be monopolized by outsiders who don't contribute anything to the local economy."

Solving the Problem

After the 1994 gray whale season ended, officials at the La Paz office of the INE were determined to resolve the conflicts over whalewatching at Puerto Adolfo López Mateos and reduce the number of pangas in the water. Government officials in the INE and PROFEPA believed whalewatching had spun out of control. However, because of the position of the INE within the Ministry of Social Development (SEDESOL)—which was committed to ensuring the victory of the ruling party in the upcoming August presidential election—regulating whalewatching was no longer about protecting gray whales. It was a social and political problem.

At the same time that federal officials were working on plans to resolve conflicts in Puerto Adolfo López Mateos, a new thirty-member tourism union formed there with the help of Alfredo Martínez, the Comondú county supervisor and a member of the opposition National Action Party (PAN). After forming the union, members began the search for whalewatching permits for the upcoming season.

Francisco Murillo was elected president of the new union and was charged with securing the necessary paperwork to obtain permits. Originally from Bahía Tortugas, north of San Ignacio Lagoon, what Francisco lacked in formal education he made up for in political savvy and determination. However, during his first trip to the La Paz INE office to inquire about whalewatching permits, he was informed in no uncertain terms that new permits would not be granted. There were too many boats in the water already. Too many boats could hurt the whales. Not everyone can be a whalewatching guide. Why not sell T-shirts or tacos? Francisco left the office demoralized. He returned to a cousin's house, where he was lodging.

By chance, a friend of his cousin stopped by who happened to be the leader of the state office of the Regional Confederation of Mexican Workers (CROM). Francisco told the labor leader about his inability to secure a permit. The labor leader told Francisco that it was outrageous that Mexican workers were denied the ability to support their families. Because the labor leader had not yet met the new SEDESOL *delegado,* he decided that it would be a good time to do so, and he invited Francisco to accompany him.

When the labor leader and Francisco arrived at the SEDESOL office and asked to see the delegado, the new chief's secretary said that he was busy. Perhaps the labor leader could come back another time. Without replying, the labor leader walked into the delegado's office, introduced himself, and was warmly greeted by the most important federal representative in Baja California Sur. The CROM leader presented his friend Francisco whom he said had the misfortune of being denied the opportunity to help feed the families of Puerto Adolfo López Mateos. Francisco, he said, was a Mexican worker and wanted the opportunity to take tourists to see Mexican whales. He had a right to do that, didn't he? asked the labor leader. Maybe the delegado could talk to the people in the INE who give out the permits and see if alternative arrangements could be made.

Grabbing the telephone, the delegado called the office next door and asked the permit granters to come over to his office immediately. The two bureaucrats sensed a problem when they entered and greeted the unsmiling delegado, Francisco, and the labor leader. The delegado told them how upset he was that they had denied Francisco, a Mexican worker, and twenty-nine other workers from Puerto Adolfo López Mateos the opportunity to feed their families. Weren't people more important than whales? The delegado made it clear that Francisco and his associates would receive a permit for 1995.

In November 1994 the new Union of Tourism Services of Puerto Adolfo López Mateos received one permit for twenty whalewatching boats for the 1995 whale season. The government granted fifty-seven boats permission to operate in the area around Puerto Adolfo López Mateos. However, each permit stipulated that only eight boats could be in the water at one time. The Acuendi Cooperative immediately informed the INE that they were unhappy with the restrictions and would not obey the permits unless the government compromised and increased the limit on the number of boats allowed in the water.

To satisfy the demands of the Acuendi Cooperative, officials at the La Paz office of the INE agreed to travel to Puerto Adolfo López Mateos for a meeting.

The Meeting

Gabriel Velásquez, an eighteen-year Baja California Sur federal agency veteran, peered across the desert in Ray-Ban aviator sunglasses as we drove north out of La Paz in late November in a white Volkswagen beetle. We were on our way to the meeting in Puerto Adolfo López Mateos. Gabriel has driven this route countless times and pointed out areas of interest—dirt tracks leading to sea turtle nesting beaches and houses belonging to families that make their living gathering mesquite for firewood.

I asked Marco Antonio Girón, the director of the Vizcaíno Biosphere Reserve, who was scrunched up behind me in the back seat, what he expected to accomplish at the meeting. "The bottom line is that everyone has to realize that they all can't drive pangas around whales," he replied. "Hopefully, different groups can get concessions for different things, like taxis, whale observation towers, boats, and taco stands. Everyone has to diversify. What we are going to do is make it harder for just anyone to work as whalewatching guides. Now the boats will have to be registered with the Ministry of Communications and Transportation [the Secretaría de Comunicaciones y Transportes, or SCT]. So when each group figures out how many boats they can legally put in the water according to their official boat registration permits, then we can work on how many boats will be allowed in the water at a time around whales."

In theory, Marco Antonio should have been 300 miles north, managing the Vizcaíno Biosphere Reserve. However, because of his experience working with communities, his superiors in La Paz instructed him to deal with whalewatching problems in Magdalena Bay. Marco Antonio was generally upbeat despite the almost insurmountable obstacles he faced in running the Vizcaíno Biosphere Reserve. He appeared to be unconcerned that he had not received a paycheck in months. His wife was expecting their first child in a few weeks. Passionate about wildlife conservation, Marco Antonio hails from the northeastern state of Coahuila.

After passing the agricultural fields of the Santo Domingo Valley, we exited the main highway at the agricultural town of Ciudad Insurgentes and turned westward on the highway that led to Puerto Adolfo López Mateos. Rows of corn merged into the dunes and cactus forest of the Magdalena plain. Twenty-five minutes later, the temperature cooled down as we drove through the sandy streets of Puerto Adolfo López Mateos. Our destination was the run-down, yellow cultural center, where all the local players in the whalewatching business were waiting.

One of the problems with a small town is that behind every conflict is a lifetime of bitterness, envy, and animosity. Marco Antonio and Gabriel knew they would be unable to resolve all the problems in Puerto Adolfo López Mateos. They were only following orders and trying to keep the issue from turning into a public brawl like the one that had erupted the previous year.

There was not really that much Marco Antonio and Gabriel could do. In a town like Puerto Adolfo López Mateos, where jobs and money are almost nonexistent and almost everyone knows how to operate an outboard engine, it is hard to expect people not to want to work as whalewatching guides. There are few alternatives.

Marco Antonio and Gabriel emerged from the Volkswagen and walked over to shake hands with local guides milling around the front of the meeting hall. After a few handshakes and smiles, they entered the dark and dirty building. Marco Antonio and Gabriel walked to the front of the room, just in front of a dilapidated wooden stage. Everyone else sat in rickety metal chairs and on wooden benches away from the stage or stood along the wall near the front door. About fifty men were present. Whalewatching is the exclusive domain of men in Puerto Adolfo López Mateos. Men create the conflicts, but women suffer the most when their husbands refuse to allow them to speak to sisters, *comadres,* and relatives married or related to business competitors.

In addition to Marco Antonio and Gabriel, other officials present included the tourism delegado for Baja California Sur, the local mayor, and two representatives from Comondú County. The presence of government representatives was intended to project an image of authority and joint decision making, but everyone in the room knew that the INE calls the shots.

Marco Antonio was the moderator. With his friendly personality and easygoing manner, he came across as a good guy who was trying to give everyone a fair shake. "I'm sorry the delegado is not here," he told the crowd. "He has other commitments and couldn't make it. Let me assure you he is very interested in addressing the concerns you have."

Miguel Palacios, a scraggly bearded fishermen turned whalewatching guide, leaned over to me and said quietly, "If the INE really wanted to make everything work, the delegado would have come. They're just trying to buy time until the whale season begins and keep everyone quiet."

Surveying the crowd and smiling, Marco Antonio continued, "We realize that most of you are unhappy about the permit situation and the regulations restricting the number of boats that can be in the water, but we are willing to work with you. What we've come up with is a requirement to have everyone register their boats with the SCT, to make sure that everyone starts out on the same foot. If your boat is registered and your papers are in order, then you will be able to work. So, before any complaints begin about how unfair the permit situation is, you will have to get everything checked out and then come back to us so that we can figure out how many boats we will allow in the water. And before you start complaining about how much business you are going to lose because of the new restrictions, we want to see proof of contracts with tourist agencies and outside outfitters before we can guarantee that we will permit an increase in the boats in the water. Everything is up to you."

Marco Antonio was buying time by increasing the paper chase. Very few fisherman had their boats and engines registered with the SCT. Getting the required approvals is a long and arduous process. By requiring everyone to present tourist agency contracts, Marco Antonio was asking them to put up or shut up.

No one appeared to be happy with this arrangement, but there was nothing anyone could do until they had cleared the new bureaucratic hurdle. Francisco, the leader of the new tourism union, piped up halfheartedly, "All we want this year is to have ten boats in the water so that we can raise some money for next year. That's all we want."

Antonio Navarro, the somber secretary of the Acuendi Cooperative and a former union official, shouted angrily, "We are going to have flights coming in everyday from Cabo San Lucas, but the agencies don't like to give us any contracts in advance because they can't guarantee how many tourists they are going to have. They usually just show up or let us know at the last minute. What are we going to do when they arrive and we can only put a couple of boats in the water?"

"It is up to you," responded Marco Antonio calmly, "to get all your boats registered and show us your contracts so that we can make the arrangements. We can't do anything until we know how many boats can actually work. But we think the best option is to consider the alternatives to whalewatching so that every group can divide up concessions for food, taxis, and observation towers."

Domingo Romero, the president of Acuendi, who is six-foot-four and who swaggered around like an aging former pro football player, said loudly, "How are we going to arrange for observation towers this winter? It's too late for that now. Kind of like quarter to midnight. Maybe next year, but not this year. If you only allow eight boats around whales, we're going to have a social conflict. We'll have a problem. You have to protect people as well as whales."

The officials squirmed in their seats and looked very uncomfortable. Marco Antonio responded, "We understand that. And that is why we are going to sit down and analyze the situation so that we can justify putting fifteen boats in the water. If the whales don't return because there are too many boats, you'll all be out of work. Whales belong to everyone in Mexico. So you are all going to have to work together to make sure that they keep coming back here. We'll work with you to develop alternatives. But the decision that will determine how many boats are allowed in the water will be based on the contracts you show us and proof that you have proper permits. Maybe we'll allow up to twenty boats. It depends on the contracts you have. In Scammon's and San Ignacio, only eight boats are allowed, and those areas have more room than here. Things have to change. Everyone will have to cooperate. PROFEPA will work with us, and the American companies will not be able to do what they did last year."

Glancing at the tourism delegado for support, Marco Antonio continued, "I'm sure that the Secretaría de Turismo will work with you to develop alternatives to whalewatching. You can get help from the Solidarity program and Comondú County. Not everyone can be satisfied. But if you want to resolve this problem, bring in your paperwork to La Paz on December 5, and you'll have a response by the following week."

Marco Antonio adjourned the meeting. The guides knew there was nothing else they could do. Marco Antonio and Gabriel ameliorated the tensions and kept the allies of the PRI at bay—at least for a few weeks. Everyone understands that red tape is a fact of life. The decision to request additional permits and then decide how many boats would be allowed in the water seemed fair. At least local groups received a response to their demands. Marco Antonio and Gabriel went through the motions of demonstrating government sympathy.

After the meeting was over, Marco Antonio and Gabriel were invited to eat lunch at the home of Hector Espinoza, a longtime fisherman who now works for an American outfitter. "Last time we were here, Hector fed us lobster. I ate four and left completely stuffed," Marco Antonio told me as we drove the few blocks to lunch. Marco Antonio is always concerned with his next meal.

Hector, sixty-six, was sitting in the backyard of his colorful plywood house at the center of town. We sat down under the vine-covered *ramada*. A cool breeze blew off the bay. Marta, Hector's wife, tended a mesquite-fired iron disco (which resembles a large *paella* dish) filled with freshly caught perch. Whole fish are cooked in oil until they are hot and crispy. There is no better way to eat fresh fish than surrounded by old fishing nets, outboard engines, rotting pangas, and salty fishermen. Members of Hector's clan—grandsons, sons, and nephews who dominate the local lobster and abalone cooperative—grabbed pieces of fish from the disk.

The word was out that Marco Antonio and Gabriel were still in town. Soon, other guides showed up to pay their respects. Gabriel left the table for a private meeting with one of the new arrivals. These rituals of obligation are designed to establish a bond between people and the government officials who can help them survive.

Hector knows that Marco Antonio and Gabriel depend on his goodwill for boat rides during the whale season to inspect tourist camps and collect information on the tourism industry. Marco Antonio and Gabriel understand that unless they establish good relationships with locals, they do not have a chance of protecting gray whales. The system is not perfect, but rules and regulations are worthless unless a web of social and political obligations exists to make them meaningful.

Into the Future

The efforts of Marco Antonio and Gabriel were a first step in a long process of collaborating with the residents of Puerto Adolfo López Mateos to improve whalewatching. The inability of government to regulate tourism in Magdalena Bay effectively is not the biggest threat faced by gray whales. Habitat development throughout the migratory route is by far the biggest threat to the long-term survival of gray whales.

Although many American outfitters and tourists become exasperated by what they perceive to be the failure of the Mexican government to clamp down and "fix" whalewatching in Magdalena Bay, they forget that in the United States and Canada, whalewatching is largely unregulated.

Mexican environmental officials and locals are committed to resolving whalewatching conflicts in Magdalena Bay, but these problems will not disappear overnight. Local conservation groups such as Pronatura have entered the fray in an attempt to find solutions that benefit both gray whales and the people of Puerto Adolfo López Mateos. There are no easy answers, but the fact that there is a commitment to working together to solve the problem is a good omen for the future. The most valuable tool that government officials used in Magdalena Bay and other sites was their empathy. They listened and attempted to draft solutions that addressed local concerns.

In San Ignacio Lagoon, locals and foreign outfitters found that building partnerships was a profitable and effective way of doing business. Conflicts between competing groups were reduced, and gray whales benefited as a business partnership evolved into a partnership for conservation. For example, the outfitters who work together in tourism collaborate with conservation organizations working to stop the San Ignacio Lagoon saltworks. Local and American outfitters also take local students to see whales.

It is ironic that residents of some of the most isolated fishing villages in North America are helping to redefine our relationship with wild animals. Americans and Europeans brought the gray whale population to the brink of extinction. The inhabitants of San Ignacio Lagoon and Magdalena Bay are helping us to celebrate their survival. For gray whales, conservation is a community affair.

8 Shaping Their Own Future

If you take care of the whales, they'll take care of you.
—A WOMAN FROM SAN IGNACIO LAGOON

Environmentalists are so used to lamenting the sad state of the planet, they rarely take time to learn from success. But who would have thought that after a ninety-year period when American and European whalers slaughtered thousands of gray whales inside their winter refuges in Baja California, the species would come back from the brink of extinction? Now that gray whales have been "saved," it is critical to continue protective measures and programs that will allow the long-term survival of the species.

There has never been a better time to develop the partnerships necessary to create conservation success stories in Mexico. Despite the negative press coverage of Mexico and hardened stereotypes in the United States, the country *is* changing. Because of opposition party control over the national legislature, one pillar of the state is no longer available to rubber-stamp ruling party edicts and budgets. The fact that the Mexican Congress formed a commission chaired by a deputy from the Green Party to investigate the proposed San Ignacio Lagoon saltworks is proof of the profundity of political change. The committee will receive support from nongovernmental and community organizations that defend gray whales. In turn, the committee will provide these groups the political space to continue their lobbying efforts. Opposition parties and conservation groups have finally learned how to use the positive political capital of the gray whale.

In rural states such as Baja California Sur, Yucatán, and Chiapas (states with some of the highest levels of biodiversity and the largest protected areas in Mexico), the ruling party controls the allocation of federal funds, impeding democratization, decentralization, and conservation. For example, to insure a PRI victory in elections in Yucatán in May 1998, Governor Cervera Pacheco, a hard-line PRIísta, bankrupted the state treasury by spending $40 million to defeat opposition candidates for municipal and state legislative posts. That sum included the cost of distributing 200,000 bicycles to campesinos. Former governor Guillermo Mercado of Baja California Sur, another old-school PRI dinosaur, bankrupted the PAN-governed county of Comondú in 1995 by withholding the delivery of state and federal funds. His obsession with the San Ignacio Lagoon saltworks was at the expense of the development of the rest of the state. Rather than spending time and money to solve problems, ruling-party leaders bankrupt the country to maintain their own power and prop up their political allies. Imagine the poverty, public health, or conservation programs that could be funded with the $40 million spent on elections in Yucatán or the $120 million proposed for the San Ignacio Lagoon saltworks.

Fortunately, ruling-party empires are slowly crumbling. Rising up to take their place is a network of groups committed to democracy *and* environmental conservation at the local and regional levels. The political system is slowly evolving out of its relic status, which will hopefully allow a more democratic system of conservation — one that encourages community-level and nongovernmental organizations to participate in decision making and to define conservation solutions for the twenty-first century. Building the effectiveness of these communities and nongovernmental organizations is the key to insuring the long-term protection of gray whales in Baja California Sur and biodiversity throughout Mexico.

A wide range of nongovernmental organizations involved in everything from conservation to public health and women's rights have forced local, state, and federal officials to open up the political process in Mexico. The most innovative and successful conservation programs and protected areas are the result of the presence of vibrant, creative, and independent nongovernmental organizations. In the state of Quintana Roo, Amigos de Sian Ka'an has taken an active role in searching for financial mechanisms such as a hotel tax to create a conservation trust fund for protected areas in the region. The nonprofit organization successfully spearheaded a three-nation effort (Mexico, Guatemala, and Belize) to protect the Great Maya Reef, the world's second largest barrier reef. In Loreto, Baja California Sur, a local citizen's group, Grupo Ecologísta Antares, successfully pressured President Zedillo to create the 500,000-acre Loreto Bay National Park as a way of outlawing industrial fishing near the town. In Baja California, Pro Esteros, a grassroots conservation organization, collaborated with the Natural Resources Defense Council to develop a peninsulawide coalition to lobby against the San Ignacio Lagoon saltworks. The disassembling of the PRI's stranglehold on power in Mexico will only further spur nonprofit and community-level organizations to take the lead in resolving Mexico's environmental problems. The willingness of nongovernmental conservation groups to enter the conservation arena is a good sign that there is a desire to find common ground and solutions that keep the gray whale conservation agenda alive.

The biggest challenge in gray whale conservation is the long-term preservation of winter refuges in Baja California Sur. However, of the three nations that host migrating gray whales, only Mexico is expected to subsidize protective measures while sacrificing economic growth. Tourists spend approximately $30 million a year to catch a glimpse of gray whales off the west coast of North America. Why not establish an international trust fund for gray whale conservation programs in Mexico? Funds could support the management of the Vizcaíno Biosphere Reserve, the hiring of park rangers to halt the epidemic of resource piracy in gray whale lagoons, environmental education programs, and sustainable economic development (e.g., private-sector aquaculture ventures, local ecotourism ventures).

Unless ecotourism directly benefits and involves local communities, the majority of local people will accept whatever offer of employment comes along. Maintaining gray whale conservation in Mexico will require continued dialogue among people who live around whales, outfitters who profit from the cetaceans, conservation groups, and government officials charged with protecting the environment.

The best indication that Mexico is still ahead of its First World neighbor in terms of commitment to gray whale conservation is government support of local community efforts to benefit from the growing whalewatching industry. Despite conflicts in Magdalena Bay over rights to whalewatching permits, it is important to recognize that local people are fighting over the right to take tourists to observe whales rather than kill them. The growing involvement of local communities with gray whales and the whalewatching industry in Baja California has fostered a significant shift in popular sentiment toward these marine mammals and is a hopeful sign for the growing conservation movement in Mexico. Further, it is concrete evidence that economic incentives can help to create conservation attitudes among natural resource–dependent communities.

In contrast, fishing communities in Russia, Norway, Japan, and the United States pressure their governments and the IWC to permit them to slaughter whales. The Mexican government takes note of the hypocrisy of American environmental groups pointing the finger over the San Ignacio Lagoon saltworks while the U.S. government sanctions the killing of gray whales by the Makah Indians. Why not engage Indian communities of the Pacific Northwest in a symbolic harvest of gray whales through a sustainable tribal whalewatching industry? A North American gray whale conservation trust fund could finance conservation and sustainable development activities in Mexico and provide incentives for native communities in the United States, Canada, and Russia not to kill whales. Conservation in the twenty-first century means thinking creatively about problem solving rather than just hurling slogans across international boundaries.

Ultimately gray whales are their own ambassadors for goodwill. Few people who encounter these primeval leviathans leave unchanged. No other animals in Mexico are capable of eliciting the type of support that gray whales have. Consequently, these cetaceans will shape their own future.

Hotel Hacienda Beach Resort

CABO SAN LUCAS BAJA SUR MEXICO

Fecha / Date

No de Toallas: / No. of Towels: 3 Hab.: / Room: 109

Recibí de HOTEL HACIENDA las toallas mencionadas arriba, mismas que devolveré antes de las 19:00 horas. De lo contrario, autorizo a que me sean cargados $20.00 U.S. por cada una.

I received from HACIENDA HOTEL the above mentioned towels, which I will return before 7:00 p.m. If not returned, I will be charged for each one $20.00 U.S.

20 00 c.s

Firma
Signature Katrina Jessen

NOTE: DEAR GUEST
WHEN RETURNING YOUR TOWELS REQUEST THIS CARD, OTHERWISE, WE WILL NOT PROVIDE TOWELS BY NOT SHOWING THIS CARD.

DO NOT DESTROY IT!

Notes

Chapter 1. Mexican by Birth

1. Charles Scammon, *The Marine Mammals of the North-western Coast of North America Described and Illustrated Together with an Account of the American Whale-Fishery* (1874, reprint, with an introduction by Victor B. Scheffer, New York: Dover Publications, 1968), 28.

2. In Mexico, Scammon's Lagoon is known as Laguna Ojo de Liebre or Jack Rabbit Spring Lagoon, after a famous spring located east of the lagoon.

3. "Endangered and Threatened Wildlife and Plants: Final Rule to Remove the Eastern North Pacific Population of the Gray Whale from the List of Endangered Species," *Federal Register* 59, no. 115 (1994): 31094–31095.

4. Gray whales are viewed in Mexico as having Mexican nationality. The best example of this is the color comic book on gray whales *Mexicanas por nacimiento* (Mexicans by birth) distributed throughout Mexico by the Ministry of Fisheries (Secretaría de Pesca, 1993). The pamphlet discusses the natural history of gray whales and Mexico's role in their protection.

Chapter 2. Natural History and Human Exploitation

1. "Endangered and Threatened Wildlife and Plants."

2. David Gordon and Alan Baldridge, *Gray Whales* (Monterey: Monterey Bay Aquarium, 1991), 51.

3. Steven Swartz and Mary Lou Jones, "Gray Whales at Play in Baja's San Ignacio Lagoon," *National Geographic* 171 (1987): 758, 764.

4. Mary Lou Jones and Steven Swartz, *Demography and Phenology of Gray Whales and Evaluation of Whale-Watching Activities in Laguna San Ignacio, Baja California Sur, Mexico, 1978–1982* (U.S. Department of Commerce NTIS PB 86-2190778, 1986), 54–56.

5. Luis Fleischer, Javier Contreras, and E. Michel, "La ballena gris (*Eschrichtius robustus*) en la region norte de Bahía de Magdalena, B.C.S., Mexico," in *Memoria de la IX Reunión internacional para el estudio de los mamíferos marinos* (La Paz: Universidad Autónoma de Baja California Sur, 1984), 40.

6. Jones and Swartz, "Gray Whales at Play," 49.

7. Luis Fleischer, "Aerial Surveys of Gray Whales (*Eschrichtius robustus*) in Mexican Waters (1980–1990)" (paper presented to the Scientific Committee of the International

Whaling Commission at the Special Meeting for the Comprehensive Assessment of the Gray Whale, Seattle, Washington, 1990).

8. David Cambell and Melba Cambell, "Surf-Riding by the California Gray Whale," *Bull. South. Calif. Acad. Sciences* 62, pt. 2 (1963): 99.

9. Scammon, *The Marine Mammals,* 24.

10. Marilyn Dalheim, "A Comparison of the Acoustical Environments and Activities of the Gray Whale (*Eschrichtius robustus*) in the Bering Sea, Alaska, and Baja California, Mexico," in *Memoria del X reunión internacional sobre mamíferos marinos* (La Paz: Secretaría de Pesca and Universidad Autónoma de Baja California Sur, 1985), 42.

11. Ibid.

12. Ibid.

13. Swartz and Jones, "Gray Whales at Play," 761.

14. Ibid., 764.

15. Raymond Gilmore to Dale Rice, 10 March 1976, box 42, file 33, Gilmore Collection, San Diego Natural History Museum Library, San Diego, California. According to Mary Lou Jones and Steven Swartz, a 1960s chart of Scammon's Lagoon they found at the San Diego Natural History Museum, prepared by a Santa Barbara pharmacist, noted "curious and friendly whales" in the lagoon. See Mary Lou Jones and Steven Swartz, "Demography and Phenology of Gray Whales and Evaluation of Human Activities in Laguna San Ignacio, Baja California Sur, Mexico," in *The Gray Whale,* ed. Mary Lou Jones, Steven Swartz, and Stephen Leatherwood (Orlando: Academic Press, 1984), 370.

16. Mary Lou Jones, Steven Swartz and Stephen Leatherwood, "Introduction," *The Gray Whale,* 14.

17. Jones and Swartz, "Demography and Phenology of Gray Whales and Evaluation of Human Activities," 351.

18. Ibid.

19. Swartz and Jones, "Gray Whales at Play," 770.

20. Dalheim, "A Comparison of the Acoustical," 45.

21. See David Henderson, *Men and Whales at Scammon's Lagoon* (Los Angeles: Dawson's Book Shop, 1972) for an extended discussion of the exploitation of marine mammals off the coast of Baja California by Indians.

22. Stephen Reilly, "Population assessment and population dynamics of the California Gray Whale (*Eschrichtius robustus*)," (Ph.D. diss., University of Washington, Seattle, 1981) cited in Randall Reeves and Edward Mitchell, "Current Status of the Gray Whale, *Eschrichtius robustus,*" *Canadian Field-Naturalist* 102, no. 2 (1988): 378.

23. David Henderson, "Nineteenth Century Gray Whaling: Grounds, Catches, and Kills, Practices and Depletion of the Whale Population," in *The Gray Whale,* 163.

24. Scammon, *The Marine Mammals,* 24.

25. Henderson, *Men and Whales,* 138.

26. Henderson "Nineteenth Century," 169.

27. Henderson, *Men and Whales,* 134.

28. Henderson, "Nineteenth Century," 165.

29. Whalers divided Magdalena Bay into three zones. The South Zone was called Lee Bay. The Central Zone was Weather or Main Bay. The Boca de Soledad area in the North Zone was known as the Estero de Santo Domingo. The Central and South Zones were also called Marguerita Bay. See Henderson, "Nineteenth Century," 165.

30. Charles Scammon, "Report of Captain C. Scammon, of the U.S. Revenue Service, on the West Coast of Lower California," in *Resources of the Pacific Slope,* ed. J. Ross Browne (New York: D. Appleton and Company, 1869), 127.

31. Lyndall Landauer, *Scammon: Beyond the Lagoon* (San Francisco: Associates of the J. Porter Shaw Library, 1986), 36.

32. Henderson, *Men and Whales,* 151.

33. Scammon, *The Marine Mammals,* 260.

34. Henderson, *Men and Whales,* 126.

35. J. Ross Browne, *Explorations in Lower California* (1868, reprint, Tucson: Arizona Silhouettes, 1952), 19.

36. Scammon, "Report of Captain," 125.

37. Henderson, "Nineteenth Century," 167.

38. The average yield per whale was approximately 35 barrels. See Henderson, *Men and Whales,* 260.

39. Ballenas Bay includes the area outside the main lagoon entrance northward to Punta Abreojos. See Henderson, "Nineteenth Century," 169.

40. Scammon, "Report of Captain," 126.

41. Mary Lou Jones, Steven Swartz, and Marilyn Dalheim, *Census of Gray Whale Abundance in San Ignacio Lagoon: A Follow-up Study in Response to Low Whale Counts Recorded During an Acoustic Playback Study of Noise-Effects on Gray Whales* (U.S. Department of Commerce NTIS PB94-195062, 1994), 2.

Noise associated with whaling also caused whales to flee Magdalena Bay in 1848. According to Captain Scammon (in *The Marine Mammals,* 268), the "deafening noise" of fifty ships, "coopering their oil," along with "the chase and capture of the animals, the staving of boats, and the smoke and the blaze from try-works by night soon drove the whales to the outside shores."

42. From 1864 to 1933, five American companies received concessions to Magdalena Bay and much of the Pacific coast of the peninsula. See chapter 37 of Pablo L. Martínez, *Historia de Baja California* (1956, reprint, La Paz, Consejo Editorial del Gobierno del Estado de B.C.S., 1991).

43. El Coronel Jefe de las Armas, Gobierno Político Militar del Distrito Sur de la Baja California, 8 January 1904, 334:V337:Exp. 60, Pablo L. Martínez State Historical Archives of Baja California Sur, La Paz.

44. Secretaría de Estado y del Despacho de Guerra y Marina to Jefe de la Secretaría de Guerra, 10 May 1904, 334:V374:Exp. 60, Pablo L. Martínez Archives.

45. Subsecretario del Estado y del Despacho de Guerra y Marina de México to Jefe Político y Militar del Distrito Sur de la Baja California, 10 May 1904, 334:V374:Exp. 60, Pablo L. Martínez Archives.

46. Subsecretario del Estado y del Despacho de Guerra y Marina de Mexico to Jefe

Político y Militar del Distrito Sur de la Baja California, 11 August 1904, 334:V374:Exp. 60, Pablo L. Martínez Archives.

47. The presence of so many American ships caused Díaz to send the governor of the southern district of Baja California, Coronel Agustín Sangines, to Magdalena Bay to remind the Americans that they were still in Mexico. Díaz's fears were realized when Sangines notified him in a letter written on March 11 that a U.S. naval commander had informed him that he was sure that Magdalena Bay belonged to the United States, because the U.S. consul in Trinidad told him it did. Sangines monitored the activities of the fleet and reminded them from his headquarters aboard the *Tampico* that Magdalena Bay was indeed Mexican territory. Although Sangines provided detailed reports to Díaz with fleet and ammunition statistics, he made a great effort to avoid mentioning the effect of gunnery activities. Perhaps fear of angering the dictator deterred Sangines from telling Díaz what was really happening in Magdalena Bay. See Agustín Sangines, Jefe de la Armas to Secretaría General de Guerra y Marina, 19 April 1908, 546:V471bis:Exp. 36, Pablo L. Martínez Archives.

48. Samuel Carter III, *The Incredible Great White Fleet* (New York: Crowell-Collier Press, 1971), 68.

49. Various communications about ships, 1909, 571:V500:Exp. 112, Pablo L. Martínez Archives.

50. Joh. N. Tønnessen and Arne Odd Johnsen, *The History of Modern Whaling,* trans. R. I. Christophersen (Berkeley and Los Angeles: University of California Press, 1982), 205.

51. Dale Rice and Allan Wolman, *The Life History and Ecology of the Gray Whale (Eschrichtius robustus),* Spec. Publ., The American Society of Mammalogists, no. 3 (1971), 123.

52. Randall Reeves, "Modern Commercial Pelagic Whaling for Gray Whales," in *The Gray Whale,* 191.

53. Raymundo Lucero Murillo, conversation with author, 6 July 1994, Puerto Adolfo López Mateos, Baja California Sur. Lucero is one of Magdalena Bay's oldest living fishermen.

54. Tønnessen and Johnsen, *The History of Modern Whaling,* 327.

55. Testimony of Juan Zuñiga regarding whales, 16 February Box 41, file 54, Hubbs Papers, Scripps Institution of Oceanography Library, La Jolla, California.

56. Mark Derr, "To Whale or Not to Whale," *Atlantic* (October 1998), p. 24.

57. "Commerical Use of Gray Whales Confirmed," *American Cetacean Society–San Diego Chapter Newsletter* (October 1998).

Chapter 3. People and Gray Whales in Baja California Sur

1. There is no federal or state government program to protect the five species of sea turtles (green, black, loggerhead, leatherback, and olive ridley) that inhabit the waters of Baja California Sur. Federal authorities have arrested sea turtle poachers in the Vizcaíno Biosphere Reserve and in Loreto Bay National Park in the Sea of Cortez. The

staff of Loreto Bay National Park and a Loreto conservation group, Grupo Ecologísta Antares, are working with University of Arizona doctoral student Wallace J. Nichols to develop a pilot sea turtle conservation program. A local conservation organization in Cabo San Lucas carries out sea turtle conservation programs in the Cape region. Bighorn sheep receive some attention because the federal government receives revenues from bighorn sheep hunting permits. Due to poaching and habitat loss, the subspecies of pronghorn found in the Vizcaíno Desert is close to extinction despite a captive-breeding program managed by the Vizcaíno Biosphere Reserve.

2. Luis Fleischer and Octavio Maravilla, "Presence of Gray Whales (*Eschrichtius robustus*) in the Gulf of California" (paper presented to the Scientific Committee of the International Whaling Commission at the Special Meeting for the Comprehensive Assessment of the Gray Whale, Seattle, Washington, 1990).

3. Since 1992 the majority of population increase in the state has been in the Los Cabos region (San José del Cabo and Cabo San Lucas). See Eliseo Zuloaga, "Alto crecimiento poblacional se registra en la entidad," *Diario Peninsular* (La Paz), 14 July 1998, p. 3.

4. See Victoria Chenault, *Los pescadores de Baja California* (Mexico City, Centro de Investigaciónes y Estudios Superiores en Antropología Social, 1985). For an overview of the ranching culture that has heavily influenced local attitudes toward marine resources, see Harry W. Crosby's beatifully written and photographed *Last of the Californios* (ed. Richard F. Pourade, San Diego: Copley Press, 1981).

5. R. E. Viñas, A. Sarria, and V. Rubio, "Repertorio temático de la pintura rupestre de la Sierra de San Francisco, Baja California (Mexico)," *Ars Praehistorica,* III/IV (1984/1985): 201. The ancient rock art of the Sierra de San Francisco illustrates how the resources of the region have been exploited by humans for many centuries. The peninsula of Baja California has been described by some American popular authors and by the eco-tourist industry as a "wilderness" ruined by its current inhabitants. In *Conservation and Development in the Gray Whale Lagoons of Baja California Sur, Mexico* (U.S. Dept. of Commerce NTIS PB96-113154 1995, 12), Emily Young and I argue that, "A major obstacle to understanding the complexity of nature-society issues along the Baja California peninsula is that a 'pristine myth' has been established by popular U.S. authors who have written about the peninsula. This myth de-emphasizes historic human impacts to the peninsula, glorifying a depopulated and unscarred landscape, while ignoring a vibrant human geography that has existed since pre-Columbian times." The best example of a work that typifies the pristine myth is Joseph Wood Krutch's *Baja California and the Geography of Hope* (ed. Kenneth Brower, foreward by David Brower, New York: Sierra Club and Ballantine Books, 1967). The book depicts a peninsula void of humans. The most complete discussions on the geography and complexity of human settlement in Baja California can be found in Homer Aschmann, *The Central Desert of Baja California: Demography and Ecology* (Berkeley and Los Angeles: University of California Press, 1959); Miguel del Barco, *Historia natural y crónica de la Antigua California [Adiciones y correcciones a la Noticia de Miguel Venegas],* edición, estudio preliminar, notas, y apéndices: Miguel León-Portilla (Mexico City: Universidad Nacio-

nal Autónoma de México, 1973); Martha Micheline Cariño Olvera, *Historia de la relaciones hombre naturaleza en Baja California Sur, 1500–1940* (La Paz: Universidad Autónoma de Baja California Sur, 1996); Harry W. Crosby, *Antigua California: Mission and Colony on the Peninsular Frontier, 1697–1768* (Albuquerque: University of New Mexico Press, 1994); David Henderson, *Men and Whales*; Peveril Meigs, *The Dominican Mission Frontier of Lower California* (Berkeley: University of California Press, 1935); and Peveril Meigs, *The Kiliwa Indians of Lower California* (Berkeley: University of California Press, 1939).

6. This story is from Leonardo Reyes Silva, *El molino de viento: Leyendas, costumbres y narraciones sudcalifornianas* (La Paz: Consejo Editorial del Gobierno del Estado de Baja California Sur, 1992), 107–110.

7. Jefe de Aduana, Bahía Magdalena to General Brigadier Felix Ortega, Jefe Político de La Paz, Baja California, 29 March 1915, 662:V648:Exp. 15, Pablo L. Martínez Archives.

8. Secretario de General Brigadier Felix Ortega Jefe Polito del Distrito Sur de la Baja Calfornia, 6 April 1915, 662:V648:Exp. 15, Pablo L. Martínez Archives.

9. Residents of Bahía Magdalena to Jefe Político Militar de Distrito Sur, 15 September 1915, 662:V648:Exp. 15, Pablo L. Martínez Archives.

10. The residents of San Ignacio are referred to as panzas dulces or sweet-bellies for their fondness for sweets made from the dates and other sweet fruits grown around town.

11. Tønnessen and Johnsen, *The History of Modern Whaling*, 327.

Chapter 4. The Origins of Gray Whale Conservation in Mexico

1. Aurora Breceda et al., "Conservacion y areas protegidas en Baja California Sur," in *La Reserva de la Biósfera El Vizcaíno en la península de Baja California*, ed. Alfredo Ortega and Laura Arriaga (La Paz: Centro de Investigaciónes Biológicas de Baja California Sur, 1990), 29.

2. Teodoro Riveroll, Informe sobre el estado en que se halla la Peninsula de la Baja California, en su calidad de Territorio, presentado por el funcionario que suscribe al Exm. Senor Presidente de la Republica, 1861, Pablo L. Martínez Archives.

3. Jokes are still told about these surveys: One day the mayor of Todos Santos received a telegram from the governor asking for information about flora and fauna. The mayor didn't know anything so decided to ask the police captain for help. "Say Captain," the mayor asked. "Do you know anything about flora or fauna?" The captain thought for a minute and replied, "Well, I don't know who Fauna is, but Flora—she moved to Ensenada."

4. Municipalidad de Comondú. Informe sobre la flora y fauna de la Municipalidad de Comondú, 1910, 536:V501bis:Exp28, Pablo L. Martínez Archives.

5. Subprefecto Político de San José y Santiago to Secretaría de la Jefatura Política, La Paz, 15 April 1910, 536:V501bis:Exp. 28, Pablo L. Martínez Archives.

6. Presidente Municipal de La Paz to Secretario del Gobierno del Distrito de Baja

California, 19 April 1910, 536:V501bis:Exp. 28, Pablo L. Martínez Archives. The governor's office compiled a master list of the flora and fauna of the southern district of the peninsula and rated the abundance of each species. The species of the order cetacea were all listed as abundant. Zoología y botánica del Distrito Sur de la Baja California, 28 July 1910, 536:V501bis:Fxp. 28, Pablo L. Martínez Archives.

7. Secretaría de Estado y del Despacho de Fomento Colonización e Industria to Jefe Político, Distrito Sur de la Baja California, 22 June 1912, V548bis:Exp. 16, Pablo L. Martínez Archives.

8. Subrefecto Político to Secretario de Gobierno de La Paz, 13 March 1913, 548bis:Exp. 16, Pablo L. Martínez Archives.

9. Copy of 17 July 1917 decree regarding natural resources emitted by Venustiano Carranza, Secretaría de Fomento, 1 August 1917, V666:Exp. sin número, Pablo L. Martínez Archives.

10. Roberto Arroyo C. to Enrique Moreno, Jefe Politico de Baja California Sur, 26 January 1917, V683:Exp. 50, Pablo L. Martínez Archives.

11. Dirección de Estudios Biológicos to the Gobernador del Distrito Sur de la Baja California, 4 September 1920, V744:Exp. 49, Pablo L. Martínez Archives; Gobernador del Distrito to the Secretaría de Agricultura y Fomento, 12 October 1920, V744:Exp. 49., Pablo L. Martínez Archives.

12. Secretario de Gobierno del Distrito Sur de la Baja California to Presidente Municipal de La Paz, 11 June 1926, V880:Exp. sin número, Pablo L. Martínez Archives.

13. P. Diaz Bonilla, Datos sobre las diferencias especies de peces, cetaceos y tesaceos que estistanen las aguas que bañan las costas del Distrito Sur de la Baja California, 21 February 1927, V880:Exp. sin número, Pablo L. Martínez Archives.

14. See Lane Simonian, *Defending the Land of the Jaguar* (Austin: University of Texas Press, 1995), for a comprehensive history of twentieth century national-level conservation initiatives in Mexico.

15. For a detailed description of the conservation policies and efforts of Lázaro Cárdenas to establish national parks in Mexico see Simonian, *Defending the Land of the Jaguar,* 94–100, and Fernando Vargas, *Parques nacionales de México y reservas equivalentes: Pasado, presente y futuro* (Mexico City: Instituto de Investigaciónes Económicas–UNAM, 1984), 46. According to Enrique Krauze in *Mexico: Biography of Power* (trans. by Hank Heifetz; New York: HarperCollins 1997), one of the two pillars of the regime of President Lázaro Cárdenas was "defending natural resources" (p. 652).

16. Secretaría de Pesca, *El programa nacional de investigación y conservación de mamíferos marinos de Mexico* (Mexico City, 1987).

17. "Decreto por el cual se reforma la prevención reglamentaria de 25 de Noviembre de 1921, que establece veda absoluta para la pesca de manatí," *Diario Oficial,* 22 August 1929, p. 3.

18. "Acuerdo que establece veda para la captura del manatí o vaca marina." *Diario Oficial,* 1 August 1934, p. 531; "Acuerdo que establece relativa, general y definitiva para la pesca en toda la Republica del manatí o vaca marina (Manatus americanus),"

Diario Oficial, 27 February 1945, p. 5; "Acuerdo que establece veda para la especie manatí (Trichechus manatus) en la República Mexicana," *Diario Oficial,* 26 October 1981, p. 33.

19. G. D. Hanna, "Expedition to Guadalupe Island Mexico," in *Proceedings of the California Academy of Sciences,* 24 (1925): 217–275. The initial period of marine mammal conservation coincided with an extraordinary period of legislation signed by President Álvaro Obregón from 1920 to 1924. The *hacendado* from Sonora took a great interest in the state of the peninsula's wildlife, enacting a succession of decrees to preserve its fauna from indiscriminate hunting. In 1923, hunting inspector Eustolio Guajardo reported that "so many skins of deer and antelope, etc. are for sale as well as the dried meat of these animals, that I believe these are purely commercial enterprises." Guajardo believed that the hunting of big game and the sale of skins and meat had become so ingrained that only with "coercive" measures would rampant poaching be stopped. See Subsecretario Encargado del Despacho, Sec. de Agricultura to Gobernador del Distrito Sur de Baja California, La Paz, 23 October 1923, 577:V837:Exp. 45, Pablo L. Martínez Archives.

20. "Acuerdo que establece veda para la captura de elefante marino y foca fina," *Diario Oficial,* 24 April 1933, p. 648.

21. See for example, "Contrato celebrado con el señor Nicolas Fossum para el establecimiento de una fabrica de producción de la ballena," *Diario Oficial,* 4 September 1920, pp. 86–89; "Acuerdo declarando caduco el contrato celebrado con el señor Magnus Kenow, para la explotación de la ballena en el littoral occidental de la Baja California," *Diario Oficial,* 20 February 1926, pp. 834–835; Contrato celebrado entre C. Ramon de Negri, Secretaría de Agricultura y Fomento en representacion del Ejecutivo Federal, y el señor Gunnar M. Vik, para la explotación de ballena en aguas del litoral occidental de Baja California, 1924, 545:V837:Exp. 16, Pablo L. Martínez Archives.

22. Tønnessen and Johnsen, *The History of Modern Whaling,* 400.

23. "Decreto que aprueba el Convenio Internacional para la reglamentación de la caza de ballena," *Diario Oficial,* 23 February 1938, pp. 1–2. Argentina, Australia, Germany, the United Kingdom, Ireland, New Zealand, Norway, South Africa, and the United States signed the agreement.

24. Reeves, "Modern Commercial Pelagic Whaling for Gray Whales," 189.

25. Tønnessen and Johnsen, *The History of Modern Whaling,* 499.

26. "Convención Internacional para la Reglamentación de la Caza de la Ballena," *Diario Oficial,* 6 December 1949, pp. 5–10.

27. Reeves, "Modern Commercial Pelagic Whaling for Gray Whales," 190.

28. Alexey Yablokov, "Validity of Whaling Data," *Nature* 367 (13 January 1994): 108.

29. Fleischer was kicked out of the Mexican Society for the Study of Marine Mammals in 1995.

30. Carl Hubbs to Santiago A. Campbell, Consul of Mexico in San Diego, 29 February 1952, Box 56, file 4, Hubbs Papers.

31. Julio Berdegue, "Ultimo censo de la ballena gris, Rhachianectes glaucus (Cope), en aguas de Baja California," *Ciencia* 16 (1956): 103.

32. J. Bunker, "Experts Fear End of Gray Whale if Pact's Broken," *San Diego Evening Tribune,* 21 June 1965, p. 1.

33. Ibid.

34. Ian Moore to Gustavo Díaz Ordaz, President of Mexico, 22 June 1965, Box 56, file, 41, Hubbs Papers.

35. "Mexican Plans to Hunt Whales off Baja Assailed," *San Diego Union,* 11 September 1965, Box 56, file 41, Hubbs Papers.

36. H. Y. Jones, "Mexican Denies Whale Hunt Plans" *San Diego Union,* 12 September 1965, p. A2.

37. Ibid.

38. It is no coincidence that renewed interest in whaling, rather than formal attempts at gray whale conservation, occurred during the term of President Gustavo Díaz Ordaz (1964–1970), who had little interest in environmental issues or protected areas. See Vargas, *Parques nacionales de México,* 49. Data on whaling obtained from Rice and Wolman, *The Life History,* 127.

39. George Lindsay to Ralph C. Baker, Director Bureau of Commercial Fisheries, U.S. Fish and Wildlife Service, 18 July 1967, Box 56, file 31, Hubbs Papers.

40. Raymond Gilmore to Paul Paulbitski, 26 March 1970, Box 42, file 1. Gilmore Collection.

41. Alan Merridew, "Whale Harvesting Turmoil Bubbles," *San Diego Evening Tribune,* 23 October 1971, Box 56, file 17, Hubbs Papers.

42. Tønnessen and Johnsen, *The History of Modern Whaling,* 673.

43. Carl Hubbs, "Observations on California Gray Whales, etc., on Flight of PBM II:12:1947 about 7:30–17:30," Box 55, file 27, Hubbs Papers.

44. David Day to Raymond Gilmore, 27 November 1956, Box 42, file 78, Gilmore Collection.

45. Ed Ainsworth. "Scientists Spy on Birth and Mating of Whales," *Los Angeles Times,* 26 February 1954, p. I-6. 1954.

46. Carl Hubbs to Errol Flynn, 24 December 1947, Box 42, file 49, Hubbs Papers.

47. Randall Reeves, *The Problem of Gray Whale (Eschrichtius robustus) Harassment at the Breeding Lagoons and during Migration* (U.S. Dept. of Commerce, NTIS PB-272-506, 1977), 12; Carl Hubbs, First draft of mss, The Gray Whale, 1968, Box 55, file 26, Hubbs Papers.

48. See Paul White, Samuel Mathews, and J. Baylor Roberts, "Hunting the Heartbeat of a Whale," *National Geographic* 110, no. 1 (1956): 49–64.

49. Reeves, *The Problem of Gray Whale,* 12.

50. See Eleanor Coerr and William E. Evans, *Gigi, a Baby Whale Borrowed for Science and Returned to the Sea* (New York: G. P. Putnam's Sons and Evans, 1980). Sea World in San Diego also retrieved a rescued gray whale calf in 1997, helping to nurse it back to health. The animal was later returned to the ocean.

51. Bryant Evans, "Gray Whale Found in Larger Part of Gulf of California," *San*

Diego Union, 13 February 1954, Box 56, file 13, Hubbs Papers; Raymond M. Gilmore, Robert L. Brownell, James G. Mills, and Al Harrison, "Gray Whales near Yavaros Southern Sonora, Golfo de California, Mexico," *Trans. San Diego Nat. Hist. Soc.* 14, no. 16 (1967): 197–204.

52. Carl Hubbs to Santiago A. Campbell, Consul of Mexico in San Diego, 29 February 1952, Box 56, file 41, Hubbs Papers.

53. Berdegue, "Ultimo censo de la ballena gris."

54. Raymond Gilmore to Dr. Roger R. Revelle, Director, Scripps Institution of Oceanography, 2 August 1956, Box 42, file 108, Gilmore Collection.

55. See Secretaría de Pesca, *El programa nacional,* 10.

56. Hubbs to Campbell, Hubbs Papers.

57. Carl Hubbs to Enrique Beltrán, 31 July 1956, Box 56, file 26, Hubbs Papers. Hubbs's premonition about Guerrero Negro Lagoon and Magdalena Bay came true. As a result of salt company–related boat traffic, gray whales abandoned the lagoon for a period of about ten years, returning only after salt operations had ceased there. In 1962, Raymond Gilmore argued that Guerrero Negro Lagoon "would be lost to the gray whale" from salt company dredging (Raymond Gilmore to David E. Day, 18 February 1962, Box 42, file 78, Gilmore Collection). A phosphorite mine was developed east of the Boca de Soledad in Magdalena Bay in the early 1980s. The mine was never completed but raised the concern of marine mammal researchers in Mexico, who thought that related boat traffic and dredging would cause gray whales to abandon the Boca de Soledad. See Félix Córdoba, "La ballena gris y la explotación de fosforita en Baja California Sur," in *Reunión nacional sobre la ballena gris: Aspectos biológicos, socioeconomicos, y legales,* ed. Jorge A. Vargas (Mexico City: Centro de Estudios Económicos y Sociales del Tercer Mundo, 1981), 5–11.

58. Berdegue, "Ultimo censo de la ballena gris," 104.

59. "Civilization Seen as Peril to Whales: Scripps Scientist Asks for Breeding Preserves," newspaper article, 17 January 1957, Box 56, file 14, Hubbs Papers, 1957.

60. "Baja California Port Plan Told," *San Diego Union,* 27 October 1959, Box 56, file 14, Hubbs Papers.

61. "New Peril Is Seen to Gray Whales," *San Diego Union,* 9 April 1967, p. A5.

62. Rodolfo Hernández to A. Starker Leopold, 13 October 1969, Box 41, file 62, Hubbs Papers.

63. Carl Hubbs to A. Starker Leopold, 2 October 1969, Box 41, file 62, Hubbs Papers.

64. "Mexico Creates Whale Sanctuary," *San Diego Union,* 10 February 1972, Box 56, file 17, Hubbs Papers.

65. Gustavo Díaz Ordaz was concerned with neither the environment nor human rights. A brutal ruler, Díaz Ordaz, along with Luis Echeverría, was responsible for the massacre of hundreds of students in Mexico City in 1968. See chaper 21 of Krauze, *Mexico: Biography of Power.*

66. Manuel Tello, *La política exterior de México (1970–1974)* (Mexico City: Fondo de Cultural Económica, 1975), 103.

67. Luis Echeverría, conversation with author, Mexico City, 14 September 1994.

68. "Decreto que declara zona de refugio para ballenas y ballenatos, las aguas del area de la Laguna Ojo de Liebre, al sur de la Bahía de Sebastian Vizcaíno, en el Litoral del Oceano Pacífico, Territorio de Baja California," *Diario Oficial,* 14 January 1972, pp. 4–5; "Decreto por el que se declara zona de reserva y refugio de aves migratorias y de la fauna silvestre, la constituida por la laguna Ojo de Liebre y San Ignacio, dentro del area que comprende la Bahía de San Sebastian Vizcaíno, en la costa del Territorio Sur de Baja California," *Diario Oficial,* 11 September 1972, pp. 4–5.

69. See Secretaría de Desarrollo Urbano y Ecología, Reserva de la Biósfera "Sebastian Vizcaíno" Baja California Sur, Mexico City, 1984.

70. Secretaría de Desarrollo Urbano y Ecología, Budgets for 1984 to 1988, La Paz.

71. Aradít Castellanos, Programa refugio natural de aves acuaticas migratorias en Bahía de Sebastian Vizcaíno: Informe técnico, Secretaría de Agricultura y Recursos Hidráulicos, Guerrero Negro, 1979.

72. Secretaría de Desarrollo Urbano y Ecología, Press release no. 88-099, 16 February 1988, Mexico City.

73. See Intituto Nacional de Ecología, Programa de manejo de la Reserva de la Biósfera El Vizcaíno, B.C.S., Mexico City, 1994.

74. "Decreto por el que se declara la Reserva de la 'Biósfera El Vizcaíno', Ubicada en el Municipio de Mulege, BCS," *Diario Oficial,* 30 November 1988, pp. 2–26.

75. Aradít Castellanos, conversation with author, La Paz, 27 May 1994. According to Castellanos, it was the pressure from Group of 100 president Homero Aridjis that finally convinced de la Madrid to approve the reserve decree. See also Grupo de los Cien to Manuel Camacho Solís, 10 February 1988.

76. See Agenda of the Workshop on The Management of Marine and Coastal Resources in Baja California: Research Needs and Priorities, 1974, Box 41, file 69, Hubbs Papers.

77. The First International Symposium on the Gray Whale, 1977, Box 56, file 48, Hubbs Papers.

78. Secretaría de Pesca, *El programa nacional,* 12.

Chapter 5. Gray Whales and Mexican Politics

1. The first federal environmental policy act in Mexico was the 1971 revision of Article 73 of the Mexican Constitution to include a reference to environmental pollution. That same year Echeverría enacted the Federal Pollution Prevention and Control Law which gave the executive branch the authority to establish environmental regulations. Echeverría established the Subsecretariat of Environmental Improvement in 1972 to administer environmental laws. See Stephen P. Mumme, C. Richard Bath, and Valerie J. Assetto, "Political Development and Environmental Policy in Mexico," *Latin American Research Review* 23 (1988): 12. The 1982 Federal Law for Environmental Protection was a weak precursor to the 1988 General Law of Ecological Balance and Environmental Protection.

2. Established in 1985 and dismantled in 1992, SEDUE was the first cabinet-level federal agency that combined efforts to integrate pollution control with the conservation of natural resources. SEDUE was also in charge of the national system of protected areas and protecting flora and fauna.

3. Mumme, Bath and Assetto, "Political Development", 20.

4. After leaving INE in 1997, Quadri was rewarded for his anti-environmental campaigning by being appointed the director of the corporate interest group, Centro de Estudios del Sector Privado para el Desarrollo Sustentable or CESPEDES (Center for Private Sector Studies for Sustainable Development). The organization is part of a larger corporate group, Consejo Coordinador Empresarial (Business Coordinating Council). Juan Bezaury, e-mail communication with author, 4 September 1998.

5. The federal government issued a modified Federal Law of Administrative Procedures on December 24, 1996. Article 6 of the new law grants the Ministry of Commerce and Industry the discretion to require Regulatory Impact Assessments. Juan Bezaury, e-mail communication with author, 2 November 1998.

6. See "Carece de experiencia política la mayor parte del nuevo gabinete," *La Jornada* (Mexico City), 1 December 1994, p. 5–7.

7. See Instituto Nacional de Ecología, *Conservación de la biodiversidad en areas naturales protegidas selectas de México* (Mexico City, 1993), 5.

8. See Global Environmental Facilities Program, *Quarterly Operational Report* (Washington, D.C., November 1994), 12. Composed of municipal, state, and federal representatives, as well as sectors of the corporate state, the Vizcaíno Biosphere Reserve TAC is a mirror of the top-down, hierarchical structure of the Mexican government with little influence on the management of the reserve. The Nature Conservancy is currently working with INE and protected area staff throughout Mexico to develop a system of TACS that serve as "Friends of the Park" organizations that help to secure long-term funding for conservation activities. This type of committee is being developed in the Pinacate Biosphere Reserve in northern Sonora.

9. Pronatura A.C. and The Nature Conservancy, *Mexico Protected Areas Project: An Independent Analysis of the World Bank Global Environmental Facility* (Mexico City and Arlington, Virginia, 1995): ii.

10. "Environmental Fines," *The News* (Mexico City), 28 February 1995, p. 13.

11. See Arturo Nieves, "Diagnóstico PROFEPA sobre la ballena," *Sudcaliforniano,* 22 March 1994, p. 1A; Alejandra Estrada, "Protección y cuidado se ofrece a la Ballena Gris: PROFEPA," *Sudcaliforniano,* 16 February 1995, p. 1A, 6C.

Chapter 6. The Battle over San Ignacio Lagoon

1. CorpWatch, web site, 24 March 1998, www.corpwatch.org/trac/greenwash/mitsubishi.html.

2. Gabriel Quadri de la Torre to Juan Bremer, 27 February 1995.

3. "Declaratoria de incorporación al patrimonio de la Comisión de Fomento Minero,

de una franja de terreno a lo largo de la costa occidental de la península en Mulege, Distrito de Baja California, para explotar sal marina." *Diario Oficial,* 2 October 1953, p. 6.

4. Juan Bremer conversation with author, 26 April 1994, Guerrero Negro; "Acuerdo por el que se cancelan las asignaciones de la Comisión de Fomento Minero por las salinas de San Ignacio, Abreojos y Ramales, en Baja California Sur, y se asigna a la Exportadora de Sal, S.A. de C.V., la zona San Ignacio, para la exploración y explotación de sal comun," *Diario Oficial,* 25 August 1992, pp. 14–16.

5. Victor Octavio García, "ABCdario," *Diario Peninsular* (La Paz), 3 July 1998, p.7.

6. Information on the proposed San Ignacio Lagoon salt project was obtained from the following sources: Juan Bremer conversation with author, 26 April 1994; Exportadora de Sal, web site, 13 September 1998, http://www.bajasalt.com/main.html; Bruce Mate, "A Report to the Marine Mammal Commission on Proposed Salt Production Facilities at San Ignacio Lagoon, Baja California" (1995); Mark Spalding, "Laguna San Ignacio Briefing Book" prepared for the Natural Resources Defense Council (NRDC) and the International Fund for Animal Welfare (IFAW) (February 1997)," Natural Resources Defense Council, web site, 13 September 1998, http://www.nrdc.org.

7. Juan Bremer, conversation with author; "Manifestación de impacto ambiental modalidad intermedia, Proyecto salitrales de San Ignacio," (La Paz, Centro de Investigaciónes Biológicas de Baja California Sur, 1994), 11.

8. See Luis A. Fuentes and Consuelo Soto, "Las salinas de Guerrero Negro en Baja California Sur, Mexico," *Geografía* 5 (1993): 60; Mark Spalding, "Laguna San Ignacio Briefing Book."

9. Juan Bremer, conversation with author.

10. Mark Spalding, "Laguna San Ignacio Briefing Book."

11. According to Mark Spalding in "Laguna San Ignacio Briefing Book," although "approximately 208 jobs will be created, it is estimated only half will be available to Mexican nationals. Moreover, none of the salt processing jobs will be in Mexico."

12. Tali Nauman, "La ballena gris, en peligro de extinción en la laguna de San Ignacio," *El Financiero,* 24 February 1995, p. 60.

13. Homero Aridjis, "Las salinas y el tercer socio," *Reforma* (Mexico City), 10 March 1996, p. 18A.

14. Juan Bremer, conversation with author.

15. Victor Octavio García, "ABCdiario."

16. Francisco Guzmán Lazo, statement, Mexico City, 29 February 1996.

17. Homero Aridjis, "Las salinas y el tercer socio."

18. Tim Golden, "Salinas Brother Is Tied by Swiss to Drug Trade," *New York Times,* 19 September 1998, pp. A1, A6. An e-mail message from an anonymous individual (most likely an Exportadora de Sal employee or a federal agency employee with access to insider project information, including a list of Cedros Island fishing cooperative members) to the Environment in Latin America Network electronic mail listserv on April 3, 1996, disparaged Aridjis for suggesting Salinas might be involved in the project.

Donzante@aol.com, the message author, used the original Bremer justification for the project—to reduce costs by eliminating expensive double handling at Cedros Island—to justify the project. The message stated that, "According to the company, it cost more to produce salt at Gro. [sic] Negro than it is worth delivered to Japan. The point is that there is a reason for the proposed new salt works. If the old one is losing money much of it will have to be closed." The extensive use of the Internet in the ongoing controversy illustrates just how powerful a tool this medium has become for opening up a political process normally closed to the public.

19. Exportadora de Sal, web site.

20. Peter J. Bryant, Christopher M. Lafferty, and Susan K. Lafferty, "Reoccupation of Laguna Guerrero Negro, Baja California, Mexico, by Gray Whales," in *The Gray Whale,* 375–376.

21. "Manifestación de impacto ambiental," 94.

22. Holly Payne conversation with author, 23 March 1998, Ensenada.

23. Ibid.

24. Alfonso Gavito González, "La cooperativa Punta Abreojos retira su respaldo a la expansión de la salinera," *Diario Peninsular* (La Paz), 19 May 1998, p. 9. For a detailed examination of fisheries policies in the region and resource piracy see chapter 3 of Emily Young, "Linking Local Needs to Nature Protection in the Coastal Lagoons of Baja California Sur, Mexico" (Ph.D. diss., University of Texas at Austin, 1995).

25. Instituto Nacional de Ecología, *Programa de Manejo Reserva de Biósfera El Vizcaíno* (Guerrero Negro 1997).

26. Exportadora de Sal, web site. A photo of Victor Sanchez appears on the Exportadora de Sal web site pointing to existing pumps for the Scammon's Lagoon facility. The photo caption contains a quote by Sanchez, "A great number of whales gather at the bottom of the lagoon that apparently are not disturbed by any noise produced by the pumps."

27. "Decreto por el que se declara la Reserva de la Biósfera 'El Vizcaíno,' Ubicada en el Municipio de Mulege, BCS," *Diario Oficial,* 30 November 1988, p. 23.

28. Mark Spalding, "Laguna San Ignacio Briefing Book."

29. Gabriel Quadri de la Torre to Juan Bremer, 27 February 1995.

30. "Avanzan los propósitos de la nueva salina en San Ignacio," *Sudcaliforniano,* 2 January 1993, p.1.

31. "Manifestación de impacto ambiental," p. 434.

32. Fernando Jaramillo, Aradít Castellanos and Jorge Cancino, "El berrendo de Baja California, su situacion actual y perspectivas de manejo," Delegación SEDUE en Baja California Sur, La Paz (1985), pp. 8–9.

33. Armando Masao, "Intereses internacionales pretenden frenar el proyecto salinero," *Sudcaliforniano,* 18 April 1995, pp. 1.

34. During the 1980s CIBNOR (then known as CIB) sponsored a public meeting to discuss the potential environmental impacts of a mine being excavated along the shore of Magdalena Bay. See F. Córdoba, Ibid.

35. Breceda et al., "Conservación y areas protegidas," p. 29.

36. Homero Aridjis, introduction to *La Reserva de la Biósfera El Vizcaíno en la península de Baja California,* p. 13.

37. Exportadora de Sal, ad, *New York Times,* 26 June 1995. Mitsubishi also placed an ad in the *New York Times* about the salt project the following day (27 June 1995).

38. "Mexican Government request for an IWC role in assisting the review process for a proposed additional commercial salt producing operation in Baja California," IWC/47/29 Agenda Item 31 (International Whaling Commission, 1995).

39. Instituto Nacional de Ecología, "Salitrales de San Ignacio, BCS," Nota Informativa (Mexico City, 29 May 1985).

40. Copies of the first environmental impact assessment were made available through the efforts of an American scientist who was given a copy by a Vizcaíno Biosphere Reserve employee in January 1995. The scientist then distributed copies to individuals in Mexico and the United States. The study was never made available to the public in Mexico.

41. See Secretaría de Medio Ambiente, Recurso Naturales y la Pesca, "Salitrales de San Ignacio, B.C.S," (Mexico City, 1996). The committee is composed of Gonzalo Halffter Salar (committee chair) (Mexico), Exequiel Ezcurra Real de Azua (Mexico), Bruce Mate (U.S.), Steven Swartz (U.S.), Stephen Reilly (U.S.), Victor Marin Briano (Chile), and Manuel Enrique Figueroa Clemente (Spain). All seven are biologists. The addition of a social scientist would have strengthened the committee's understanding of the socioeconomic context of saltworks development. The terms of reference were also posted on the Internet.

42. Mark Spalding, "Laguna San Ignacio Briefing Book."

43. Elizabeth Velasco, "Vetan la explotación de Salinas de San Ignacio, BC, por razones ecológicas," *Excelsior* (Mexico City), 1 March 1995, p. A-38.

44. Jesús Chavez, "GMR rechaza que haya impacto ambiental negativo en la Laguna de San Ignacio," *Sudcaliforniano,* 1 March 1995, p. 1A.

45. Armando Masao, "Dicen no al proyecto salinera de Laguna San Ignacio," *Sudcaliforniano,* 4 March 1995, p.1A.

46. "El proyecto de ampliación de la salinera, no esta cancelado: GRM," *Sudcaliforniano,* 7 March 1995, p. 7-A.

47. Alejandra Estrada, "Frenar la expansión de la salinera, es atentar contra el desarrollo de vario rubrios productivos: Flores Yee," *Sudcaliforniano,* 8 March 1995, p. 1.

48. "FEDOCOPE pide al INE que rectifique su decision de no paralizar el proyecto de la salinera de GN," *Sudcaliforniano,* 9 March 1995, p. 1A.

49. "La ampliación salinera colocaría a nuestro país a la vanguardia del mercado mundial, dijó el Secretario de Comercio y Fomento Industrial." *Sudcaliforniano,* 9 March 1995, p. 1A.

50. "Legisladores sudcalifornianos se unen para defender la salina," *Sudcaliforniano,* 25 April 1995, p. 1A.

51. Armando Masao, "Diputados y campesinos defienden el proyecto salinero. Los ecologistas que se openen defienden oscuros y mezquinos intereses: Ejidatarios," *Sudcaliforniano,* 11 May 1995, p. 1A.

52. Oscar Canton et al. to Julia Carabias, 17 May 1995.

53. "El congreso de la unión decidirá la ampliación de la salinera: JCO," *Diario Peninsular* (La Paz), 26 June 1998, pp. 1, 10.

54. Grupo de los Cien to Manuel Camacho Solís, 10 February 1988.

55. On February 4, 1995, *Reforma* published a response to the article from the Instituto Nacional de la Pesca (National Fisheries Institute—a subagency of Pesca) of SEMARNAP, stating that the agency supports projects such as the saltworks and negating any adverse impacts from project development. See Grupo de los Cien, "Cronología, compañía Exportadora de Sal vs. la ballena gris y la Reserva de la Biósfera del Desierto del Vizcaíno" (Mexico City, 1995).

56. Homero Aridjis, "El silencio de las ballenas," *Reforma* (Mexico City), 21 February 1995, p. 8A.

57. Grupo de los Cien and Partido Verde Ecologísta de México, "Se solicita require la manifestación de impacto ambiental que se indica," 21 August 1995.

58. Mark Spalding, "Vizcaíno Biosphere Reserve," Environment in Latin America Network listserv, elan@csf.colorado.edu, 13 May 1996.

59. Jacob Scherr, telephone conversation with author, 19 September 1998.

60. See "Inside Story: Saving the Whales," *Hello!,* 29 March 1997; Ruben García Fernández, "Fin de Semana con las ballenas," *Reforma* (Mexico City), 5 March 1997, p.1E (Gente).

61. José Sota Molina, "Ecodesarrollo en Vizcaíno," *Sudcaliforniano,* 22 April 1995, pp. 5A, 10A.

62. Comisariado Ejidales of Ejido San Ignacio and N.C.P.E. Luis Echeverría Alvarez to President Ernesto Zedillo Ponce de León, 23 January 1995.

63. "Se mostraron accesibles los pescadores del Ejido Echeverría con la expansion de la salinera GN," *Sudcaliforniano,* 9 July 1995, p. 1A. It is common for government officials, politicians, and ruling party leaders in Baja California Sur to plant articles in the press claiming the support of rural organizations that do not have access to newspapers and therefore cannot complain about fabricated stories.

Chapter 7. Fishing Communities and Gray Whale Conservation

1. I also interviewed fishermen who informed me that this practice also occurs in the Sea of Cortez. However, I have never talked to anyone who actually witnessed a fisherman spear a dolphin with a pitchfork. The meat is allegedly used for bait. Fishermen in Baja California Sur generally enjoy the company of dolphins and porpoises.

2. Pata rajada or cracked foot is a common name for natives of Cabo San Lucas and the surrounding Cape region (most likely due to their traditional use of handmade huaraches). They are also referred to as *pata saladas* or salty feet.

3. Arthur North, *Camp and Camino in Lower California* (1910, reprint, Glorieta, New Mexico: Rio Grande Press, 1977), 253.

4. North, *Camp and Camino,* 249.

5. Michael Mathes, introduction to *Clemente Guíllen Explorer of the South: Diaries of the Overland Expeditions to Bahia Magdalena and La Paz, 1719, 1720–1721,* ed. and trans. Michael Mathes (Los Angeles: Dawson's Book Shop, 1979), 15.

6. Martínez, *Historia de Baja California,* 403.

7. Browne, *Explorations in Lower California,* 23.

8. See Eugene K. Chamberlin, "Explotación de la orchilla, Bahía Magdalena," in *Baja California: Textos de su historia,* vol.2, ed. Miguel Mathes (Mexico City: Instituto de Investigaciónes Dr. José María Luis Mora, 1988), 46–50.

9. Martínez, *Historia de Baja California,* 408.

10. "The Lower California Revolution," *Daily Union* (San Diego), 25 November 1871, Special Collections, University of California–San Diego Library.

11. Martínez, *Historia de la Baja California,* 409.

12. Chamberlin, "Explotación de la orchilla."

13. John F. Janes, *The Adventures of Stickeen in Lower California, 1874,* ed. Anna Marie Hagar (Los Angeles: Dawson's Book Shop, 1972), 84.

14. Administrado de Aduana to Gobernador del Distrito Sur de Baja California, 10 December 1917, V683:Exp. 61, Pablo L. Martínez Archives.

15. Fabio Martínez, "Historia de Bahia Tortugas: La Pesca y el cooperativísmo," in *Memoria XI semana de informacion historíca de Baja California Sur* (La Paz: Gobierno de Baja California Sur, Direccion de Cultura, 1986), 37–64.

16. Jefe del Puerto, Bahía Magdalena, to General Brigadier, La Paz, Baja California, 12 December 1910, 626:V532:Exp. 7, Pablo L. Martínez Archives.

17. Francis J. Manno and Richard Bednarcick, "El Japón en Bahía Magdalena, 1911," in *Baja California, Textos de su historia,* vol. 1, ed. Miguel Mathes (Mexico City: Instituto de Investigaciónes Dr. José María Luis Mora, 1988), 428.

18. Jesús Chavez, "Puerto San Carlos ventana natural de nuestro país, para el movimiento de la cuenca del Pacífico y TLC." *Sudcaliforniano* 31 January, 1994, p. 1-A.

19. See Dedina and Young, *Conservation and Development in the Gray Whale Lagoons of Baja California Sur, Mexico,* 28–29. We found that foreign outfitters that operated package tours to both Magdalena Bay (Puerto Adolfo López Mateos) and San Ignacio Lagoon earned gross revenues of approximately $8 million in 1994. We estimated that only about $59,000, or less than 1 percent, was spent on local salaries and supplies. However, outfitters estimated that between 50 and 65 percent of their gross income from gray whale tourism was spent on direct operating costs in Mexico. For additional discussion of whalewatching in Baja California Sur, see chapter 4 of Emily Young, "Elusive Edens."

20. Later, a total of fifty-eight skiffs operated in the area around Puerto Adolfo López Mateos at one time. This included an extra twenty-seven local boats given permission by the INE to operate, five "pirate" skiffs that operated on the weekends, and thirteen

skiffs owned by foreign outfitters that operated without permits. This situation received extensive coverage in the *Sudcaliforniano.* In a January 22, 1994, English language column of the *Sudcaliforiano,* Jane Firstenfeld argued that "Panga skippers in Magdalena Bay . . . call for the ouster of luxury ships. Shouldn't someone point out to them that (foreign) vessels . . . are not their competition." On January 18, 1994, an alternative view appeared in the caption of a front-page photo in the *Sucaliforniano* of a large luxury tour vessel that read, "(the boat) does not permit local tourism operators to work."

Bibliography

"Acuerdo declarando caduco el contrato celebrado con el señor Magnus Kenow, para la explotación de la ballena en el littoral occidental de la Baja California." *Diario Oficial,* 20 February 1926, pp. 834–835.

"Acuerdo por el que se cancelan las asignaciones de la Comisión de Fomento Minero por las salinas de San Ignacio, Abreojos y Ramales, en Baja California Sur, y se asigna a la Exportadora de Sal, S.A. de C.V., la zona San Ignacio, para la exploración y explotación de sal comun." *Diario Oficial,* 25 August 1992, pp. 14–16.

"Acuerdo que establece relativa, general y definitiva para la pesca en toda la Republica del manatí o vaca marina (*Manatus americanus*)." *Diario Oficial,* 27 February 1945, p. 5.

"Acuerdo que establece veda para la captura de elefante marino y foca fina." *Diario Oficial,* 24 April 1933, p. 648.

"Acuerdo que establece veda para la captura del manatí o vaca marina." *Diario Oficial,* 1 August 1934, p. 531.

"Acuerdo que establece veda para la especie manatí (*Trichechus manatus*) en la República Mexicana, *Diario Oficial,* 26 October 1981, p. 33.

Ainsworth, Ed. "Scientists Spy on Birth and Mating of Whales." *Los Angeles Times,* 26 February 1954, p. I-6.

"La ampliación salinera colocaría a nuestro país a la vanguardia del mercado mundial, dijó el Secretario de Comercio y Fomento Industrial." *Sudcaliforniano,* 9 March 1995, p. 1A.

Aridjis, Homero. Introduction to *La Reserva de la Biósfera El Vizcaíno en la península de Baja California,* edited by Alfredo Ortega and Laura Arriaga, p. 13. La Paz: Centro de Investigaciónes Biológicas de Baja California Sur, 1990.

———. "Las salinas y el tercer socio." *Reforma* (Mexico City), 10 March 1996, p. 18A.

———. "El silencio de las ballenas." *Reforma* (Mexico City), 21 February 1995, p. 8A.

Aschmann, Homer. *The Central Desert of Baja California: Demography and Ecology.* Berkeley: University of California Press, 1959.

"Avanzan los propósitos de la nueva salina en San Ignacio." *Sudcaliforniano,* 2 January 1993, p. 1.

Barco, Miguel del. *Historia natural y crónica de la Antigua California [Adiciones y correcciones a la Noticia de Miguel Venegas].* Edición, estudio preliminar, notas, y apéndices: Miguel León-Portilla. Mexico City: Universidad Nacional Autónoma de México, 1973.

Berdegue, Julio. "Ultimo censo de la ballena gris, Rhachianectes glaucus (Cope), en aguas de Baja California." *Ciencia* 16 (1956): 99–109.

Breceda, Aurora, et al., "Conservacion y areas protegidas en Baja California Sur." In *La Reserva de la Biósfera El Vizcaíno en la península de Baja California,* edited by Alfredo Ortega and Laura Arriaga. La Paz: Centro de Investigaciónes Biológicas de Baja California Sur, 1990.

Bremer, Juan. Conversation with the author, 26 April 1994, Guerrero Negro.

Browne, J. Ross. *Explorations in Lower California.* 1868. Reprint, Tucson: Arizona Silhouettes, 1952.

Bryant, Peter J., Christopher M. Lafferty, and Susan K. Lafferty, "Reoccupation of Laguna Guerrero Negro, Baja California, Mexico, by Gray Whales." In *The Gray Whale,* edited by Mary Lou Jones, Steven Swartz, and Stephen Leatherwood, pp. 375–387. Orlando, Fla.: Academic Press, 1984.

Buckland, S. T., J. M. Breiwick, K. L. Cattanach, and J. L. Laake. "Estimated Population Size of the California Gray Whale." *Marine Mammal Science* 9 (1993): 235–249.

Bunker, J. "Experts Fear End of Gray Whale If Pact's Broken." *San Diego Evening Tribune,* 21 June 1965, p. 1.

Cambell, David, and Melba Cambell. "Surf-Riding by the California Gray Whale." *Bull. South. Calif. Acad. Sciences* 62, pt. 2 (1963): 99.

Canton, Oscar, et al. to Julia Carabias, 17 May 1995.

"Carece de experiencia política la mayor parte del nuevo gabinete." *La Jornada* (Mexico City), 1 December 1994, pp. 5–7.

Cariño Olvera, Martha Micheline. *Historia de la relaciones hombre naturaleza en Baja California Sur, 1500–1940.* La Paz: Universidad Autónoma de Baja California Sur, 1996.

Carter, Samuel, III. *The Incredible Great White Fleet.* New York: Crowell-Collier Press, 1971.

Castellanos, Aradít. Programa refugio natural de aves acuaticas migratorias en Bahía de Sebastian Vizcaíno: Informe técnico, Secretaría de Agricultura y Recursos Hidráulicos, Guerrero Negro, 1979.

Chamberlin, Eugene K. "Explotación de la orchilla, Bahía Magdalena." In *Baja California: Textos de su historia.* Edited by Miguel Mathes. Vol. 2, pp. 46–50. Mexico City: Instituto de Investigaciónes Dr. José María Luis Mora, 1988.

Chavez, Jesús. "GMR rechaza que haya impacto ambiental negativo en la Laguna de San Ignacio." *Sudcaliforniano,* 1 March 1995, p. 1A.

———. "Puerto San Carlos ventana natural de nuestro país, para el movimiento de la cuenca del Pacífico y TLC." *Sudcaliforniano,* 31 January, p. 1-A.

Chenault, Victoria. *Los pescadores de Baja California.* Mexico City: Centro de Investigaciónes y Estudios Superiores en Antropología Social, Museo Nacional de Culturas Populares, 1985.

Coerr, Eleanor, and William E. Evans. *Gigi: A Baby Whale Borrowed for Science and Returned to the Sea.* New York: G. P. Putnam's Sons and Evans, 1980.

Comisariado Ejidales of Ejido San Ignacio and N.C.P.E. Luis Echeverría Alvarez to President Ernesto Zedillo Ponce de León, 23 January 1995.

"Commercial Use of Gray Whales Confirmed." *American Cetacean Society–San Diego Chapter Newsletter* (October 1998).

"El Congreso de la unión decidirá la ampliación de la salinera: JCO." *Diario Peninsular* (La Paz), 26 June 1998, pp. 1, 10.

"Contrato celebrado con el señor Nicolas Fossum para el establecimiento de una fabrica de producción de la ballena. *Diario Oficial,* 4 September 1920, pp. 86–89.

"Convención Internacional para la Reglamentación de la Caza de la Ballena." *Diario Oficial,* 6 December 1949, pp. 5–10.

Córdoba, Félix. "La ballena gris y la explotación de fosforita en Baja California Sur." In *Reunión nacional sobre la ballena gris: Aspectos biológicos, socioeconomicos, y legales,* edited by Jorge A. Vargas, 5–11. Mexico City: Centro de Estudios Económicos y Sociales del Tercer Mundo, 1981.

CorpWatch. Web page, 24 March 1998. www.corpwatch.org/trac/greenwash/mitsubishi.html.

Crosby, Harry W. *Antigua California: Mission and Colony on the Peninsular Frontier, 1697–1768.* Albuquerque: University of New Mexico Press, 1994.

——. *The Last of the Californios.* Edited by Richard F. Pourade. San Diego: Copley Press, 1981.

Dalheim, Marilyn. "A Comparison of the Acoustical Environments and Activities of the Gray Whale (*Eschrichtius Robustus*) in the Bering Sea, Alaska, and Baja California, Mexico." In *Memoria del X reunión internacional sobre mamíferos marinos,* 37–70. La Paz: Secretaría de Pesca and Universidad Autónoma de Baja California Sur, 1985.

"Declaratoria de incorporación al patrimonio de la Comisión de Fomento Minero, de una franja de terreno a lo largo de la costa occidental de la península en Mulege, Distrito de Baja California, para explotar sal marina." *Diario Oficial,* 2 October 1953, p. 6.

"Decreto por el cual se reforma la prevención reglamentaria de 25 de Noviembre de 1921, que establece veda absoluta para la pesca de manatí." *Diario Oficial,* 22 August 1929, p. 3.

"Decreto por el que se declara la Reserva de la Biósfera 'El Vizcaíno,' Ubicada en el Municipio de Mulege, BCS." *Diario Oficial,* 30 November 1988, pp. 2–26.

"Decreto por el que se declara zona de reserva y refugio de aves migratorias y de la fauna silvestre, la constituida por la laguna Ojo de Liebre y San Ignacio, dentro del area que comprende la Bahía de San Sebastian Vizcaíno, en la costa del Territorio Sur de Baja California." *Diario Oficial,* 11 September 1972, pp. 4–5.

"Decreto que aprueba el Convenio Internacional para la reglamentación de la caza de ballena." *Diario Oficial,* 23 February 1938, pp. 1–2.

"Decreto que declara zona de refugio para ballenas y ballenatos, las aguas del area de la Laguna Ojo de Liebre, al sur de la Bahía de Sebastian Vizcaíno, en el Litoral del Oceano Pacífico, Territorio de Baja California." *Diario Oficial,* 14 January 1972, pp. 4–5.

Dedina, Serge, and Emily Young. *Conservation and Development in the Gray Whale*

Lagoons of Baja California Sur, Mexico. U.S. Dept. of Commerce NTIS PB96-113154, 1995.

Derr, Mark. "To Whale or Not to Whale." *Atlantic,* October 1998, 24–26.

"Endangered and Threatened Wildlife and Plants: Final Rule to Remove the Eastern North Pacific Population of the Gray Whale from the List of Endangered Species." *Federal Register* 59, no. 115 (1994): 31,094–31,095.

"Environmental Fines." *The News* (Mexico City), 28 February 1995, p. 13.

Estrada, Alejandra. "Frenar la expansión de la salinera, es atentar contra el desarrollo de vario rubrios productivos: Flores Yee." *Sudcaliforniano,* 8 March 1995, p. 1.

——. "Protección y cuidado se ofrece a la Ballena Gris: PROFEPA." *Sudcaliforniano,* 16 February 1995, p. 1A, 6C.

Evans, Bryant. "Gray Whale Found in Larger Part of Gulf of California." *San Diego Union,* 13 February 1954. Carl L. Hubbs Papers about Baja California and gray whales, 1947–1977, Hubbs Collection, Scripps Institution of Oceanography Library, La Jolla, California.

Exportadora de Sal. Advertisement. *New York Times,* 26 June 1995.

——. *Project Plans for Proyecto Laguna de San Ignacio.* 28 July 1992. Guerrero Negro.

——. Web site, 13 September 1998, http://www.bajasalt.com/main.html.

"FEDOCOPE pide al INE que rectifique su decision de no paralizar el proyecto de la salinera de GN." *Sudcaliforniano,* 9 March 1995, p. 1A.

Fleischer, Luis. "Aerial Surveys of Gray Whales (*Eschrichtius robustus*) in Mexican Waters (1980–1990)." Paper presented to the Scientific Committee of the International Whaling Commission at the Special Meeting for the Comprehensive Assessment of the Gray Whale, Seattle, Washington, 1990.

Fleischer, Luis, and J. Beddington. Seasonal Abundance, Reproduction and Early Mortality Rates of Gray Whales (*Eschrichtius robustus*) in Mexican Waters (1980–1985). Paper SC/A90/G29 presented to the Scientific Committee of the International Whaling Commission, 1985.

Fleischer, Luis, Javier Contreras, and E. Michel. "La ballena gris (*Eschrichtius robustus*) en la region norte de Bahía de Magdalena, B.C.S., Mexico." In *Memoria de la IX Reunión internacional para el estudio de los mamíferos marinos.* La Paz: Universidad Autónoma de Baja California Sur, 1984.

Fleischer, Luis, and Octavio Maravilla. "Presence of Gray Whales (*Eschrichtius robustus*) in the Gulf of California." Paper presented to the Scientific Committee of the International Whaling Commission at the Special Meeting for the Comprehensive Assessment of the Gray Whale, Seattle, Washington, 1990.

Fuentes, Luis A., and Consuelo Soto. "Las salinas de Guerrero Negro en Baja California Sur, Mexico." *Geografía* 5 (1993): 54–61.

García, Ruben. "Fin de Semana con las ballenas." *Reforma* (Mexico City), 5 March 1997, p. 1E (Gente).

García, Victor Octavio. "ABCdario." *Diario Peninsular* (La Paz), 3 July 1998, p. 7.

Gard, Richard. "Aerial Census of the Gray Whale in Baja California Lagoons, 1970 and

1973, with Notes on Behavior, Mortality and Conservation." *California Fish and Game* 60 (1974): 132–134.

Gavito, Alfonso. "La cooperativa Punta Abreojos retira su respaldo a la expansión de la salinera." *Diario Peninsular* (La Paz), 19 May 1998, p. 9.

Gilmore, Raymond M. "A Census of the California Gray Whale." In U.S. Fish and Wildlife Service, Spec. Sci. Rep. Fish. 342 (1960): 1–30.

———. Papers about Baja California and gray whales, 1956–1976. San Diego Natural History Museum, San Diego, California.

Gilmore, Raymond M., Robert L. Brownell, James G. Mills, and Al Harrison. "Gray Whales near Yavaros, Southern Sonora, Golfo de California, Mexico." *Trans. San Diego Nat. Hist. Soc.* 14, no. 16 (1967): 197–204.

Global Environmental Facilities Program. *Quarterly Operational Report*. Washington, D.C., November 1994.

Golden, Tim. "Salinas Brother Is Tied by Swiss to Drug Trade." *New York Times*, 19 September 1998, pp. A1, A6.

Gordon, David, and Alan Baldridge. *Gray Whales*. Monterey: Monterey Bay Aquarium, 1991.

Grupo de los Cien. "Cronología, compañía exportadora de sal vs. la ballena gris y la Reserva de la Biósfera del Desierto del Vizcaíno." Mexico City, 1995.

Grupo de los Cien and Partido Verde Ecologísta de México. "Se solicita require la manifestación de impacto ambiental que se indica." 21 August 1995.

Grupo de los Cien to Manuel Camacho Solís, 10 February 1988.

Hanna, G. D. "Expedition to Guadalupe Island, Mexico." *Proceedings of the California Academy of Sciences* 24 (1925): 217–275.

Henderson, David. *Men and Whales at Scammon's Lagoon*. Los Angeles: Dawson's Book Shop, 1972.

———. "Nineteenth Century Gray Whaling: Grounds, Catches, and Kills, Practices and Depletion of the Whale Population." In *The Gray Whale*, edited by Mary Lou Jones, Steven Swartz, and Stephen Leatherwood, pp. 159–186. Orlando: Academic Press, 1984.

Hubbs, Carl L. Papers about Baja California and gray whales, 1947–1977. Hubbs Collection, Scripps Institution of Oceanography Library, La Jolla, California.

"Inside Story: Saving the Whales." *Hello!* 29 March 1997.

Instituto Nacional de Ecología. *Conservación de la biodiversidad en areas naturales protegidas selectas de México*. Mexico City, 1993.

———. *Programa de Manejo de la Reserva de la Biósfera El Vizcaíno*. Guerrero Negro, 1997.

———. *Programa de Manejo de la Reserva de la Biósfera El Vizcaíno, B.C.S.* Mexico City, 1994.

———. "Salitrales de San Ignacio, BCS." Nota Informativa, Mexico City, 29 May 1985.

Janes, John F. *The Adventures of Stickeen in Lower California, 1874*. Edited by Anna Marie Hagar. Los Angeles: Dawson's Book Shop, 1972.

Jaramillo, Fernando, Aradít Castellanos, and Jorge Cancino. El berrendo de Baja California, su situacion actual y perspectivas de manejo. Delegación SEDUE en Baja California Sur, La Paz, 1985.

Jones, H. Y. "Mexican Denies Whale Hunt Plans." *San Diego Union,* 12 September 1965, p. A2.

Jones, Mary Lou, and Steven Swartz. "Demography and Phenology of Gray Whales and Evaluation of Human Activities in Laguna San Ignacio, Baja California Sur, Mexico." In *The Gray Whale,* edited by Mary Lou Jones, Steven Swartz, and Stephen Leatherwood, pp. 309–374. Orlando: Academic Press, 1984.

——. *Demography and Phenology of Gray Whales and Evaluation of Whale-Watching Activities in Laguna San Ignacio, Baja California Sur, Mexico, 1978–1982.* U.S. Department of Commerce NTIS PB 86-2190778, 1986.

Jones, Mary Lou, Steven Swartz, and Marilyn Dalheim, *Census of Gray Whale Abundance in San Ignacio Lagoon: A Follow-up Study in Response to Low Whale Counts Recorded during an Acoustic Playback Study of Noise-Effects on Gray Whales.* U.S. Department of Commerce NTIS PB94-195062, 1994.

Krauze, Enrique. *Mexico: Biography of Power.* Translated by Hank Heifetz. New York: HarperCollins, 1997.

Krutch, Joseph Wood. *Baja California and the Geography of Hope.* Edited by Kenneth Brower, with a foreward by David Brower. New York: Sierra Club and Ballantine Books, 1967.

Landauer, Lyndall. *Scammon: Beyond the Lagoon.* San Francisco: Associates of the J. Porter Shaw Library, 1986.

"Legisladores sudcalifornianos se unen para defender la salina." *Sudcaliforniano,* 25 April 1995, p. 1A.

"The Lower California Revolution." *Daily Union* (San Diego), 25 November 1871. Special Collections, University of California–San Diego Library.

"Manifestación de impacto ambiental modalidad intermedia, Proyecto Salitrales de San Ignacio." La Paz: Centro de Investigaciónes Biológicas de Baja California Sur, 1994.

Manno, Francis J., and Richard Bednarcick. "El Japón en Bahía Magdalena, 1911." In *Baja California: Textos de su historia.* Edited by Miguel Mathes. Vol. 1, pp. 416–432. Mexico City: Instituto de Investigaciónes Dr. José María Luis Mora, 1988.

Martínez, Fabio. "Historia de Bahia Tortugas: La Pesca y el cooperativísmo." In *Memoria XI semana de informacion historíca de Baja California Sur,* pp. 37–64. La Paz: Gobierno de Baja California Sur, Direccion de Cultura, 1986.

Martínez, Pablo L. *Historia de Baja California.* 1956. Reprint. La Paz: Consejo Editorial del Gobierno del Estado de B.C.S., 1991.

Masao, Armando. "Dicen no al proyecto salinera de Laguna San Ignacio." *Sudcaliforniano,* 4 March 1995, p. 1A.

——. "Diputados y campesinos defienden el proyecto salinero: Los ecologistas que se openen defienden oscuros y mezquinos intereses; Ejidatarios." *Sudcaliforniano,* 11 May 1995, p. 1A.

——. "Intereses internacionales pretenden frenar el proyecto salinero." *Sudcaliforniano,* 18 April 1995, p. 1.

Mate, Bruce. A Report to the Marine Mammal Commission on Proposed Salt Production Facilities at San Ignacio Lagoon, Baja California, 1995.

Mathes, Michael. Introduction to *Clemente Guíllen: Explorer of the South; Diaries of the Overland Expeditions to Bahia Magdalena and La Paz, 1719, 1720–1721*. Edited and translated by Michael Mathes. Los Angeles: Dawson's Book Shop, 1979.

Meigs, Peveril. *The Dominican Mission Frontier of Lower California*. Berkeley: University of California Press, 1935.

——. *The Kiliwa Indians of Lower California*. Berkeley: University of California Press, 1939.

"Mexican Government request for an IWC role in assisting the review process for a proposed additional commercial salt producing operation in Baja California." IWC/47/29 Agenda Item 31. International Whaling Commission, 1995.

Mumme, Stephen P., C. Richard Bath, and Valerie J. Assetto, "Political Development and Environmental Policy in Mexico." *Latin American Research Review* 23 (1988): 7–34.

Nauman, Tali. "La ballena gris, en peligro de extinción en la laguna de San Ignacio." *El Financiero,* 24 February 1995, p. 60.

"New Peril Is Seen to Gray Whales." *San Diego Union,* 9 April 1967, p. A5.

Nieves, Arturo. "Diagnóstico PROFEPA sobre la ballena." *Sudcaliforniano,* 22 March 1994, p. 1A.

North, Arthur. *Camp and Camino in Lower California*. 1910. Reprint, Glorieta, N.M.: Rio Grande Press, 1977.

Ortega, Alfredo, and Laura Arriaga (eds.). *La Reserva de la Biosfera El Vizcaíno en la península de Baja California*. La Paz: Centro de Investigaciones Biológicas, 1991.

Pablo L. Martínez State Historical Archives of Baja California Sur, La Paz. Papers about natural history, Magdalena Bay, and San Ignacio Lagoon.

Pronatura A.C. and The Nature Conservancy. *Mexico Protected Areas Project: An Independent Analysis of the World Bank Global Environmental Facility*. Mexico City and Arlington, Va., 1995.

"El Proyecto de ampliación de la salinera, no esta cancelado: GRM." *Sudcaliforniano,* 7 March 1995, p. 7-A.

Quadri de la Torre, Gabriel, to Juan Bremer, 27 February 1995.

Reeves, Randall. "Modern Commercial Pelagic Whaling for Gray Whales." in *The Gray Whale,* edited by Mary Lou Jones, Steven Swartz, and Stephen Leatherwood, 187–202. Orlando: Academic Press, 1984.

——. *The Problem of Gray Whale (Eschrichtius robustus) Harassment at the Breeding Lagoons and during Migration*. U.S. Dept. of Commerce, NTIS PB-272-506, 1977.

Reeves, Randall, and Edward Mitchell. "Current Status of the Gray Whale, *Eschrichtius robustus*." *Canadian Field-Naturalist* 102, no. 2 (1988): 369–390.

Reilly, Stephen. "Population Assessment and Population Dynamics of the California Gray Whale (*Eschrichtius robustus*)." Ph.D. diss., University of Washington, Seattle, 1981.

Reilly, Stephen, Dale Rice, and Alan Wolman. "Population Assessment of the Gray Whale, *Eschrichtius robustus* from California Shore Censuses, 1967–1980." *Fish. Bull.* 81 (1983): 267–281.

Reyes Silva, Leonardo. *El molino de viento: Leyendas, costumbres y narraciones sud-californianas*. La Paz: Consejo Editorial del Gobierno del Estado de Baja California Sur, 1992.

Rice, Dale, and Allan Wolman. *The Life History and Ecology of the Gray Whale (*Eschrichtius robustus*)*. Special Publication, no. 3. American Society of Mammalogists, 1971.

Scammon, Charles. *The Marine Mammals of the North-western Coast of North America Described and Illustrated Together with an Account of the American Whale-Fishery*. 1874. Reprint, with an introduction by Victor B. Scheffer. New York: Dover Publications, 1968.

———. "Report of Captain C. Scammon, of the U.S. Revenue Service, on the West Coast of Lower California." In *Resources of the Pacific Slope,* edited by J. Ross Browne, 123–131. New York: D. Appleton and Company, 1869.

"Se mostraron accesibles los pescadores del Ejido Echeverría con la expansion de la salinera GN." *Sudcaliforniano,* 9 July 1995, p. 1A.

Secretaría de Desarrollo Urbano y Ecología. Budgets for 1984 to 1988, La Paz.

———. Press release no. 88-099, 16 February 1988, Mexico City.

———. Reserva de la Biósfera "Sebastian Vizcaíno" Baja California Sur, Mexico City, 1984.

Secretaría de Medio Ambiente, Recurso Naturales y la Pesca. "Salitrales de San Ignacio, B.C.S." Mexico City, 1996.

Secretaría de Pesca. *El programa nacional de investigación y conservación de mamíferos marinos de Mexico*. Mexico City, 1987.

———. *Mexicanas por nacimiento*. Mexico City, 1993.

Simonian, Lane. *Defending the Land of the Jaguar*. Austin: University of Texas Press, 1995.

Sota Molina, Jóse. "Ecodesarrollo en Vizcaíno." *Sudcaliforniano,* 22 April 1995, pp. 5A, 10A.

Spalding, Mark. Laguna San Ignacio Briefing Book, Prepared for NRDC and IFAW, February 1997. Natural Resources Defense Council, web site, 13 September 1998, http://www.nrdc.org.

———. "Vizcaíno Biosphere Reserve." Environment in Latin America Network listserv, elancsf.colorado.edu, 13 May 1996.

Swartz, Steven, and Mary Lou Jones, "Gray Whales at Play in Baja's San Ignacio Lagoon." *National Geographic* 171 (1987): 755–771.

Tello, Manuel. *La política exterior de México (1970–1974)*. Mexico City: Fondo de Cultural Económica, 1975.

Tønnessen, Joh. N. and Arne Odd Johnsen. *The History of Modern Whaling*. Translated by R. I. Christophersen. Berkeley and Los Angeles: University of California Press, 1982.

Vargas, Fernando. *Parques nacionales de México y reservas equivalentes: Pasado, presente y futuro*. Mexico City: Instituto de Investigaciónes Económicas-UNAM, 1984.

Velasco, Elizabeth. "Vetan la explotación de Salinas de San Ignacio, BC, por razones ecológicas." *Excelsior* (Mexico City), 1 March 1995, p. A-38.

Viñas, R. E., A. Sarria, and V. Rubio. "Repertorio temático de la pintura rupestre de la Sierra de San Francisco, Baja California (Mexico)." *Ars Praehistorica*, 3/4 (1984/1985): 201–232.

White, Paul, Samuel Mathews, and J. Baylor Roberts, "Hunting the Heartbeat of a Whale." *National Geographic* 110 (1956): 49–64.

Yablokov, Alexey. "Validity of Whaling Data." *Nature* 367 (13 January 1994): 108.

Young, Emily. "Elusive Edens: Linking Local Needs to Nature Protection in the Coastal Lagoons of Baja California Sur, Mexico." Ph.D. diss., University of Texas at Austin, 1995.

Zuloaga, Eliseo. "Alto crecimiento poblacional se registra en la entidad." *Diario Peninsular* (La Paz), 14 July 1998, p. 3.

Illustration Credits

The political cartoons used in this book are reproduced courtesy of Jorge Eloy Teran Torres.

The advertisement by the Grupo del los Cien is reproduced courtesy of the Grupo del los Cien and the Public Media Center.

All the color photographs are reproduced courtesy of Marilyn Kazmers/ SharkSong.

Index

About the Author

Serge Dedina grew up next to the U.S.–Mexico border in San Diego and has spent the last twenty years traipsing the back roads of Baja California. He spent two years in Baja California Sur during the course of his dissertation research on gray whale conservation. Dedina received a bachelor of arts degree in political science from the University of California–San Diego in 1987 and a master of science degree in geography from the University of Wisconsin–Madison in 1991. He received his Ph.D in geography from the University of Texas at Austin in 1996. Dedina worked as an ocean lifeguard for twelve years in California and as an environmental planner in the United States and Mexico. He is currently Executive Director of WildCoast, an international conservation team preserving the last coastal wildlands of the Californias, and formerly was the director of the Baja California/Sea of Cortez Program for The Nature Conservancy. He divides his time between Tucson and Mexico with his wife, Emily Young, and sons, Daniel and Israel.

Dedina's publications include "People of the Mangroves." *Surfer's Journal* 4 (4) (1995): 98–105; *Conservation and Development in the Gray Whale Lagoons of Baja California Sur, Mexico* (Washington, D.C.: U.S. Department of Commerce, NTIS Publication, 1995) (coauthor); "Conservation as Communication: Local People and Gray Whale Tourism in Baja California Sur, Mexico." *Whalewatcher* 29 (2) (1995): 8–15 (coauthor); and "The Political Ecology of Transboundary Development: Land Use, Flood Control and Politics in the Tijuana River Valley." *Journal of Borderland Studies* 10 (1) (1995): 89–110.